ANGLICAN CHURCHES IN COLONIAL SOUTH CAROLINA

ANGLICAN CHURCHES IN COLONIAL SOUTH CAROLINA
Their History and Architecture

Suzanne Cameron Linder

WYRICK & COMPANY
CHARLESTON

Published by Wyrick & Company
Post Office Box 89
Charleston, South Carolina 29402

Copyright © 2000 by The Protestant Episcopal Diocese of South Carolina

All rights reserved. No part of this book may be reproduced in any form
or by any electronic or mechanical means, including
information storage and retrieval systems, without written permission.

Printed and bound in Hong Kong by C&C Offset Printing Co., Ltd.

Photo credits: ©Gibbes Museum of Art/Carolina Art Association, 14 (top), 20 (top),
32 (top), 40 and front jacket, 90, 94 (top), 97; Historic American
Buildings Survey (HABS), National Park Service, 11 (Schwartz), 13 (Schwartz),
23 (left), 23 (right, Boucher), 36 (top, Waterman), 107 (lower left and right),
132 (Schwartz), 133, back jacket (Waterman, upper right); Punkin Moser, 128;
South Carolina Department of Archives and History, 44; South Carolina
Historical Society, 3, 8; South Caroliniana Library, 16, 84 (Carl Julian);
Marta Thacker, maps on pp. viii, xi, xii; Courtesy, The Winterthur Library:
Printed Book and Periodical Collection, 37; all other photos by Suzanne Cameron Linder

Library of Congress Cataloging-in-Publication Data

Linder, Suzanne Cameron.
Anglican churches in colonial South Carolina : their history and architecture /
Suzanne Cameron Linder.
p. cm.
Includes bibliographical references and index.
ISBN 0-941711-45-5
1. Episcopal Church--South Carolina--History--17th century. 2. South Carolina--
Church history--17th century. 3. Episcopal Church--South Carolina--History--18th century.
4. South Carolina--Church history--18th century. I. Title.
BX5917.S6 L56 1999
283'.757'09033--dc21   99-059040

CONTENTS

Dedication, vi

Foreword, vii

Acknowledgments, ix

Introduction, 1

St. Philip's Parish, 7

St. Andrew's Parish, 15

St. James' Parish, Goose Creek, 21

Christ Church Parish, 27

St. Thomas' and St. Denis' Parish (Pompion Hill and Chapel of Ease), 33

St. Bartholomew's Parish (Pon Pon Chapel), 41

St. Paul's Parish, 47

St. James' Parish, Santee, 51

St. John's Parish, Berkeley (Biggin Church and Strawberry Chapel), 57

St. Helena's Parish, 67

St. George's Parish, Dorchester, 73

Prince George's Parish, Winyah, 79

Prince Frederick's Parish, 85

St. John's Parish, Colleton, 91

Prince William's Parish, 95

St. Peter's Parish, 101

St. Stephen's Parish, 105

St. David's Parish, 111

St. Mark's Parish, 119

St. Matthew's Parish, 123

All Saints' Parish, Waccamaw, 127

St. Luke's Parish, 129

St. Michael's Parish, 131

Epilogue, 137

Index, 139

DEDICATION

A history of the colonial parish churches of South Carolina would not be possible without the foresight and commitment of those individuals who throughout the centuries have preserved, recorded, and cared for the church buildings, their liturgical fittings and their written records.

This chronicle of church history is made possible by the inspiration, guidance and contributions of devoted individuals who saw the need to bring the parish histories together for the edification and enjoyment of all who view the past as prologue to the future.

To them we give special thanks and the dedication of this book.

Mr. and Mrs. William J. Detyens, Jr.
Mr. and Mrs. James L. Ferguson
Mr. and Mrs. Hugh C. Lane
Mills Bee Lane Memorial Foundation

FOREWORD

The potential for the "Province of Carolina" emerged in the year 1662, when eight noblemen applied to Charles II for a grant of extensive territory in North America. A charter was granted by the king on the 24th of March, 1662/63. The third and the eighteenth articles of the charter sought the increase of the Christian religion within the province and allowed for the building and founding of "churches, chapels, and oratories" according to the "Ecclesiastical laws of our Kingdom of England" as well as offering "indulgencies and dispensations" for those who in conscience' sake could not conform to "said Liturgy and Ceremony."

The second charter, granted on the 30th of June, 1665, and the Fundamental Constitutions (1669) anticipated that the Church of England would be established in Carolina. The ninety-sixth article of the latter stated that it shall belong to the Carolina parliament "to take care of the building of churches and the public maintenance of divines …according to the Church of England."

The first divine of the Church to arrive in Charleston was the Reverend Atkin Williamson. He was here in 1680. In 1710-11, the General Assembly appropriated £30 per annum for his support, but he later died in poverty at an advanced age.

The first Anglican church in the colony was built sometime between 1681 and 1692 at the southeast corner of Broad and Meeting Streets, the present location of St. Michael's. It was a large and stately structure built of black cypress on a brick foundation and was surrounded by a white palisade. An Act of the Assembly was passed on March 1, 1710/11, for the building of a new church of brick on Church Street, the present location of St. Philip's Church.

The Episcopal Church of today rests upon this strong and historic foundation from the very beginning of the Carolina colony. In a desire to strengthen this legacy from the past, I asked Mrs. Esther Ferguson to lead in the formation of a foundation to own an official Episcopal Residence, as the church did from Bishop Thomas's time (1934) until 1967, when it was sold. The absence of an official residence is a serious drain on diocesan finances and diverts money from much-needed mission. Mrs. Ferguson enlisted the partnership of Mr. Hugh Lane, Sr., who for many years had been interested in the preservation of the colonial Anglican churches and who was actively working to document their significance. Through their vision and significant financial support a pictorial book about early Carolina churches was envisioned as a way to engage the interest of the diocese, as well as to seek to discover forgotten information and details about the earliest parishes and churches.

Mr. Lane engaged a research specialist, who journeyed to England and was able to discover significant facts long since forgotten. Using this material and the results of her own researches, Dr. Suzanne Linder has written not only a lovely and historic book about the parishes established by the Church Act of 1706 and other subsequent acts but also a work of major significance in South Carolina colonial historiography. She has written about the original buildings which survive and the others which still exist in one form or another; more importantly, she has given the reader a clear window into church life in the colonial period.

To Mr. and Mrs. William J. Detyens, Mr. and Mrs. James L. Ferguson, and Mr. and Mrs. Hugh C. Lane, I want to express my deep gratitude for their vision, their dedication, and their financial support for the writing and publication of this volume. We are thereby encouraged to build for the future upon this ancient foundation. As all proceeds from this publication will be applied to the purchase of an episcopal residence, my hope is that each member of the diocese will become a partner in this endeavor.

Edward L. Salmon, Jr.
XIII Bishop of South Carolina

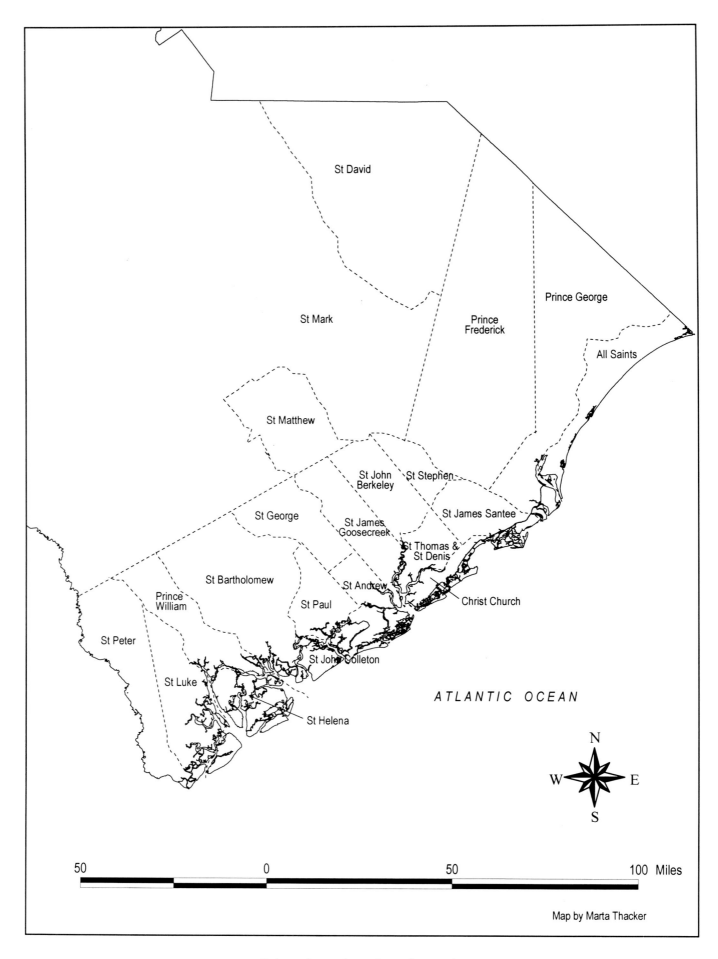

Colonial parishes of South Carolina

ACKNOWLEDGEMENTS

Writing a book is an experience in personal enrichment. This book has been especially rewarding because of the many people who have contributed their time and talents to the final product. The Reverend Canon Michael Malone of the Diocese of South Carolina has been a guiding force. His knowledge of church history and his pursuit of excellence have contributed to the quality of the work.

Louis P. Nelson, a doctoral candidate in the Department of Art History at the University of Delaware, conducted a study of the architecture of the colonial Anglican parishes in the lowcountry outside of Charleston. This included about fourteen of the twenty-four colonial parishes in South Carolina. His expert analysis of architecture within the context of Anglican tradition was most helpful. He kindly consented to allow me to use his manuscript, and I have documented this use in the notes. I sincerely appreciate his thorough research and coordination of ideas which made my work much easier.

One of my greatest pleasures in preparing a book is exploring the locations to see where history actually happened. South Carolina's colonial churches and their churchyards must be among the most beautiful and peaceful places in the entire South. Among the dignified tombstones and Spanish moss, time seems to stand still. An added bonus was meeting the people who take responsibility for caring for the churches. Agnes Baldwin kindly invited me to participate in the annual picnic at St. James' Church, Santee. As the congregation gathered in the churchyard for a generous dinner after the service, one was struck with a sense of continuity. Members of some of the same families have been gathering there for some two centuries to share a repast and renew friendships and family ties. I am indebted to Agnes Baldwin for reading the essay on St. James' Parish, Santee and offering suggestions. I also enjoyed talking with Oran Baldwin and William McG. Morrison about the parish. I was able to speak briefly with Anne Bridges and Roy Williams, and I found their book, *St. James Santee: Plantation Parish*, to be a most valuable resource.

I was honored to have a member of the Ball family, which played such an important part in the history of Strawberry Chapel, show me this gem of a site. Robert Ball kindly opened the chapel and shared with me family stories of events that had transpired there. In St. Thomas' and St. Denis' Parish, John Slayton showed me the parish church, which he maintains with great interest. Richard Coen made arrangements for me to visit Pompion Hill Chapel, and Rodney Mooneyham opened the church and waited patiently while I made photographs. John Barnwell made arrangements for me to visit St. James' Church, Goose Creek, and Ethel Simmons showed me around and told me about the church. Members of her family have acted as custodians for several generations. Debbie Swearingin was my friendly hostess at Christ Church Parish. At St. Stephen's, Elaine Phillips opened the church for me on two occasions. The Reverend George Tompkins, an accomplished church historian, graciously made available to me his history of St. Andrew's Church, which greatly simplified my research. Jack Boineau made arrangements for me to visit the location of the colonial St. Paul's Parish Church and showed me the way. George Cormeny, property manager at St. Michael's, shared his extensive knowledge of the building's history and accompanied me to the tower to photograph the magnificent bells. George Townsend talked with me about All Saints' Parish, and we discussed the church history by Henry DeSaussure Bull, which has been updated by Townsend, Alberta Lachicotte Quattlebaum, and Katherine Wells. The Reverend Charles Walton kindly sent information about St. John's Parish, Colleton. Richard Marks, contractor, and Martha Zierden, archaeologist with the Charleston Museum, spoke with me about their observations about the building at St. James' Goose Creek. I am indebted to all of these people for their cooperation and willingness to help. Many of them are actively involved in efforts to preserve the historic buildings. When I looked at old photographs of the churches, I was struck with how much their appearance has improved in recent years. Only the interest and care of individuals could have brought about this change.

Debbie Roland of the Calhoun County Museum made information on St. Matthew's Parish available from the museum archives and took several hours from her busy schedule to discuss the history of the region with me. She also introduced me to Charles Richard Banks, the noted photographer who illustrated Albert S. Thomas's *Protestant Episcopal Church in South Carolina* and other books. Mr. Banks shared his ideas about photographing colonial churches and helped me with some special problems.

I was fortunate in having an expert in local history as well as an active member of St. David's Church in Cheraw to advise me about St. David's Parish. Sarah Spruill, Director of Historic Cheraw Foundation, has been actively involved in historic preservation in Cheraw. She gathered information for me and constructively criticized my manuscript on St. David's. Lawrence Roland and Alexander Moore discussed Prince William's Parish with me, and I found valuable material in the *History of Beaufort County*, which they co-authored with the late George Rogers. Gerhard Spieler gave me a guided tour of St. Helena's Parish Church in Beaufort and shared with me the *History of the Parish Church of St. Helena*, of which he was co-author. Other books which were especially valuable were *Heritage Passed On* by Sarah Parker Lumpkin (Prince George's Parish, Winyah), *St. Stephen's Episcopal Church* by Jane Searles Misenhelter, and George W. Williams's *St. Michael's, Charleston*. I found Rebecca Talbert Fouché's University of South Carolina master's thesis on St. Philip's Church to be an excellent resource, and George Terry's Ph.D. Dissertation at the University, "Champaign Country," on St. John's Parish, Berkeley gave information on the entire culture of the community. *Historic Goose Creek, South Carolina, 1670-1980* by Michael Heitzler contained hard facts and wonderful stories about the parish church, and Anne King Gregorie's study of Christ Church was based on thorough research.

I am grateful to Bonita McLaurin, Roy McKaughan, John Harden, and Richard Watkins for accompanying me on visits to churches in remote areas and to Bryant Sapp, Emily Garner, and Marta Thacker for research assistance. Marta was particularly helpful in preparing the maps for this volume. Julie Epting shared her vast knowledge of hymnody and offered friendly encouragement.

A historian could not work without the aid of archivists and librarians. I am indebted to Steve Tuttle, Robert McIntosh, Wade Dorsey, Patrick McCawley, Yvette Lebby, Paul Begley and Sharmila Bhatia at the South Carolina Archives Center and to Allen Stokes, Robin Copp, Thelma Hayes, Laura Costello, Beth Bilderback, and Henry Fulmer at the South Caroliniana Library at the University of South Carolina. I also appreciate the help of Anne Schneider at the State Library, Elizabeth Steedly at the Institute for Southern Studies, and the staff of the World Methodist Museum at Lake Junaluska, North Carolina. Scott Zetrouer of the Gibbes Museum in Charleston was most helpful in finding historic paintings of colonial churches.

In black and white photography, pushing the shutter button is only the first step. Much of the truly creative work is done in the dark room. Mary Ellen Rice of Columbia Photo spent many hours developing and printing the photographs, most of which were taken the old-fashioned way with a Mamiya 645 medium format camera and a hand-held light meter.

I am most grateful to Dr. Walter Edgar, author of *South Carolina: A History* and Director of the Institute for Southern Studies at the University of South Carolina, for reading the manuscript and offering suggestions. I especially appreciate the appointment as Research Fellow, which makes the outstanding university libraries and the scholarly associations and programs of the Institute for Southern Studies available to me.

Finally, Hugh Lane had the vision of preserving a written and photographic history of South Carolina's colonial parishes which would focus on the buildings, but would also include the spirit that motivated their founding. To Hugh and Beverly Lane and Esther and James Ferguson for their guidance and encouragement and for making the project possible through the Episcopal Foundation Fund, I am profoundly appreciative. My sincere thanks go to Mr. and Mrs. William Detyens for their contribution. I am also grateful to Bishop Edward L. Salmon for his support of the project.

Suzanne Cameron Linder
Columbia, South Carolina

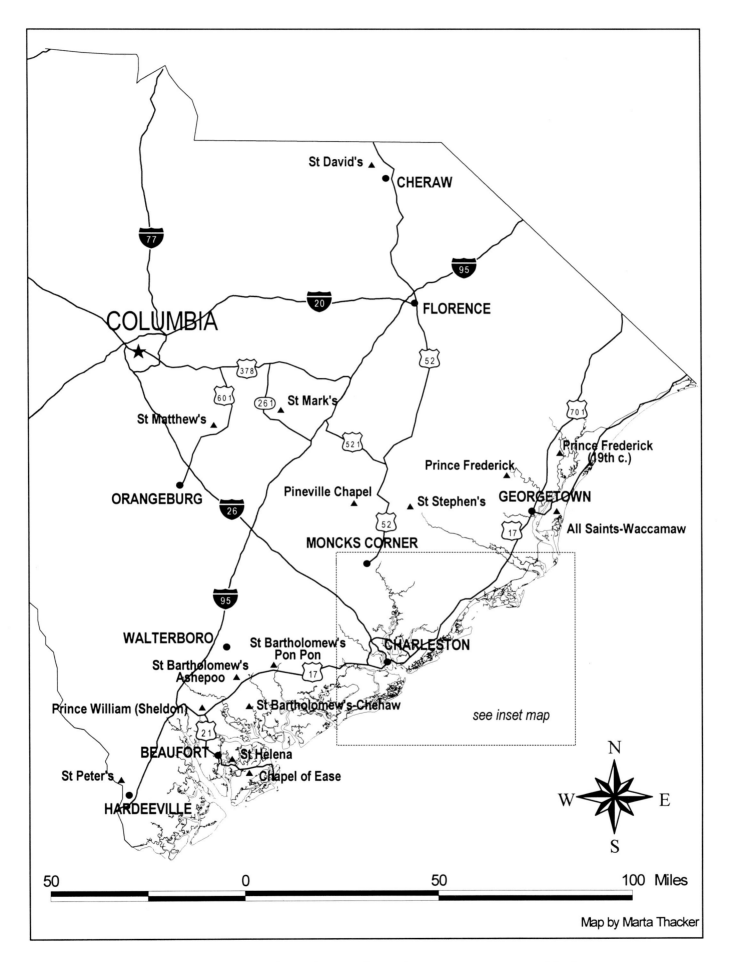

Locations of the colonial parishes in relationship to current cities and highways

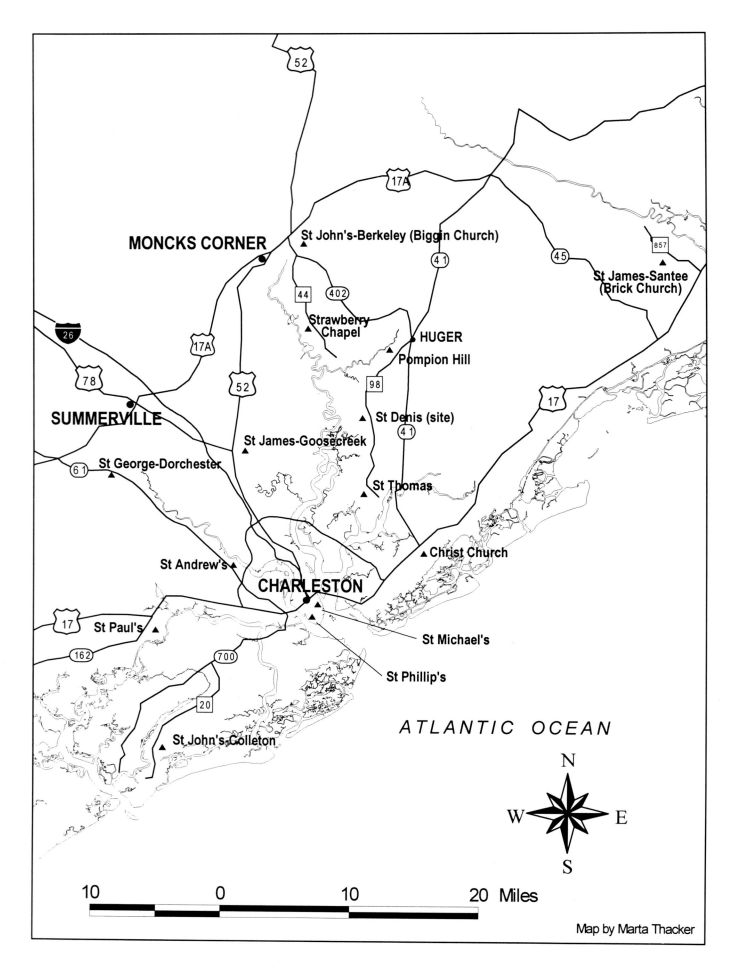

Parishes in relationship to the colonial capital of Charleston

INTRODUCTION

Each Sunday, the congregation gathers at old St. Andrew's Church on the Ashley River to worship in a building that colonial settlers began in 1706. For nearly three centuries, the graceful and dignified church has welcomed people of strong faith along with those in search of some initial contact with the Divine. South Carolina is fortunate in having a number of colonial churches which still stand. They are valuable for their contributions to religious, regional, family, architectural, and political history. It is the purpose of this book to identify those parishes which existed prior to the American Revolution, when South Carolina was a colony of Great Britain, to provide photographs and locations, and to place the early churches within the historical context in which they functioned. Even if the original building has not survived, information about the parish is a part of history. Although painstakingly documented, the study does not attempt to be comprehensive either in architectural analysis or historical context. The book is designed for the layman who has an interest in how these churches came to be and what significance they might hold for the modern age.

A church is more than bricks and mortar. It is the collective spirit of those who come together to worship, and it can be a manifestation of God's spirit working through his people. The spirit of a church can only be suggested on the printed page, but for people whose families have received the rites of baptism, communion, marriage, and burial from the same altar for generations, the spirit of the place is very real. A place where people have come together to worship for centuries has a special atmosphere of reverence which can become apparent to native South Carolinians as well as to those who visit the state for the first time.

As the process of change has accelerated, hectic lifestyles and secular pursuits have challenged the position of religion in the family and in the community. Perhaps a look at the churches of those who came before us can offer a perspective for considering our present state and our hopes for the future.

In order to avoid repeating basic background material in each chapter, information that relates to all the parishes is given below.

RELIGIOUS BACKGROUND

The Anglican Church, or Church of England, was the established church—which meant that it received funding and direction from the government. The Church *in* England became the Church *of* England in 1534, when Henry VIII cut ecclesiastical, canonical, legal, and financial ties with the Papacy because the pope refused to authorize his divorce from Katharine of Aragón. From that time on, the Anglican Church was independent from Catholic rule. The monarch appointed English bishops, who in turn administered the affairs of the church. When English settlers immigrated to South Carolina, they brought with them the idea of an official state religion supported by public funds. Some of them wanted to perpetuate an established church, while Protestants other than Anglicans (called dissenters) did not.

The Fundamental Constitutions of Carolina, although never officially ratified, provided for freedom of religion as well as for support of the established church. The Lords Proprietors and the Crown encouraged both Anglicans and dissenters to come to South Carolina in an attempt to populate the colony. In 1704, the provincial assembly passed a law which effectively outlawed dissenters from office holding and made the Church of England the established church in South Carolina. After active lobbying by the dissenters, the House of Lords and Queen Anne disallowed the 1704 act. In the Church Act of 1706, the South Carolina Assembly allowed for the political participation of dissenters but also provided for establishing the Anglican Church. The Church Act of 1706 created ten parishes and allocated funds from the tax on skins and furs for building churches and paying ministers. The names of the parishes show the strong influence of those who had settled first on the island of

Barbados in the Caribbean, for six of the ten parishes have the same names as parishes in Barbados.[1]

Because no Anglican bishop resided in America, the colonies fell under the authority of the Bishop of London. Ordination of a minister could only be performed by a bishop, so no ministers could be ordained in South Carolina. After ordination, the Bishop of London would issue a license. Unlike dissenting ministers, many of whom were not formally trained, Anglicans had to be educated and to receive sanction by the Bishop of London. This system meant that often parishes had trouble finding a minister to fill their pulpits, but on the other hand, when they did find one, he was sometimes also employed as schoolmaster. Serving as schoolmaster was a way to supplement the meager salaries offered by most parishes.[2]

The bishop's representative, or commissary, supervised all Anglican clergy in South Carolina. In the Church of England, a commissary was appointed by a bishop to exercise ecclesiastical jurisdiction in a particular part of the diocese, to hold visitations, and to superintend the conduct of the clergy.[3]

FUNCTIONS OF THE PARISH

Parishioners were to meet on Easter Monday of each year to elect seven members of the vestry and two churchwardens to administer the business of the parish. The Church Act also directed that a register be chosen to keep a record of births, deaths, and marriages. This was the only provision for keeping vital statistics, and the parish register book became the official record. The parish could also select a clerk to participate in the service by reading scripture or prayers and a sexton to keep the church clean and in repair. In actual practice, the duties of these three officers were sometimes combined in one position.[4]

According to "An Act for the Better Observation of the Lord's Day," passed in 1712, the churchwardens were responsible for enforcing what modern people might call "blue laws." It was mandatory to attend the church of one's choice, and those who did not attend could be fined five shillings. The law allowed no work or selling of goods other than food. People were not permitted to travel by land or water (except to go to church or in extenuating circumstances) or to engage in "publick sports or pastimes, as bear-baiting, foot-ball playing, horse raceing, enterludes or common plays...." Public houses or taverns could house strangers but could not permit idle drinking by inhabitants. Within the city of Charleston, the law required that the churchwardens walk through the town in morning and afternoon on Sundays to apprehend anyone not following the law.[5]

Before 1716, people could vote in elections only in Charleston, but after that date, churchwardens in each parish organized the election process. The wardens had to appear personally before the Assembly in Charleston to report the election results. The position of churchwarden could be a political stepping-stone for a young man, offering a chance for him to prove himself and become acquainted with people of influence in the province.

In addition to elections, the parish officers maintained the church, rectory, chapels of ease, and schools, if such existed. They also had charge of the glebe lands. A glebe was land owned by the parish and set aside for the maintenance of the minister and the church. It was necessary to have a place to gather firewood for both heating and cooking, and in some country parishes where there was no market, the minister had to grow his own food. Occasionally, in colonial South Carolina, the parish provided slaves to work the glebe.[6]

Parish officials also had charge of assessing, collecting, and distributing funds to help the poor. Many parishes built small vestry houses so they would not have to conduct business matters in the church. The parish officers functioned as the only local government in the province. Specific functions—such as road maintenance, clearing rivers for navigation, fighting fires, or monitoring the sale of wood and coal—were handled by commissions appointed for that purpose. Neither Charleston nor small towns were incorporated. Since any legislation had to go through the provincial assembly, the legislative body of South Carolina set a precedent for holding the reins of power which would last well into the twentieth century and have far-reaching consequences for the colony and, later, the state. It was not until 1975 that county governments could independently enact ordinances.[7]

THE SOCIETY FOR THE PROPAGATION OF THE GOSPEL

Finding able ministers who were willing to

brave a dangerous sea voyage of several months and settle in a relatively unknown land was not an easy task. In 1700, the Reverend Thomas Bray, an English clergyman who had served as the bishop's representative in Maryland, persuaded Henry Compton, Bishop of London, and Thomas Tenison, Archbishop of Canterbury, that a new society was needed to sponsor clergy for the colonies. In June 1701, William III granted a charter for the Society for the Propagation of the Gospel in Foreign Parts. In practice, the long name was soon shortened to SPG. The purpose of the society was to receive contributions and support orthodox ministers of the Anglican Church in the English colonies overseas through salary supplements. The charter provided that both Archbishops, the Bishops of London and Ely, the Deans of Westminster and St. Paul's, the Archdeacon of London, and the Regius and Lady Margaret Professors of Divinity of Oxford and Cambridge Universities should be members of the Society. Thus, the officials of the established church and representatives of the universities were united in support of the organization. The seal of the society shows a ship approaching land with a minister standing in the prow with an open Bible in his hand. People on the shore are waiting and their words are expressed in Latin: *Transiens Adjuva Nos* ("Come over and help us"). The policy of the SPG was to send missionaries only to people who requested them. The SPG played an important role in supplying clergymen for South Carolina, and the reports that the missionaries sent back to the Society provide valuable historical information about colonial South Carolina.[8]

Samuel Thomas, the first missionary, arrived in 1702 and served until his death four years later. Between 1706 and 1716, the Society sent ten missionaries and supplied each a salary of £50 which the colonial government supplemented. Through the efforts of Bishop Henry Compton, another six clergymen came to South Carolina; three arrived independently; and one local Presbyterian went to England for ordination. Of the total, about twenty percent died within three or four years of their arrival in the colony. Several narrowly escaped massacre by the Indians in the Yamassee War.[9]

A primary concern of the SPG was the conversion of Indians and slaves. The Society sent Samuel Thomas with the original intention that he would minister to the Yamassee Indians. The colonial governor, Nathaniel Johnson, had other ideas. He sent Thomas to his own neighborhood of Goose Creek. Thomas pointed out that the Indian villages were unsafe and that the language barrier made missionary work among the Indians impossible. Francis LeJau, Thomas's successor, said of the Indians, "They make us ashamed by their life, Conversation, and Sense of Religion quite different from ours; ours consists in words and appearance, their [*sic*] in reality." Given the treatment the Indians received from unscrupulous traders, it can hardly be surprising that they were not interested in the white man's religion.[10]

The seal of the Society for the Propagation of the Gospel in Foreign Parts.

LeJau and others made a sincere effort at religious instruction of slaves, but the opposition of the masters was a major obstacle. After all, how could one deny the humanity of a Christian brother? LeJau quoted a lady who inquired of him, "Is it possible that any of my slaves could go to Heaven and must I see them there?" Peter Kalm, an astute Swedish visitor to America, wrote that the opposition arose partly through the conceit of its being shameful to have a Christian brother or sister among slaves, partly by thinking masters would not be able to keep their slaves subjected afterwards, and partly through fear of the slaves considering themselves on the same level with their masters in religious matters.[11]

About 1740, George Whitefield, a leader of the evangelical movement known as the Great Awakening, insisted on humane treatment of slaves as well as their religious instruction. Whitefield's plans to educate blacks may have motivated his archrival, Alexander Garden, the Anglican commissary in Charleston, to contact the SPG about starting a school. The Society purchased two young black men and trained them to teach. One of them, Harry, administered the school for slaves which operated in Charleston from about 1743 to 1768, when it disbanded. Yearly enrollment was from thirty to about seventy students, which overall was an extremely small number.

Historian Peter Wood suggested that if widespread baptism had been undertaken at an early date so that English masters were forced to concede full humanity through use of a European ritual, later Afro-American history could have been significantly different. Francis LeJau, the missionary who served first on St. Christopher's Island in the Caribbean and later at St. James' Goose Creek, said the planters objected that baptism would set the Negroes free, but he believed the real objection was that they "would be obliged to look upon 'em as Christian Brethren, and use 'em with humanity." Wood concluded that "initial efforts to propagate the Christian faith among the Negroes in Carolina had for them a direct impact which was almost negligible and indirect effects which were less than fortunate."[12] On the other hand, an argument could be made that what was in the heart and soul of the master was more influential than any ritual imposed upon an African who may have had strong beliefs in his or her own religion.

THE YAMASSEE WAR

Trade with the Indians, particularly for deerskins, was one of the most lucrative aspects of the South Carolina economy in the early eighteenth century. A problem arose because unscrupulous traders took advantage of the Indians and cheated them at every opportunity. They also captured Indians and sold them as slaves. The provincial government created a Commission on Indian Affairs which attempted to regulate the trade, but uniform enforcement was impossible. Whites were encroaching on lands set aside for the Yamassee in St. Helena's Parish near present-day Pocotaligo. The Yamassees succeeded in forming an alliance with most of the tribes of the southeast, including Creeks, Choctaws, and Catawbas. The Indians attacked on April 15, 1715, and by June had killed ninety percent of the traders among them, sometimes through brutal torture. In all, about 400 colonists (about six percent of all settlers) died in the war. Indians raided isolated plantations, so colonists sought refuge in Charleston, leaving half the cultivated land in the colony deserted. Skirmishes with the Indians continued until 1728. North Carolina sent token assistance; Virginia, even less; and Massachusetts sent weapons. An alliance with the powerful Cherokees kept them from joining the Yamassees and possibly prevented the total annihilation of the colonists. The Lords Proprietors refused help, so colonists, mostly South Carolinians, defeated the Indian alliance practically alone.[13]

Although the colonists achieved a military victory, they lost a large portion of the very lucrative Indian trade. Almost as devastating was the monetary inflation that resulted when the government printed paper currency to try to pay for the war. Prices soared, and clergymen on a fixed salary had a very difficult time. The SPG agreed to advance half a year's salary to its missionaries and to make a gift of £30 each to two French ministers who were not affiliated with the Society. The missionaries had never had much success in Christianizing the Indians, and the war stopped even the meager attempts that were underway.[14]

THE ARCHITECTURAL SETTING FOR ANGLICAN WORSHIP

Worship in the Anglican Church was based on the liturgy as defined by the Book of Common Prayer. Members valued the ritual, order, and regularity of the service. The design of an Anglican church reflected the requirements of the worship service. Interior elements of churches included the altar, the pulpit and reading desk and clerk's desk (sometimes combined), the baptismal font, and the pews. The altar, usually a simple wooden table at the east end of the building, was the location of the communion service. A railing set off the chancel area to preserve it from irreverence or profanation. Some churches had a window behind the altar, while other more elaborate sanctuaries boasted a reredos or paneled altarpiece displaying the Lord's

Prayer, the Decalogue (Ten Commandments), and the Creed.[15]

Anglican canon law provided that a font for administering baptism should be provided and set up near the door as a reminder that baptism is the entrance to the Christian life. In America, the location of the font could vary, and it frequently appeared near the altar. The pulpit and reading desk were very important in eighteenth-century churches, because the minister read the greatest part of the liturgy from that point. Whereas the Catholic service was in Latin, the Anglican service was in English and was designed for participation. Placement of the pulpit reflected the need for the priest to be heard, so it often stood near the center of one of the long sides of the church. The pulpit was traditionally set on a pedestal accessible by stairs and topped by a sounding board.[16]

Pews were of two types, the ordinary kind used today, known as "slip pews," and the square or box pews with high sides and a door at the aisle. The vestry sold the pews for prices which could differ according to the desirability of the location. Preference of choice often went to those who contributed most to the building fund of the church. Families who owned pews had their own particular place in church, and it is possible that this contributed to an enhanced sense of family and community. It probably also contributed to an awareness of social hierarchy. Pews in the gallery, usually of the slip type, were sometimes available for servants or strangers. As a rule, it was not until the nineteenth century that slaves sat in the gallery.[17]

Documentary records do not identify any architects in colonial South Carolina with the building of Anglican churches. Likewise, there is no evidence that English architects provided specific designs for South Carolina sanctuaries.[18] Various laymen, craftsmen, and clergy participated in designing and creating the worship setting. The buildings which survive and the vestry minutes which describe how they came to be offer a glimpse into the spiritual aspirations and the culture of eighteenth-century Anglican colonists. The churches exhibit elements of regularity demanded by the Anglican liturgy but also aspects of originality that reflect the tastes and preferences of the congregations and craftsmen who built them.

---

[1] See Walter Edgar, *South Carolina, A History* (Columbia: University of South Carolina Press, 1996), pp. 120-130, passim; Thomas Cooper, ed., *Statutes at Large of South Carolina* (Columbia: A. S. Johnston, 1838), II, 282-294.

[2] Stephen P. Dorsey, *Early English Churches in America, 1607-1807* (New York: Oxford University Press, 1952), p.8; S. Charles Bolton, *Southern Anglicanism: The Church of England in Colonial South Carolina* (Westport, Connecticut: Greenwood Press, 1982), pp. 11-12.

[3] Frederick Dalcho, *An Historical Account of the Protestant Episcopal Church in South Carolina* (Charleston: E. Thayer, 1820; rpt. New York: Arno Press, 1970), p. 78.

[4] *Ibid.* See also chapter on St. David's Parish, this volume.

[5] *Statutes*, II, 396-399. Charles Town became Charleston in 1783, but the modern spelling is used throughout this book.

[6] Dalcho, *Protestant Episcopal Church in South Carolina*, pp. 371-372. For definition of terms, see glossary.

[7] Edgar, *History of South Carolina*, pp. 125-130, 551.

[8] Dorsey, *Early English Churches in America*, pp. 6-7; Bolton, *Southern Anglicanism*, p. 20. Transcripts of the South Carolina reports to the SPG are available on microfilm in the Library of Congress and in the South Carolina Department of Archives and History.

[9] Bolton, pp. 29, 166-167.

[10] Bolton, *Southern Anglicanism*, pp. 102-104, 120.

[11] Winthrop D. Jordan, *White over Black* (New York: W. W. Norton, 1977), pp. 182-183.

[12] Bolton, *Southern Anglicanism*, pp. 115-119; Francis LeJau, *The Carolina Chronicle of Dr. Francis LeJau, 1706-1717*, ed. Frank Klingberg (Millwood, NY: Kraus Reprint, 1980), p. 11; Peter Wood, *Black Majority: Negroes in Colonial South Carolina from 1670 through the Stono Rebellion* (New York: W.W. Norton, 1974), p. 142. Wood points out that no one can deny the later importance of Protestant sects among black Americans. Significant mission work in the nineteenth century is described in W. P. Harrison, *The Gospel Among the Slaves* (Nashville, Tenn.: Methodist Church, South, 1893).

[13] Verner W. Crane, *The Southern Frontier, 1670-1732* (Ann Arbor: University of Michigan Press, 1956), pp. 162-186, passim; Edgar, *History of South Carolina*, pp. 100-102.

[14] Gideon Johnston to the SPG, January 27, 1715/16 as cited in Frank J. Klingberg, *Carolina Chronicle: The Papers of Commissary Gideon Johnston 1707-1716* (Berkeley: University of California Press, 1946), pp. 154-155; Bolton, *Southern Anglicanism*, p. 107.

[15] Dorsey, *Early English Churches in America*, pp. 15-19.

[16] *Ibid.*, pp. 26-30.

[17] *Ibid.*, pp. 22-23.

[18] Louis P. Nelson, "South Carolina Anglican: the architecture of the Lowcountry plantation parishes," Draft of Nov. 17, 1997, Diocese of South Carolina, pp. 8-9.

St. Philip's Parish Church in Charleston. Construction of the current church took place between 1835 and 1850.

ST. PHILIP'S PARISH

Where cross the crowded ways of life, Where sound the cries of race and clan,
Above the noise of selfish strife, We hear thy voice, O son of man.

O Master, from the mountain side, Make haste to heal these hearts of pain;
Among these restless throngs abide, O tread the city's streets again;

Till sons of men shall learn thy love, And follow where thy feet have trod;
Till glorious from thy heav'n above, Shall come the city of our God.

- Frank Mason North, 1905

The location of St. Philip's Church, protruding into Church Street in downtown Charleston, is an announcement that the church intends to dominate the comings and goings of the parishioners. The builders of the colonial St. Philip's chose to place the church with the axis of its steeple right down the center of the street so that it could serve the people by showing its clock face and letting its bells sound down the thoroughfare. The placement was also to remind people to attend church, for it was impossible to pass the building without noticing it. When the church was rebuilt in 1835, the Commission for the Widening and Straightening of Streets asked the vestry to push back the location in order to implement traffic flow. The vestry replied that people should slow down and quiet down when passing a holy building. The result was a compromise in which the vestry agreed to move the portico back eighteen feet, but it still extended well into the street.[1]

St. Philip's is the mother church of all the Anglican congregations in South Carolina. Its beginnings date back to the time before comprehensive records are available. On January 14, 1680/81,[2] Originall Jackson and his wife, Millicent, executed a deed of gift donating four acres of land, "being excited with a pious zeal and in consideration of Divine Service (according to the form and Liturgy of the Church of England now established) to be duly and solemnly done and performed by Atkin Williamson, Cleric,...in our Church, or House of Worship to be erected, and built upon our piece, or parcel of ground."[3] It is not certain where the Jacksons' land was, but since there were no settlements outside of Charleston in 1680, it seems reasonable that the donated acres were in the town. Sometime between 1681 and 1692, Anglicans built a sanctuary of black cypress on a brick foundation at the southeast corner of Broad and Meeting streets, the site originally designed for it in the model of the town.[4]

In a letter to the SPG in 1710, Commissary Gideon Johnston said, "Mr Atkins Williamson has lived here under the Notion and Character of a Minister 29 Years, but the Inhabitants have not thought fit to take up with him as a settled Minister in any part of this Province during that time." According to Johnston, Williamson had no credentials, and the commissary asked the SPG to check on his authenticity as an ordained Anglican. Part of the problem stemmed from the story that pranksters, knowing Williamson had a problem with strong drink, conspired to get him drunk and then presented a baby bear, which Williamson accordingly christened. The kindly Francis LeJau, pastor of St. James' Goose Creek, refused to believe the story in spite of affidavits to its authenticity.[5] Williamson ministered in the province some thirty years, and when he became old and infirm, the Assembly appropriated £30 per year for his support.[6]

By 1696, the English church in Charleston had a fully licensed "amiable, learned, and pious" minister in the Reverend Samuel Marshall. Because election as rector included life tenure, he served on a trial basis for two years. Then, in recognition of his conduct and talents, the Assembly passed "an Act to settle a maintenance on a Minister of the Church of

England in Charles-Town," in 1698. The act provided a salary of £150 per year and directed that a Negro man and woman, and four cows and calves be purchased for his use. Affra Coming, widow of John Coming, bequeathed seventeen acres adjoining the town for a glebe in 1698.[7]

Samuel Marshall died in an epidemic of what was probably yellow fever in 1699. In a letter from the governor and council to the Lords Proprietors dated January 17, 1699/1700, the Carolinians reported "a most infectious, pestilential and mortal distemper" which had killed about 160 people in Charleston. Not being aware of the mosquito vector, the colonists remarked on the fact that several people contracted the disease in Charleston and went home to their families in the country, yet none of the relatives became infected.[8]

Of Samuel Marshall, the governor and council said, "By his sound doctrine, the weak sons of our Church, he confirmed.... By his prudent and obliging way of living, and manner of practice, he had gained the esteem of all persons."[9] Following such an exemplary minister must have been difficult. His successor, Edward Marston, was not so fondly remembered. He openly criticized the Assembly and asserted that he had only to answer to ecclesiastical authority. Apparently he forgot who was paying his salary, and he found himself without a job in 1705. He preached briefly at Bermuda Town in Christ Church Parish and eventually left the province.[10]

Richard Marsden had recently come to Charleston from Maryland. Although he had no appointment from the Bishop of London, he took over the pulpit at St. Philip's and proved to be very popular. When Commissary Gideon Johnston arrived in 1707 with credentials from the bishop, Marsden moved on to Christ Church Parish, where he soon got into trouble.[11]

Johnston was an Irish clergyman of the highest recommendations. His arrival in Charleston was inauspicious. After a tedious passage, his ship arrived off Charleston harbor, but had to anchor and wait for high tide in order to cross the bar. Johnston embarked in a small boat for the town, but a sudden squall caused the boat to capsize. Johnston, a sailor, and a merchant were marooned on a small island without meat or drink for twelve days. When a search party finally located them, they were nearly dead from starvation and exposure. Johnston said it took him a fortnight to recover his

The second St. Philip's, begun in 1711 and completed by 1733. It burned in 1835.

strength. It is not surprising that he began a letter to a good friend by saying, "I never repented so much of any thing, my Sins only excepted, as my coming to this Place, nor has ever man been treated with less humanity and Compassion, considering how much I had suffered in my Passage, than I have been since my Arrival in it."[12]

Johnston found it very difficult to support his family of eleven on his meager salary, and he found the Carolinians difficult to deal with. Having succeeded in making their own way in the wilderness, they were suspect of any authoritarian power, including that of the established church. Johnston found them "the most factious and Seditious people in the whole World."[13]

Nevertheless, the commissary proved to be an apt and able administrator who earned the respect of both churchmen and government officials. His wife, Henrietta Johnston, helped to support the family by drawing pastel portraits, many of which survive to illustrate the appearance of the more affluent South Carolinians of the early eighteenth century. Unfortunately, she soon exhausted the materials she brought from England and could not get any more in Charleston. She was likely the earliest woman painter in North America, and the first of either sex to work in pastels.[14]

Gideon Johnston's voluminous letters to the SPG from 1707 to 1716 give a valuable first-hand account of the early years of South Carolina history. The letters emphasize the constant struggle with sickness experienced by the colonists. Quinine to treat malaria was not available in the eighteenth century, and for many settlers the disease was a chronic condition. Johnston said that in order to write, he had to hold his right hand with his left to keep it from shaking.[15]

Despite his hardships and longing for his homeland, Johnston had a rare determination to persevere. A freak accident abruptly terminated his career. On April 23, 1716, Governor Charles Craven set sail for England. The commissary was one of thirty-two people who intended to sail out to the bar to see the governor off. A sudden gust of wind overturned the sloop, and, according to a contemporary, "they all Escaped by singular Providence but Mr. Comissary, who through weakness of Body could not come out of the Hold and was drowned there." One other person drowned while trying to swim to a rescue boat, but all the others survived.[16]

Ironically, the sloop washed ashore on the same island where Johnston had been marooned when he first came to South Carolina. Some fishermen found what was left of his body in the hold of the sloop and buried it on the island. Later, Francis LeJau wrote to the Bishop of London, "I think it is my duty to Let Your Lordship know that with much difficulty Mr. Commrys corps was brought this day to this town & we are going to Bury him as decently as we can." Henrietta Johnston remained in Charleston until her death in March 1729.[17]

Under Johnston's leadership, the province had begun a new church. On March 1, 1711, the Assembly passed an act to build a new brick church with a steeple and a ring of bells together with a cemetery or churchyard to be enclosed by a brick wall. Along with Gideon Johnston, other church commissioners were William Rhett, Alexander Parris, William Gibbon, John Bee, and Jacob Satur.[18] The plan chosen was an ambitious and expensive one, and was probably based on the baroque church of St. Ignatius in Antwerp (now called St. Charles Borromée). When the building was nearly complete, a massive storm, probably a hurricane, caused extensive damage and delayed construction. In 1720, the Assembly passed another act for completing the church. To pay for the building, the Assembly levied a tax on rum and brandy and another tax on importing slaves and merchandise. The act specified that there would be a pew reserved for the governor and council, a pew for the members of the Assembly, and another large pew for strangers.[19]

With funds provided, and with leadership from Alexander Garden, who arrived to become minister of St. Philip's in 1719 or early 1720, the church soon reached completion. The new location on Church Street between Queen and Cumberland provided a larger space for a churchyard and also presented a fortified stronghold at the edge of the town limits. Cumberland Street was a creek at that time, which made this location more accessible for parish members who arrived from their plantations by boat.[20]

Services commenced sometime between 1723 and 1728, and the steeple was finally completed in 1733. Vestry minutes which survive from 1732 indicate that the church was in use at that time, and the gallery was "lately erected."[21] The architect Robert Mills described St. Philip's as built of brick and stuccoed to resemble stone. He said it exhibited "more of design in its arrangement than any other of our ancient buildings erected here." The general outline of the plan was in the form of a cross, seventy-four feet long and sixty-two feet wide. "The arms form the vestibule, tower, and porticoes at each end, projecting twelve feet beyond the sides, and surmounted by a pediment." The head of the cross was a portico of four massive square pillars with arches between and surmounted with a regular entablature and crowned with a pediment. Over the portico rose two sections of an octagonal tower, the lower section containing the bells, the upper the clock, all crowned with a dome and quadrangular lantern and weather vane in the form of a cock. The sides of the edifice were ornamented with a series of pilasters. Each of the spaces contained a single lofty window.

The interior of the church presented an elevation of a lofty double arcade, supporting a vaulted ceiling. The piers were ornamented with fluted Corinthian pilasters rising to arches. Cherubim sculptured in relief ornamented the keystones of the arches. On the south side were some figures in heraldic form, representing the infant colony imploring the protection of the king with the motto of the church, *Propius res aspice nostras* ("Look closer at our affairs"). On the north side over the middle arch was the inscription *Deus mihi Sol* ("God is as the sun to me") with armorial bearings. Beautiful pieces of monumental sculpture, some with bas-relief and some with full figures, ornamented the faces of the pillars. According to Robert Mills, these were "finely executed by the first artists in England and this country."

Master architect that he was, Mills found it regrettable that the galleries, which were added by the 1730s but were not a part of the original design, disturbed the grandeur of the massive arcades. Nevertheless, he found that the effect produced upon the mind in viewing the edifice was that of solemnity and awe, from its massive character. He said, "When you enter under its roof, the lofty arches, porticoes, arcades, and pillars which support it, cast a sombre shade over the whole interior, and induce the mind to serious contemplation and religious reverence."[22]

In the 1730s, the church accumulated such luxurious accouterments as a black velvet funeral pall, a kneeling cushion of crimson damask with silk fringe, two large fine damask tablecloths, and seven surplices to be worn by the clergy. The communion silver included two large flagons, a cup, and a basin—all marked with the King's arms; a flagon, gilt cup and cover, and a basin donated by Colonel William Rhett; a salver given by Francis Fidling in 1702; and a paten in a heart shape of Spanish make. In addition to the rector and an assistant minister, the church employed Peter Morgue to keep the clock, and Herreford, a slave, for "blowing of the organ." John Salter was organist in 1735, and after his death, Charles Theodore Pachelbel played the organ beginning in 1739. By 1765, the church had a "great organ" with sixteen stops and a "choir organ" with eight.[23]

The Reverend Alexander Garden, minister from 1720 until his retirement in 1753, proved more than equal to the task of presiding in one of the finest, if not the finest, of the Anglican churches in the American colonies. The South Carolina clergy in a letter to the SPG called it "a Work of ...Magnitude Regularity Beauty, & Solidity...not paralleled in his Majestys Domminions in America." Garden held a master's degree from the University of Aberdeen. Before coming to South Carolina, he was a curate at the prestigious Barking Church in London. He was an able administrator, and he also served as commissary from 1728 to 1748, when the position was abolished.[24]

Garden had to discipline other clergymen from time to time in his capacity as commissary, and many of these instances are discussed in essays on other parishes. One of the most famous controversies concerned George Whitefield, who was an ordained Anglican minister and a leader of the evangelical movement called the Great Awakening. Problems began when Whitefield, having been refused permission to preach in St. Philip's Church, proceeded to preach in the dissenters' meetinghouse and at the Huguenot church. Whitefield preached extemporaneously and sometimes did not use the Prayer Book in his services. His refusal to do things in what Anglicans considered a decent and orderly manner disenchanted the establishment. Church leaders did not appreciate the emotionalism which they felt he encouraged. He also vociferously criticized the Anglican establishment and dared to assert that the Archbishop of Canterbury, John Tillotson, knew no more about Christianity than Mohammed.

Alexander Garden first talked with Whitefield privately, to no avail. He then convened an ecclesiastical court composed of himself and other Anglican ministers. Whitefield refused to acknowledge the jurisdiction of the court, which then suspended his office of priesthood in the Anglican Church. Whitefield and his follower, Hugh Bryan, encouraged preaching to the slaves. Since the province was still shaken by the Stono Rebellion, a slave revolt which occurred in 1739, any assembly of blacks was an occasion for fear. Eventually, Whitefield was arrested for libeling the Church of England, and while free on bail, left the province. The letter to the newspaper which was considered libelous asserted that the recent fire in Charleston was God's judgment against his wayward people.[25]

St. Philip's response to the disastrous fire of November 18, 1740, which destroyed more than 300 homes and numerous mercantile establishments, was to spearhead relief efforts to help the victims. The church officers met almost daily for two weeks. They received nearly £2000 in donations and provided immediate assistance to those in need. On November 23 alone, collections at the church door totaled £683/12/6. The Assembly allocated £1500 to the vestry for distribution, and St. George's Dorchester gave nineteen barrels of rice. The vestry

The interior of the third St. Philip's featured a double arcade supporting a vaulted ceiling. The piers were ornamented with fluted Corinthian pilasters.

had experience in providing for the poor of the parish, and they were prepared to provide relief to victims of the fire.[26]

Shortly after the fire and the Whitefield controversy and possibly somewhat motivated by Whitefield's insistence on Christianizing slaves, Alexander Garden proposed a school for educating blacks in Charleston. The SPG authorized the purchase of two suitable black youths to be trained to teach. Harry and Andrew, aged fourteen and fifteen, came from the estate of Alexander Skene, a communicant at St. Andrew's and later St. George's Dorchester who had been diligent in instructing his servants in religion. Andrew proved disappointing academically, but Harry progressed under Garden's teaching. Late in 1743, the school opened, and Harry soon had thirty pupils. By 1746, the school had seventy students, including children by day and adults at night. It enjoyed considerable success until 1768, when the St. Philip's vestry "Ordered that Harry, the Negroe that keeps School at the Parsonage (for repeated Transgressions) be sent to the Work house, And to be put into the Mad house, there to be kept till Orders from the Vestry to take him out." Harry was only forty and had been teaching for twenty-five years. There must have been significant stress attached to being a slave teacher of slaves, and, whatever the cause, it is sad that Harry ended his career in the madhouse.[27]

Alexander Garden's career ended on a much pleasanter note. In October 1753, at age sixty-eight, and after thirty-three years of service, Garden resigned as rector of St. Philip's. He had not only succeeded in conducting an admirable personal ministry, but he directed charitable efforts including a school for blacks, provided leadership to other clergymen, and endeavored to create an effective working arrangement between the clergy of the established church and the political leaders of the colony. He was an effective mediator between the Anglican establishment, the SPG, provincial government, and the people.

The church building where Garden officiated burned in 1835, and parishioners began rebuilding as soon as possible. The steeple was finally complete by 1850. In his final sermon, Garden gave his blessing, which might be considered a blessing to St. Philip's Parish in perpetuity:

> May the ever blessed and glorious Trinity bless you in the *City*, and in the *Field*; in the fruit of your *Body*, the fruit of your *Cattle*, and the fruit of your *Ground*; Bless you in your *Basket*, and in your *Store*, and in all that you set your Hand unto:
>
> Bless you with all the temporal blessings, of Health, peace, and prosperity; but above all, and as the Source of all, bless you with truly faithful and obedient hearts, and finally, conduct you safe to the Blessed Regions of Glory and Immortality.[28]

[1] Samuel Gaillard Stoney, *Colonial Church Architecture in South Carolina* (Charleston: Dalcho Historical Society, 1953), p. 9.

[2] For explanation of dates, see glossary.

[3] Frederick Dalcho, *An Historical Account of the Protestant Episcopal Church in South Carolina* (Charleston: E. Thayer, 1820; rpt., New York: Arno Press, 1970), p. 26. Records of the Register of the Province, January 14, 1680, Book G, p. 117, South Carolina Department of Archives and History. The Jacksons received a warrant for land in 1672 stating that they arrived in the first fleet to Carolina. A. S. Salley, Jr., *Warrants for Lands in South Carolina 1672-1711* (Columbia: University of South Carolina Press, 1973), p. 46.

[4] Dalcho, *Protestant Episcopal Church*, p. 27.

[5] Gideon Johnston, *Carolina Chronicle: The Papers of Commissary Gideon Johnston, 1707-1716*, ed. Frank J. Klingberg (Berkeley: University of California Press, 1946; rpt. Millwood, NY: Kraus Reprint, 1974), p. 57; Robert Stevens to SPG, February 3, 1707/8, SPG MS, A4 #19; John Wright to Robert Stevens, forwarded to the SPG, December 10, 1707, A4 #21, Mf., South Carolina Department of Archives and History; A. S. Salley, "A Letter by the Second Landgrave Smith," January 16, 1708, *South Carolina Historical Magazine*, XXXII, 61-63; Francis LeJau, *The Carolina Chronicle of Dr. Francis LeJau 1706-1717*, ed. Frank Klingberg (Berkeley: University of California Press, 1956; rpt., Millwood, NY: Kraus Reprint, 1980), pp. 72-73.

[6] Dalcho, p. 32. Thomas Cooper, ed., *Statutes at Large of South Carolina* (Columbia: A. S. Johnston: 1838), VII, 57.

[7] Dalcho, pp. 32, 34-35. Dalcho cites an act of October 8, 1698, but states that the act was partially consumed by vermin. A search for it was unproductive, but the Journal of the Assembly stated that "Doctr Samuell Marshall shall have a Suffieent maineaineance allowed him." See *Journals of the Commons House of Assembly of South Carolina, 1698*, ed. A. S. Salley, Jr. (Columbia: Historical Commission of South Carolina, 1914), p. 14. Will of Affra Coming, 1698, WPA Wills, 1(1687-1710), p. 14, South Carolina Department of Archives and History.

[8] Dalcho, pp. 35-36; Joseph Waring listed the epidemic of 1699 as yellow fever. See Joseph Ioor Waring, *A History of Medicine in South Carolina, 1670-1825* (Columbia: South Carolina Medical Association, 1964), p. 371.

[9] Dalcho, p. 37.

[10] Dalcho, pp. 37, 73.

[11] Dalcho, p. 73. See also the chapter on Christ Church Parish, this volume.

[12] Dalcho, pp. 77-78; Gideon Johnston to Gilbert Burnet, Bishop of Sarum, September 20, 1708, *Carolina Chronicle*, p. 21.

[13] Johnston, *Ibid.*, p. 22.

[14] *Dictionary of American Biography*, ed. Dumas Malone (New York: Charles Scribners, 1933), X, 141; Margaret Simons Middleton, *Henrietta Johnston: America's First Pastellist* (Columbia: University of South Carolina Press, 1966), passim.

[15] Gideon Johnston to the SPG, July 5, 1710, *Chronicles*, p. 35.

[16] South Carolina Clergy to the Society, May 31, 1716, in Johnston, *Chronicles*, pp. 167-168.

[17] Francis LeJau to John Robinson, Bishop of London, June 7, 1716, in *Chronicles*, p. 169; *Dictionary of American Biography*, X, 141.

[18] *Statutes*, VII, 56.

[19] The act is listed in *Statutes*, III, 111, but the text is omitted. Dalcho published the entire text of the act on pp. 458-459. In 1765, Charles Woodmason described St. Philip's as "the most elegant Religious Edifice in British America....It was built from the model of the Jesuits Church at Antwerp." Charles Woodmason, *The Carolina Backcountry on the Eve of the Revolution: The Journal and Other Writings of Charles Woodmason, Anglican Itinerant*, ed. Richard B. Hooker (Chapel Hill: University of North Carolina Press, 1953), p. 70; Anna Wells Rutledge, "The Second St. Philip's Charleston, 1710-1835," *Journal of the Society of Architectural Historians*, 18 (October 1959), 112.

[20] Rebecca Talbert Fouché, "St. Philip's Episcopal Church, Charleston, South Carolina: The Building and Its Architectural History," Master's Thesis, University of South Carolina, 1979, p. 43.

[21] Dalcho states that the church was not opened before 1727, but Robert Mills stated that the first service was in 1723. See Dalcho, p.120; Robert Mills, *Statistics of South Carolina* (Charleston: Hurlbut and Lloyd, 1826), p. 23; Minutes of the Vestry of St. Philip's Church, August 28, 1732, p. 5, WPA Typescript, Mf. SCDAH.

[22] Mills, *Statistics*, p. 23.

[23] Minutes of the Vestry, July 17, 1732, p. 4; April 25, 1737, p. 26; July 14, 1736, p. 19; December 31, 1735, p. 17; February 27, 1737, p. 33; February 25, 1739, p. 48; Woodmason, *Carolina Backcountry*, p. 70.

[24] S. Charles Bolton, *Southern Anglicanism: The Church of England in Colonial South Carolina* (Westport, CN: Greenwood Press, 1982), pp. 42-43, 60; Letter of clergy, n.d., A16: 76-78, as cited in Bolton, p. 42.

[25] Bolton, *Southern Anglicanism*, pp. 50-55; Dalcho, *Protestant Episcopal Church*, 129-145, passim. On the Stono Rebellion, see Peter Wood, *Black Majority* (New York: W. W. Norton, 1974), p. 308.

[26] Bolton, *Southern Anglicanism*, p. 54; Minutes of the Vestry, pp. 58-72; J. H. Easterby and Ruth S. Green, eds., *The Colonial Records of South Carolina, Series I: The Journal of the Commons House of Assembly, 1736-1750*, 9 vols. (Columbia: South Carolina Historical Commission, 1951-62), 2: 408-409.

[27] Bolton, *Southern Anglicanism*, pp.116-119.

[28] Fouche, "St. Philip's," pp. 65, 78-80; Dalcho, *Protestant Episcopal Church*, p. 171.

One of three principal entrances leading to the church tower and sanctuary of St. Philip's Church.

(Top) The Church in St. Andrew's Parish, *watercolor by Charles Fraser, April, 1800.*
(Bottom) The church, on the west bank of the Ashley River, is the oldest extant Anglican church in South Carolina.

ST. ANDREW'S PARISH

Almighty God, who gave such grace to your apostle Andrew that he readily obeyed the call of your Son Jesus Christ, and brought his brother with him: Give us, who are called by your holy Word, grace to follow him without delay, and to bring those near to us into his gracious presence; who lives and reigns with you and the Holy Spirit, one God, now and for ever. Amen.

Prayer for St. Andrew's Day, Book of Common Prayer

On St. Andrew's Day, November 30, 1706, the Assembly of South Carolina passed "An Act for the Establishment of Religious Worship...according to the Church of England...." The act included provisions for erecting churches, maintaining ministers, and building convenient houses for them. Among the parishes created by the act was "One upon Ashley River, which shall be called by the name of St. Andrew's," and so it happened that the parish honoring the Apostle Andrew was established on the day set aside to honor him. The parish extended from the Atlantic Ocean to the northwest boundary of Berkeley County, north to the boundary of St. James' Goose Creek Parish, and south to Colleton County.[1]

Parishioners apparently began building the church prior to the ratification of the act on July 30, 1707. Church historian Frederick Dalcho reported in 1820 that a red tile over the door opposite the chancel showed the inscription J.F.: T.R., SUPER. VI, 1706, signifying that Jonathan Fitch and Thomas Rose supervised the construction. Due to later repairs, the tile is no longer visible.[2]

Fitch had inherited "Andrews," a plantation on the Ashley, from his father, who immigrated prior to 1678, and he later obtained other substantial tracts. A member of the Assembly which passed the Church Act, Fitch became one of the commissioners appointed to implement it. There were several men named Thomas Rose in the province in the early 1700s. It is likely that the building supervisor was an Ashley River planter, and it is not known whether he was also the Thomas Rose who served as clerk of the Assembly from 1692 to 1705.[3]

The original brick building of St. Andrew's Church was forty feet by twenty-five feet with a roof made of pine. It had five small square windows which suggest an arrangement of two casement windows on each side and one at the chancel end. The inside was not finely finished, but the parish boasted seven acres adjoining the church to be used as a cemetery.[4]

The Reverend Alexander Wood, a missionary sent by the Society for the Propagation of the Gospel, arrived in 1707. Francis LeJau, a colleague in the ministry, called him "...a Gentleman of Great Parts, and Sweet humour." LeJau said, "I was very sorry when he told me that little or no care was taken of him in the parish...and twou'd be a Loss to this province that he shou'd be forced away."[5]

When Wood died within about three years, Commissary Gideon Johnston recruited Ebenezer Taylor, a Presbyterian. Taylor traveled to England for ordination, and with Johnston's recommendation, he became rector of St. Andrew's as a missionary for the Society for the Propagation of the Gospel. Somehow, Taylor could not seem to adhere to the Anglican liturgy, and his parishioners (who were accustomed to the formal language of the Book of Common Prayer) accused him of "entering into a long and unmanerly Expostulation with God Almighty, after the Method of the meanest and most ignorant of the Presbyterians." They also complained that he was "...so sordidly covetous that he is an offense to modesty...not allowing himself britches or stockings...." To the modern reader, such an accusation might sound as though the poor man couldn't keep his pants on. Actually, the vestry was probably saying that Taylor wore the loose fitting trousers of laborers rather than the fashionable knee britches with stockings favored by the gentry. A more serious accusation was his "removing the pulpit from the proper place and placing it before the communion table."[6]

The use of three distinct liturgical centers—the pulpit, the communion table, and the font—distinguished the Anglican church from the dissenter meetinghouse. Taylor's attempt at fusing two of these centers did not please his parishioners. Also, the placement of the pulpit in front of the altar was contrary to Anglican protocol. Another problem may have been that Taylor baptized fifty blacks.[7]

The parishioners did not stop by merely complaining, but proceeded to harass the minister. Taylor complained to the Society for the Propagation of the Gospel that someone drew out all the nails of the bench to his desk except one, "which he left just to keep it up." Taylor believed the deed was done on purpose so that he might fall down on the floor "...and all the People might set up a laughter at it, & I might make sport for them in the church." Taylor considered it "a very prophane & wicked trick." The parishioners also broke the pins where he hung his hat and took away his kneeling bench so that he had to kneel on the bare bricks while serving communion. He preached in fear that someone would loosen the canopy over the pulpit and it would crash down on his head. Taylor was so exasperated that he lapsed into Latin and exclaimed, "*Proh monstrum horrendum ingens cui lumen ademptum!*"[8] He continued in English, "Oh what a monstrous, horrid, great and graceless Merry Andrew's Trick was this!" The Society soon transferred Taylor to North Carolina.[9]

The next rector, William Guy, was much more popular. He had previously served as assistant rector of St. Philip's and head of the free school in Charleston. He was rector of St. Helena's in Beaufort when the Yamassee War forced his removal. After a brief residence in Narragansett,

In stark contrast to the wealth of the Ashley River planters in the antebellum period, the parish faced hard times after the Civil War.

Rhode Island, he returned to South Carolina and became rector of St. Andrew's in December 1718. Despite the fact that the upper part of the parish had been separated to form St. George's Parish, Dorchester, in 1717, St. Andrews enjoyed a period of growth and prosperity under Guy's leadership.[10]

The prosperity of the parish is reflected in the action of the Assembly which authorized a fair and markets in Ashley River Ferry Town near the church. Public markets would be open on Wednesdays and Saturdays, and fairs would open for four days in May and September. Fairs not only offered an opportunity for purchasing needed goods, but also provided sporting events such as shooting contests, bear baiting, horse racing, chasing a soaped pig, and pulling the head off a goose at full gallop. Sadly, cruelty to animals was not a consideration in that era.[11]

In 1723, prosperity also enabled parishioners to enlarge the church to the form of a cross by adding a transept, twenty-four by fifty-two feet, to the rectangular building. They also added a chancel of twelve by twenty-four feet. Builders removed the old pine roof and replaced it with cypress to match the new addition. William Guy said that it was "...well arch'd ceiled and plaister'd,...adorned and beautify'd with neat cedar pews, a large east end window, well glaz'd with two others, on each side of the communion table." Included in the remodeling plan was a gallery "design'd to be built forthwith at the west end for those people who have no pews, and the outside all to be roughcast with all convenient speed." Guy mentioned plans for a steeple, but there is no evidence that the plans ever materialized. Later documentation indicates that building the gallery may have been delayed as well. A baptismal font on a pedestal would stand just inside the entrance.[12]

The traditional location of the font at the entrance symbolized the entrance of the faithful into the community of faith through the sacrament of baptism. Since there is no door in the north transept, it is likely that the pulpit sat in the northeast corner of the crossing. The large window in the chancel marked it as the setting for Holy Communion. In his letter of 1728, William Guy did not mention the four tablets: two for the Decalogue, and one each for the Apostles' Creed and the Lord's Prayer, but it is possible that they were added during his tenure. Two of the tablets are rounded at the top.[13]

The ceiling, windows, and tablets, all arched, act in a symbolic way to identify the building as sacred space. In eighteenth-century South Carolina, arched ceilings and compass-headed windows, if not totally reserved for churches, were seldom used in secular construction. The shape of the Latin cross in the footprint of the building further sets it apart as sacred.[14]

William Guy reported that the parsonage was a small board house "in pretty good repair." Due to the generosity of William Bull and William Cattell in advancing a loan, the parish added sixty acres to the original twenty-six acre glebe, or farmland provided for the use of the minister. Guy estimated the white population of the parish in 1728 at about 800 total or 200 families along with about 1800 slaves. He could report very little effort to instruct the slaves in religion. In 1724 he said, "There are a great number of slaves, but scarce any free, all the means I use for their conversion is to show their Mrs. their obligations to this purpose, but few or none will be prevailed upon."[15]

William Guy died in 1751, and the Society sent the Reverend Charles Martyn in 1752. Martyn was very strict about keeping the Sabbath, and he complained that during the indigo season some of his parishioners profaned the Lord's day by carrying on the usual work of the plantations. Nevertheless, Eliza Pinckney, noted for encouraging the indigo industry in the province, said of Martyn, "He is a very worthy man and a Gentleman of great politeness as well as learning."[16] During Martyn's tenure, the Assembly formally recognized the chapel built by the inhabitants on James Island as an established chapel of ease for St. Andrew's Church and required the minister to preach there every fourth Sunday. The chapel had been in use at least since 1733, when William Guy reported that the chapel which had blown down in a hurricane was rebuilt. The Assembly made it an official chapel of ease in 1756.[17]

There is a long-standing tradition which is often quoted that St. Andrew's Church was destroyed by fire in 1764. Two sources add credence to the tradition. Charles Woodmason wrote an account of the churches in the South in 1765 in which he stated that St. Andrew's "was lately consum'd by Fire, but is rebuilt, and is a pretty Edifice. It has an Organ."[18] Frederick Dalcho, author of a church history pub-

Four panels—two for the Decalogue and one each for the Apostles' Creed and the Lord's Prayer—ornament the reredos behind the altar of St. Andrews's.

lished in 1820, stated that the church was destroyed by fire and rebuilt by subscriptions of the inhabitants. The Assembly passed an act on August 10, 1764, authorizing the churchwardens and vestry to sell the pews.[19] William Izard Bull of Ashley Hall plantation, vestryman and warden from 1833 to 1865, supervised the remodeling of the church in 1855. He wrote that Dalcho had been "at fault and very egregiously so, in this case, as to St. Andrew's Church, as it was never burnt." Bull's family had lived in the vicinity since the late seventeenth century, and based on family traditions and his own observations during remodeling he insisted that the church had never burned. When parishioners again restored the church between 1967 and 1970, the pavers in the floor were cracked and loosely set in sand. Upon removing them, workmen found small pavers underneath and combined the two types in the present floor. George Tompkins, the rector in 1998 and an avid historian, believes the small pavers were from the original 1706 building. Tompkins has carefully inspected the building and has found no sign of a fire. If there was a fire, it did not completely destroy the edifice. St. Andrew's is recognized as the oldest Anglican church building in South Carolina.

In stark contrast to the opulence of the Ashley River planters in the antebellum period, the parish faced hard times after the Civil War. In addition to problems brought about by war and Reconstruction, rice planters faced a major decline in their economic base.[20] The diocese classified the church as dormant in 1893. There were intermittent services through the years, and in 1955, the church regained parish status. In 1998, it is active and flourishing. The example of St. Andrew, who not only followed Christ but brought his brother with him, remains a challenge for future growth.[21]

[1] Thomas Cooper, *Statutes at Large of South Carolina* (Columbia: A. S. Johnson, 1838), II, 236; hereinafter cited as *Statutes*.

[2] Frederick Dalcho, *An Historical Account of the Protestant Episcopal Church in South Carolina* (Charleston: E. Thayer, 1820; rpt., New York: Arno Press, 1970), p. 338.

[3] Walter B. Edgar, ed., *Biographical Directory of the South Carolina House of Representatives* (Columbia: University of South Carolina Press, 1977), II, 251, 568-569.

[4] William Guy to the Secretary of the SPG, Library of Congress, Transcripts of the Papers of the SPG, pertaining to South Carolina, Series A:20 #110; microfilm South Carolina Department of Archives and History, hereinafter cited as SPG MS.

[5] Francis LeJau to the SPG, March 13, 1708, in Frank Klingsberg, ed., *The Carolina Chronicle of Dr. Francis LeJau, 1706-1717* (Berkeley: University of California Press, 1956), pp. 34-35.

[6] Frank J. Klingberg, ed., *Carolina Chronicle: The Papers of Commissary Gideon Johnston, 1707-1716* (Berkeley: University of California Press, 1946), p. 96; "Some reasons Humbly Offered...by the Parishioners of St. Andrew's Why Mr. Ebenezer Taylor Should no Longer Be Suffered to Officiate in the Said Parish," n.d., SPG Transcripts, A:13, 144-145, as cited in S. Charles Bolton, *Southern Anglicanism: The Church of England in Colonial South Carolina* (Westport, CN: Greenwood Press, 1982), p. 90.

[7] Louis P. Nelson, "South Carolina Anglican: the architecture of the Lowcountry plantation parishes," Draft of November 17, 1997, Diocese of South Carolina, p. 20; The Reverend Canon Michael T. Malone to Hugh Lane and Mills Lane, December 5, 1997, commentary on Nelson's work. The SPG encouraged conversion of slaves, but some masters objected. Taylor baptized the slaves of Alexander Skene that had been taught with his approval by his sister and others on the plantation. Bolton, *Southern Anglicanism*, p.110.

[8] Oh, alas, it was a horrible, unnatural potent by which the light was driven away.

[9] Ebenezer Taylor to the SPG, March 24, 1717, SPG MS, A:13, pp. 128-129 [letter number not given]. "Merry Andrew" was a clownlike character who performed at English fairs.

[10] George Tompkins, "A Church Shall be Built Upon Ashley River: A History of Old St. Andrew's Parish Church," MS, on file at the church; *Statutes*, III, 10; Mabel L. Webber, "Register of St. Andrews Parish, Berkeley County, South Carolina," *South Carolina Historical Magazine*, 12:172.

[11] *Statutes*, III, 217; Hennig Cohen, *The South Carolina Gazette, 1732-1775* (Columbia: University of South Carolina Press, 1953), pp. 73, 79.

[12] William Guy to the Society, January 22, 1728, SPG MS, A:20 #110, SCDAH, also quoted in H. Roy Merrens, *The Colonial South Carolina Scene* (Columbia: University of South Carolina Press, 1977), pp. 81-86. Directions are given according to liturgical practice, assuming that the nave runs east and west, and the transept north and south. Actual compass readings vary somewhat.

Tompkins, "A Church Shall be Built...," p. 1. Charles Martyn, rector, noted that the church had begun a subscription for a gallery and an organ in 1754. Dalcho, *Protestant Episcopal Church*, pp. 338, 340.

[13] Nelson, "South Carolina Anglican," p. 49.

[14] See Dell Upton, *Holy things and Profane: Anglican Parish Churches in Colonial Virginia* (The Architectural History Foundation, 1986), pp. 114-118; as cited in Nelson, "South Carolina Anglican," p. 49.

[15] William Guy to SPG, March 17, 1724, MS Copy in files of St. Andrew's Church as cited in Tompkins, "A Church Shall Be Built...," p. 7; Guy to SPG, January 22, 1728, SPG MS, A:20 #110.

[16] Elise Pinckney, ed., *The Letterbook of Eliza Lucas Pinckney, 1739-1762* (Columbia: University of South Carolina Press), p. 170.

[17] Dalcho, *An Historical Account*, pp. 339-340. This building was destroyed in the Revolution, but was rebuilt and in 1831 became St. James', James Island. Albert S. Thomas, *A Historical Account of the Protestant Episcopal Church in South Carolina 1820-1957* (Columbia: R. L. Bryan, 1957), p. 333.

[18] Charles Woodmason, *The Carolina Backcountry on the Eve of the Revolution: The Journal and Other Writings of Charles Woodmason, Anglican Itinerant*, ed. Richard J. Hooker (Chapel Hill: University of North Carolina Press, 1953), p. 71.

[19] Dalcho, *An Historical Account*, p. 342. Dalcho does not say what evidence he had that the church burned.

[20] Walter B. Edgar, *South Carolina, A History* (Columbia: University of South Carolina Press, 1998), p. 429.

[21] Tompkins, "A Church Shall Be Built...," pp. 24-25, 27, 30; also interview with the author, April 21, 1998.

(Top) A View of St. James' Church, Goose Creek, from the Parsonage, watercolor by Charles Fraser about 1800.
(Bottom) The church is decorated in the baroque style. The pelican above the door symbolized Christ's sacrifice on the cross.

ST. JAMES' PARISH, GOOSE CREEK

How firm a foundation, ye saints of the Lord,
Is laid for your faith in his excellent word!
What more can he say than to you he hath said,
To you that for refuge to Jesus have fled?

K. in John Rippon's *Selection of Hymns*, 1787

The Reverend Francis LeJau, the first missionary from the Society for the Propagation of the Gospel sent to the parish of St. James' Goose Creek, was a devout and dedicated minister who truly lived the gospel that he preached. He came from La Rochelle, a Huguenot stronghold in France, from which he and his family fled in 1685 after the revocation of the Edict of Nantes, the law that had protected Protestants from prosecution. LeJau found refuge in England and joined the Anglican Church. He received the M.A. and B.D. degrees from Trinity College, Dublin, Ireland. By 1700, he also had achieved the Doctor of Divinity degree. A master of six languages and an acknowledged scholar, he became a canon of St. Paul's Cathedral in London, and he seemed to have a bright future in the hierarchy of the English church. Instead, he chose the mission field, and in 1700 he went to the island of St. Christopher's in the Caribbean for eighteen months. There he lived in an unfinished thatched hut made of wild cane and worked with a few planters and two thousand slaves.[1]

In October 1706, LeJau arrived in South Carolina after a journey of some three months. Samuel Thomas, the first missionary to the province as a whole, had recently died. Thomas, based at Goose Creek, preached at various sites on the Cooper River, and his death left a vacancy in a well-settled part of the province. The Church Act, passed November 30, 1706, established ten parishes including one at Goose Creek, and LeJau became the first rector.[2]

The family of the lately deceased Colonel James Moore invited the Anglican missionary to stay with them until the parsonage could be prepared. Moore had served as governor of the province and was a wealthy and well-established planter. It was a comfortable beginning. LeJau wrote, "Gentility politeness and a handsome way of Living this Colony exceeds what I have seen....For this is the finest Climate I ever saw, the Soil produces everything without much trouble, and at this time the weather is finer than in Aprill with you in England."[3]

At the Moore plantation, LeJau entered the milieu of the "Goose Creek Men," a political faction dominated by Barbadian planters who opposed the proprietary government. The Barbadians had come to South Carolina with first-hand experience in plantation management, and they knew what it took to succeed. They were tough, experienced, and driven; and they could be ruthless in doing whatever would make them successful, whether it was engaging in the illicit Indian slave trade or trafficking with pirates. James Moore had arrived in South Carolina sometime before February of 1675, and by his death in 1706, he was a very wealthy man. Other Goose Creek planters had been similarly fortunate, and their accumulated wealth would enable Francis LeJau to lead his parish in building an unusually beautiful and ornate parish church in the baroque style.[4]

The baroque was popular in Europe from 1600 to 1750. The missionary was undoubtedly familiar with Sir Christopher Wren's plan for St. Paul's Cathedral, which was under construction when LeJau served as a canon there. The ornate baroque style apparently appealed to the minister's sense of what was appropriate for the house of God as well as to the expensive tastes of the wealthy Goose Creek planters.[5]

The parishioners met on Easter Monday, April 14, 1707, to organize pursuant to the church act. They elected Robert Stevens and John Sanders wardens, and the vestrymen were Ralph Izard, George Cantey, James Moore, Arthur Middleton, John Cantey, William Williams, and David Deas. By September, LeJau was writing to the SPG that the church building was "too little and not solid." He continued, "We are making bricks to build incessantly...."[6]

With LeJau's leadership, the building began in 1708, but progressed very slowly. In April 1714, he wrote to the Society that it was not likely to be finished soon. The Yamassee War broke out in 1715, and undoubtedly delayed the process, but by January 1717, he wrote that he expected the church to be finished within a few months. LeJau died in September 1717 at age 52 after a long and painful illness. Finally, in July 1719, the vestry noted that the church was completely finished and since there was no bishop in America to consecrate it, they resolved to dedicate the building and set it apart from all temporal uses.[7]

It was unfortunate that LeJau did not live to officiate in the completed sanctuary that he was very influential in building. His long and detailed letters to the Society provide a record of his ministry and also an eyewitness account of South Carolina in the decade from 1707 to 1717. LeJau described the isolation of life in the colony with difficulties of travel and communications so slow that a letter sent one year might not be answered until a year or more later. He sent a son to fight in the Yamassee War and told of the danger of attack, the shortages of food, and the terrible inflation that resulted from the war. The minister was also sensitive to the injustices to the Indians which led to the attacks.[8]

LeJau protested against the cruelties he observed, such as an Indian slave woman who was scalped at the instigation of her master and left to die in the woods. He also reported "the Cruel burning alive of a poor Negroe Woman which all of us thought to be innocent of a Crime she was accused of." When the woman's master drowned, LeJau interpreted it as God's judgement.

The missionary ministered to the slaves as best he could. On Sundays, he invited them, if their masters would permit, to stay for half an hour after worship for instruction in the Creed, the Lord's Prayer, and the Ten Commandments. About fifty participated, and he said, "I give them an entire Liberty to ask questions, I endeavour to proportion my answers and all my Instructions to their want and capacity." He noted that the most pious of the masters stayed to listen. The missionary found that "the good example of some truely Religious Masters is a check upon the others, the Alteration is so considerable of late that in general very few masters excepted, the Slaves shall be fed and provided for...."[9]

LeJau encouraged the Society to establish a school at Goose Creek. Benjamin Dennis, schoolmaster, arrived in 1711 to teach grammar, reading, and simple arithmetic. In January 1712, Dennis wrote to the Society that he had twenty-nine scholars, six of whom he taught without charge: two blacks, two Indians, and two whites. Dennis struggled with fever, ague, and a broken thigh bone. In June, he learned that his wife and children, who were on the way to join him in South Carolina, had been on board a ship that was plundered by French privateers. Having received word of their capture by a report from a passing pilot boat, Dennis wrote, "I fear [they were] either taken and carried off or Else castaway. Pray God grant me Patience to go through all my hardships and disappointments." Fortunately, by August 28, he could report, "My ffamily arrived here the 16th Instant after Suffering very much by ye ffrench and the fateagues of a tedius Voyage." Dennis's problems were not over. He served as a soldier in the Yamassee War in 1715. The war caused a dispersal of his students, and eventually he asked for a transfer to Charleston.[10]

Recovery from the Yamassee War was slow, but by 1719, the congregation could worship in the new church. The rectangular brick building is defined by quoins at the corners and generous arch-topped windows. The stucco on the exterior probably dates from 1810, when the vestry advertised in the *Charleston Courier* that they would receive proposals for roughcasting their parish church. The double doors of the west elevation are flanked by Doric pilasters, similar to columns, which support an entablature decorated with a row of flaming hearts, suggesting the utmost in religious zeal with St. Augustine often given as an example. The flaming heart might recall the disciples who met the risen

The reredos of painted plaster behind the altar dominates the interior of St. James'.

An earlier photo of the church.

Christ on the road to Emmaus and said, "Did not our hearts burn within us while he talked to us on the road, while he opened to us the scriptures?" (Luke 24:32) The flaming heart motif is also found in the devotional book of Edward Brailsford, one of the parishioners of St. James', who recorded the following prayer to be prayed when in church: "Being now in thy presence, O God, give me grace, to entertain heavenly meditations, and seriously to attend to thy sacred word, and obediently to practice the same, through Jesus Christ our Lord. Amen."[11]

The overall decoration of the church was designed to encourage such "heavenly meditations." Just over the west entrance is the "pelican in her piety." The legendary pelican has the greatest love of all creatures for its young and pierces its breast to feed them with its own blood. Based on this legend, the pelican came to symbolize Christ's sacrifice on the cross and thus also the sacrament of the Eucharist.[12] The windows on either side of the double doors are arch-topped. The winged cherub heads resting at the top of the window architraves are reminiscent of the cherub-topped arches in the nave of St. Paul's Cathedral in London as well as the decorations of the south portico. St. Paul's was nearing completion when Francis LeJau served there, but since cherubs were a common decorative feature in the baroque period, there may have been no connection.[13]

Although there is no documentary evidence to show whether or not the plaster decorations of the church are original, the fact that Francis LeJau was rector during the building process would indicate that they are. The strong faith and devotion of LeJau as well as his dedication to the ideologies of Anglican Christianity would lend credence to the assumption that he had a major influence in choosing the symbolism. The reredos of painted plaster behind the altar dominates the interior. Twin Corinthian pilasters flank a tall arched window and support an entablature and broken pediment framing the arms of the three King Georges with a lion rampant and a unicorn on either side of a shield. Tradition states that the presence of the royal arms protected the church during the Revolution, for it was the only Anglican country church in the province that the British Army did not profane. The arms of the Gibbes family with a memorial to Colonel John Gibbes, who died in 1711, appear to the right of the pulpit. The hatchment of the Izard family hangs from the gallery. In English custom, when the head of the family was buried, the hatchment or arms preceded the coffin. After the funeral the family hung the hatchment in the church.[14]

Over the chancel window are the words GLORY TO GOD ON HIGH ON EARTH PEACE GOOD WILL TOWARDS MEN. On the window ledge behind the communion table is COME UNTO ME ALL YE WHO LABOUR AND ARE HEAVY LADEN FOR I AM MEEK AND LOWLY IN HEART AND YE SHALL FIND REST UNTO YOUR SOULS. Marble tablets given by William Middleton in 1758 contain the Ten Commandments, the Apostles' Creed, and the Lord's Prayer. Just above the pilasters on either side of the altar are other scriptural texts. Facing the altar, to the left is a passage from Acts 8: 32: HE

WAS LED AS A SHEEP TO THE SLAUGHTER AND, LIKE A LAMB DUMB BEFORE HIS SHEARER, SO OPENED HE NOT HIS MOUTH. On the opposite side appear words from John 1:29: BEHOLD YE LAMB OF GOD WHO TAKEST AWAY THE SINS OF THE WORLD. Restorers rediscovered the two texts above the pilasters in 1977.[15]

The current pulpit is not original to the building. Archaeological evidence indicates that the original pulpit stood on the south side about twelve feet back from the altar end of the church. Remains of a posthole under the floor and a wrought iron hook in the ceiling that may have supported a sounding board at this location lend credence to this assumption.[16] Placement of the pulpit along the south wall would be much more consistent with eighteenth-century custom than the current location directly in front of the altar, obscuring the chancel window and the texts painted around it.

The interior of the church gives evidence that amateurs, not professional architects, designed it. Tall colonnades which support the roof run at both ends into windows. The gallery, originally for strangers or poor white people and later used by slaves, cuts into the lines of the front door. But, according to architectural historian Samuel G. Stoney, "With all these egregious neglects of proper designing the building's charm carries our minds and eyes past and over its failings."[17]

Francis LeJau, the moving force behind the building of St. James', lies buried beneath the altar. His voluminous letters provide a composite picture of pioneer efforts in South Carolina—from the ambition and wealth of the Goose Creek men to the humble needs of the exploited black and Indian slaves. LeJau met all problems with humility and compassion. His career was an example of the Anglican missionary spirit at its best.[18]

His successor was not as exemplary. Francis Merry arrived in 1720 and was delighted to find that the church was "a beautiful brick edifice" and that a contribution of Benjamin Schenckingh had provided one hundred acres of good glebe land. The vestry refused to elect Merry rector, and in 1722, Commissary William Tredwell Bull explained to the Society that Merry gave great offense by drinking to excess "which he is so frequent of withal so abusive, that He hath lost the good will of all his Friends & is become an open Scandal to his profession."[19]

The Society sent the Reverend Richard Ludlam to Goose Creek in 1723, and he became much loved and respected. He spent much of his time working with slaves and reported that his parishioners were generally sober, well disposed, and attentive to public worship. Ludlam reported to the Society in 1724 that a chapel of ease was under construction. Located at Wassamassaw about seven miles south of Strawberry Ferry, the chapel was of brick in a cruciform pattern. Ludlam planned to officiate there every three weeks. At his death in October 1728, he left his entire estate of about £2000 to establish a school.[20]

Throughout the years, a number of folk tales regarding the old church have entered the vernacular. The known graves in the cemetery date from 1757, but undoubtedly many of the earlier markers have not survived. The tombstones attest to the fact that the average male life span was thirty-eight years, and the average female life was forty years. Before the availability of modern medical instruments, it was difficult to tell the difference between deep coma and death. The story is told that a young woman was thought dead and placed in a coffin in the family vault. The slave boy who had to carry water regularly to the church heard screams in the days following the funeral, but he was too frightened to tell anyone. When he finally got the courage to tell his master, the vault was opened, and the horrified family found that the young woman had somehow pushed her way out of the coffin only to die at the door of the vault. There are no documentary records to tell who she was, but the vault opposite the west door of the church reads, "Here Lies the Body of Elizabeth Ann Smith, the Amiable and Deservedly Beloved Wife of Captain Benjamin Smith Who died the 26 March 1769 aged 27 years...."[21]

In the years preceding and during the Revolution, the Reverend Edward Ellington was rector. A contemporary account calls him pious, talented, eloquent, and zealous in his parochial duties. He was also enterprising. When the Goose Creek bridge was temporarily out, Ellington undertook to supply ferry service by procuring a flat and providing a ferryman. One wagoner complained vociferously about paying a stiff fee for such a short crossing. The next time the wagoner appeared, Ellington instructed his ferryman to take the flat up and down the creek several times. He then inquired of the wagoner if he thought he had gotten his money's worth. The minister explained that he was simply trying to help out, and anyone who wished could take the long way around.[22]

Perhaps the best known story of Goose Creek is that of the wedding of "Mad Archie" Campbell and a beautiful heiress, Paulina Philp. Campbell was a dashing British officer stationed at Charleston during the Revolution. Having wagered with his friends that he could marry the young lady within three days, Campbell asked her to go for a ride in the country. He raced his horses to Goose Creek, where he drew his pistol and forced Reverend Edward Ellington to marry them. The couple spent a year of marriage at Exeter Plantation before Captain Campbell was killed at the battle of Videau's Bridge. Their daughter, Margaret, later married Robert Deas. Paulina's descendants declared that she was madly in love with the dashing officer and never regretted the hasty marriage.[23]

St. James' Church, Goose Creek still stands today, a baroque gem in a secluded area within a densely populated part of Charleston County. Once a year friends of the parish gather for an annual service. Ethel Simons is a descendant of several generations of caretakers of the church. She lives on the premises and has devoted her life to protecting the historic sanctuary.

The old parish church is more than an important national historic monument. It is a testament to the faith and dedication to God of the early missionaries who risked shipwreck, capture by pirates, death by disease or malnutrition, and massacre by Indians to preach the Word in the wilderness and to promote the firm foundation of the Anglican Church in South Carolina. In memory of Francis LeJau and his successors, let us say, "Alleluia!"

[1]H. P. Thompson, *Into All Lands: The History of the Society for the Propagation of the Gospel in Foreign Parts, 1701-1950* (London, 1951), pp. 157-158; as cited in Francis LeJau, *The Carolina Chronicle of Dr. Francis LeJau, 1706-1717*, ed. Frank Klingberg (Millwood, NY: Kraus Reprint, 1980), pp. 4, 10-11.

[2]Frederick Dalcho, *An Historical Account of the Protestant Episcopal Church in South Carolina* (Charleston: E. Thayer, 1820; rpt. New York: Arno Press, 1970), pp. 244-245.

[3]LeJau, *Carolina Chronicle*, p. 18.

[4]Walter B. Edgar, *South Carolina, A History* (Columbia: University of South Carolina Press, 1998), pp. 84-85, 152-154; Walter B. Edgar and N. Louise Bailey, *Biographical Dictionary of the South Carolina House of Representatives* (Columbia: University of South Carolina Press, 1977), pp. 466-468.

[5]Horst W. Janson, *History of Art* (New York: Harry N. Abrams, 1984), pp. 483, 540-542. Some critics attribute the baroque to the Counter Reformation, the Catholic response to the Protestant Reformation, but it was also popular in countries that were primarily Protestant.

[6]Dalcho, *Protestant Episcopal Church*, p. 245; LeJau to the Secretary of the SPG, September 23, 1707, in *Chronicles*, p. 31.

[7]LeJau to John Chamberlain [?], and LeJau to the Secretary, both on April 20, 1714; LeJau to Secretary David Humphreys, January 3, 1717; Thomas Hasell to the Society, September 20, 1717, 204-205, in *Chronicles*, pp. 139-140, 192.

[8]LeJau, *Chronicles*, p. 205.

[9]LeJau to the Secretary, June 13, 1710, in *Chronicles*, pp. 76-78.

[10]Benjamin Dennis to the Society, June 7, 1712, SPG MS, A7 #20; July 24, 1712, A7 #21; August 28, 1712, A7 #22, Mf, South Carolina Department of Archives and History; Dalcho, *Protestant Episcopal Church*, p. 248; LeJau to the Society, November 28, 1715, in *Chronicles*, p. 170.

[11]Louis Nelson, "South Carolina Anglican: the architecture of the Lowcountry plantation parishes," Draft of November 17, 1997, Diocese of South Carolina, p. 23; *Charleston Courier*, September 26, 1810, as cited in Nelson. George Ferguson, *Signs & Symbols in Christian Art* (New York: Oxford University Press, 1958), p. 27; Devotional Book of Edward Brailsford, MS, South Caroliniana Library, University of South Carolina, p. 20.

[12]Ferguson, *Signs and Symbols*, p. 9.

[13]C. W. Shepherd, *Everyone's St. Paul's* (New York: Frederick Warne, 1966), plates 5 & 26.

[14]Nelson, "South Carolina Anglican," p. 24; Mills Lane, *Architecture of the Old South: South Carolina* (Savannah, GA: Beehive Press, 1997), pp. 17-20; Michael J. Heitzler, *Historic Goose Creek, South Carolina, 1670-1980* (Easley, SC: Southern Historical Press, 1983), pp. 178-179, 242.

[15]Nelson, "South Carolina Anglican," pp. 24-25; Richard Marks, restoration contractor, interview with the author, September 3, 1998.

[16]*Ibid.*; Martha Zierden, Archaeologist of the Charleston Museum, interview with the author, September 2, 1998. When Dalcho wrote his history in 1820, the pulpit had already been moved to the center of the chancel. See Dalcho, *Protestant Episcopal Church*, p. 250.

[17]Samuel Gaillard Stoney, *Plantations of the Carolina Low Country* (Charleston: Carolina Art Association, 1964), p. 50.

[18]See testimonials to LeJau in *Chronicles*, pp. 204-205.

[19]Francis Merry to the Society, November 3, 1722, B4-1 #127; William Tredwell Bull to the Society, October 29, 1722, SPG MS, B4-1 #126.

[20]Dalcho, *Protestant Episcopal Church*, p. 253; Heitzler, *Historic Goose Creek*, pp. 199-200; Church of England, Bishop of London, Fulham Palace Correspondence, 1703-1769, IX, #168, 1724; William Guy to the Society, January 22, 1727, SPG MS, A20, p. 115; as cited in Nelson, "South Carolina Anglican," pp. 62-62.

[21]Heitzler, *Historic Goose Creek*, p. 209.

[22]Heitzler, p. 190.

[23]Heitzler, pp. 210-212; John B. Irving and Louisa Cheves Stoney, *A Day on Cooper River* (Columbia: R. L. Bryan, 1969), p. 133; Suzanne Linder, *Historical Atlas of the Rice Plantations of the ACE River Basin, 1860,* (Columbia: South Carolina Department of Archives and History, 1995), pp. 135, 195; "Memoranda of Title to Clay Hall, etc.," Langdon Cheves Papers, South Carolina Historical Society; Marriage Settlements, III, 314, SCDAH.

Christ Church, Mt. Pleasant, South Carolina, built in 1726, was burned in both the Revolutionary and Civil Wars. It was rebuilt on the original walls.

CHRIST CHURCH PARISH

Blessed is the man that walketh not in the counsel of the ungodly,
nor standeth in the way of sinners,
nor sitteth in the seat of the scornful.
But his delight is in the law of the Lord;
and in his law doth he meditate day and night.

Psalm 1: 1-2

Christ Church Parish was very much in tune with Anglican policy. Whereas problems arose with other parishes about rules for worship such as kneeling to receive communion, having godparents for christenings, or using the Book of Common Prayer, Christ Church complied without question. Likewise, other parishes refused to elect the minister as rector because he would then have tenure and some measure of autonomy, but Christ Church regularly elected the rector unless some obvious problem existed. Despite occasional difficulties with the behavior of ministers, the regularity and stability of the Anglican religion prevailed, and South Carolina historian Anne King Gregorie aptly subtitled her informative book on Christ Church "A Plantation Parish of the South Carolina Establishment."

The Church Act of 1706 which created Christ Church simply said it was southeast of Wando River. It was just across the Cooper River from Charleston and bordered Charleston harbor, the Atlantic Ocean, Wando River, and Awendaw Creek. About thirty-six miles long and six miles wide, it comprised about 252 square miles, sparsely settled and practically without roads. The many waterways provided avenues of transportation, but the four-mile crossing of the Cooper River estuary to Charleston was difficult and dangerous.[1]

Three members of the church commission named in the original church act were residents of Christ Church Parish: Thomas Barton, George Logan, and John A. Motte. Barton and Motte were members of the Assembly, and Logan was the public receiver, or treasurer, of the province. Thus began a long series of parishioners who were prosperous leaders in the community and supporters of the establishment.[2]

The site for the church was six miles from Charleston Harbor on the path which followed the watershed between the Wando River and the sea. In later years a village grew up in the vicinity which took its name from Mount Pleasant, the plantation of Jacob Motte, son of church commissioner John Abraham Motte.[3]

The Reverend Gilbert Jones, minister from 1712 to 1721, gave a brief history of the church. The foundation of the church was laid in 1707, but neither the church building nor the parsonage was complete when Jones arrived March 20, 1711/12. At that time, the Assembly appropriated £200 in addition to the £330 originally appropriated, and members of the vestry bought 100 acres of land for a parsonage and glebe. They built a convenient house with a separate kitchen four miles from the church. In 1714, parishioners raised £67 by subscription to finish the sanctuary, but the Yamassee War interrupted progress. By 1721, Jones reported that about twelve acres of the glebe were cleared and the church, a timber building 40 feet by 24 feet, was in use but not completely finished.[4]

Jones was not the first minister of Christ Church. Edward Marston, former rector of St. Philip's in Charleston, held services within the parish in a community known as Bermuda Town in 1708, but Marston did not settle permanently. In August 1708, the parishioners unanimously elected the Reverend Richard Marsden first rector of Christ Church. A charming gentleman, Marsden had also served at St. Philip's, but he had to relinquish his position when Gideon Johnston, duly appointed representative of the Bishop of London, arrived to take charge. Marsden, a tall, handsome man in his thirties, was so popular that the parishioners of Christ Church contributed an additional £90 to his salary.

Unfortunately, Marsden was soon heavily in debt. Gideon Johnston wrote to the SPG that he was "particularly dextrous at drawing Sham Bills on Merchants and others in London and elsewhere, by which he gull'd and Cheated many of several Considerable Sums...." The wily minister told his congregation that he had to go to England to settle an estate he had inherited. He then made his escape, leaving a wife and three children behind. His wife died, and neighbors kindly took in the children.[5]

The Christ Church vestry reported their experiences with Marston and Marsden to the Society and then stated, "Therefore we make our request to your Honourable Society, that you would be pleased to send us a Minister to our Parish, who is a Person of Pious, Sober and Virtuous Life, and a good Preacher...."[6] Before the Society could send a missionary, Gilbert Jones arrived in the province, and with the permission of Commissary Gideon Johnston, the Christ Church vestry invited Jones to supply their pulpit on an interim basis. Members of the church were so pleased with Jones they elected him rector, and when the Society's nominee, Nathaniel Osborne, arrived, he moved on to St. Bartholomew's. The Society accepted Jones as its missionary to Christ Church, thus assuring him of £50 from the Society in addition to the £100 he received from the province.[7]

Jones was so conscientious that he refused contributions from his parishioners. He said that they were poor, and he feared that he should "become chargeable to them and by that means they think their religion too dear, and consequently forsake it." During the Yamassee War, the rector had more than a hundred refugees at the house where he had sought safety in Charleston. The war bypassed Christ Church parish, but Jones was left impoverished. He nevertheless continued to serve until his return to England in 1721, when he reported 107 families comprising about 400 white people and 637 slaves in the parish.[8]

Fire destroyed the small timber church in February 1725, and in the spring of 1726, John Metheringham, builder, began constructing a new brick one. The vestry made arrangements with William Elliott to plaster and roughcast the exterior. Although the building was in use prior to the ceremony, it was formally dedicated on March 28, 1727. Silver for the new church was provided by a legacy from Patrick Logan, a blind, unmarried son of Colonel George Logan, who had served as clerk, sexton, and register of the church with the help of his assistant, Anthony White. Logan died soon after he made his will in October 1726, leaving all his silver and £50 to Christ Church.

The exact plan of the original 1726 building cannot be documented. Only two doors are mentioned in the minutes of the vestry, one on the north side and one on the south. The customary plan of the day would have included a western entrance, but no evidence of that survives. The list of parishioners who bought pews in 1732 indicates that the north aisle had nine pews while the south had only seven, suggesting that a space for a pulpit was located on the south side. In a letter to the Society in December 1730, John Fulton, the missionary, reported that the church had "neither door, Pulpit, Pavement, chancel or anything in order," but that it "could scarce contain the Number of both Churchmen and Dissenters that came thither." In 1741, the vestry made changes in order to secure space for additional pews. Each new pew should have "a Pannelled front agreable to ye rest of ye Church works." It was important that the new pews closely resemble the old ones to maintain the order, regularity, and neatness characteristic of Anglican worship.[9]

Both the order and the regularity of church administration were seriously disturbed by two ministers who came after the brick church was built. John Winteley arrived with credentials from the Society on March 1, 1727, just prior to the dedication of the new church. Winteley had problems with women and strong drink. One parishioner went so far as to call him a "Whoremonger and a drunkard." Since the vestry had never elected him rector, they were free to dismiss him, but he was determined to continue. When the vestry locked the church, Winteley read prayers in the churchyard. The next time he came to church, parishioners forcibly restrained him until Commissary Alexander Garden was settled in the pulpit. After conducting the service, Garden had dinner with the vestry. He

The Christ Church interior was fitted with paneled pews that provided warmth in unheated colonial churches.

later attempted to prosecute the deposed minister for disturbing the peace.[10]

Christ Church remained without a regular minister until the arrival of the Reverend John Fulton in July 1730. Fulton also had a problem with alcohol, but the vestry was hesitant to complain lest the bishop and the Society take them for a "humoursome" and capricious people. They referred the matter to Garden, who took formal action by convening an ecclesiastical court. Serving as "assessors" with Garden as judge were William Guy, rector of St. Andrew's, and Thomas Hasell, rector of St. Thomas'. They found Fulton guilty of habitual drunkenness and suspended him for two years. He subsequently left the province.[11]

The next missionary, John Fullerton, pleased the parishioners of Christ Church, and Susannah Haddrell presented him with a surplice. It was undoubtedly hand sewn, and it is possible that Mrs. Haddrell grew the flax, spun the thread, and wove the cloth from which it was made. Clerical garb was of great distaste to the Puritans, who regarded it as a remnant of "popery." The use of the surplice at Christ Church is further evidence of the desire to conform to standard Anglican practice. The vestry expressed thanks to Mrs. Haddrell and "agreed that a good substantial Chest be made to place the said Surplice and particular things in the Church."[12]

The last SPG missionary to serve Christ Church was Levi Durand, who was unanimously elected rector on February 23, 1741. Due to the lack of dependable mail service, Durand made a practice of sending his letters to the Society in six copies by six different ships. Still, few letters from him are recorded. During his tenure, the vestry supervised the building of a new parsonage, a two-story house with a large hall and six bedchambers, three of which had fireplaces. Another addition to the parish was a brick vestry house, 22 by 14 feet, completed in 1751. It was not only used for vestry meetings, but it became a haven for coachmen and servants who had to watch the horses during worship services.[13]

The parsonage lasted nearly thirty years, but by 1769, it was necessary to build a new house. Samuel McCorkell and Jonathan Hood submitted an estimate of £2,830 to build a two-story house of yellow pine on a brick foundation 34 by 24 feet with two chimneys. The inside was to be lathed, plastered, glazed, and painted. Two piazzas eight feet wide would provide outside space to seek a breeze. Plans also included a "beaufeat," which possibly referred to a beautifully constructed china closet in the corner of the living room.[14]

Each year, Christ Church and its vestry house attract many visitors who are interested in its history. Parishioners welcome guests at an annual "tea room" to raise funds for outreach ministries. The British burned the church in the Revolutionary War, and in the Civil War the walls remained standing, but the interior was again demolished. Nevertheless, there is probably some remnant of the foundation and walls of the 1726 brick structure. The roof is distinctive and representative of southern colonial building practices in that the bellcast at the eaves is designed to throw water as far away from the foundation as possible. The cupola topped by a cross dates from the nineteenth century, but it seems to suit the spirit of the original plan. The simple, clean lines of Christ Church with its arched and shuttered windows serve as a reminder of the regularity and stability provided by the Anglican Church in the long struggle to transform a wilderness into a civilization.[15]

The Christ Church vestry house served as a meeting place for parish officials as well as a haven for coachmen during church services.

[1] Anne King Gregorie, *Christ Church, 1706-1959: A Plantation Parish of the South Carolina Establishment* (Charleston: Dalcho Historical Society, 1961), pp. 17-18; Gilbert Jones to the Society, March 28, 1717, SPG MS, B4-1 #91; Thomas Cooper, ed., *Statutes at Large of South Carolina* (Columbia: A. S. Johnston, 1838), II, 282-283.

[2] Walter B. Edgar and N. Louise Bailey, *Biographical Directory of the South Carolina House of Representatives* (Columbia: University of South Carolina Press, 1977), II, 58, 409-410, 481-482. For later examples see Gregorie, *Christ Church*, pp. 37-38, 56.

[3] Gregorie, *Christ Church*, pp. 8, 47-48.

[4] Gilbert Jones to the SPG, SPG MS, November 6, 1716, B4-1 #75; June 6, 1721, B4-1 #104; March 28, 1717, B4-1 #91.

[5] Gideon Johnston, *Carolina Chronicle: The Papers of Commissary Gideon Johnston, 1707-1716*, ed. Frank Klingberg (Berkeley: University of California Press, 1946), pp. 48-49. For the story of Marsden's long and sordid career see Fleming H. James, "Richard Marsden, Wayward Clergyman," *William and Mary Quarterly*, 3rd. ser. 11 (1954), 578-591.

[6] Frederick Dalcho, *An Historical Account of the Protestant Episcopal Church in South Carolina* (Charleston: E. Thayer, 1820; rpt. New York: Arno Press, 1970), p. 277.

[7] Nathaniel Osborne to the Society, March 27, 1712/13, SPG MS A8 #6; Gregorie, *Christ Church*, pp. 16-17.

[8] Gilbert Jones to the Society, November 5, 1716, SPG MS, B4-1 #375; Gideon Johnson to the Society, January 27, 1715/16, *Carolina Chronicle*, p. 155; Gregorie, *Christ Church*, p. 25.

[9] Gregorie, *Christ Church,* pp. 27-28; John Fulton to the Society, December 4, 1730, as cited in Gregorie, *Christ Church*, pp. 30-33; Louis P. Nelson, "South Carolina Anglican: the architecture of the Lowcountry plantation parishes," Draft of November 17, 1997, Diocese of South Carolina, pp. 55-56; Christ Church Parish, Minutes of the Vestry, 1708-1759, 1797-1847, August 31, 1732; May 22, 1732; August 30, 1740, as cited in Nelson. Owners of pews in 1732 were Charvil Wingood, Richard Fowler, Capt. George Benison, Capt. Thomas Boone, Capt. George Logan, Joseph Law and Thomas Barton, Jr., [shared pew #6], Catherine Severance, Robert Clemmons and James Allen [shared #9], John White, Capt. Hugh Hext, George Haddrell, Clergy, Andrew Quelch, John Metheringham, William Cook. See Gregorie, p. 32. Evidence is not clear as to exactly where doors were located. Anne Gregorie interpreted the vestry minutes of January 1741 as indicating that the north door was allowed to remain open with moveable pews at that location. If both the north and south doors were closed, there must have been a door at the west side, but Gregorie stated [p. 31] that Christ Church had two doors—north and south. As Dr. Gregorie observed, "...some interesting but not altogether clear decisions were made." Gregorie, p. 39.

[10] Gregorie, *Christ Church*, p. 28; S. Charles Bolton, *Southern Anglicanism: The Church of England in Colonial South Carolina* (Westport, Connecticut: Greenwood Press, 1982), pp. 42-43, 93-94.

[11] Bolton, *Southern Anglicanism*, p. 44.

[12] Gregorie, *Christ Church*, p. 33; Stephen P. Dorsey, *Early English Churches in America, 1607-1807* (New York: Oxford University Press, 1952), p. 33.

[13] Gregorie, pp. 40, 42, 44; Samuel G. Stoney, *Plantations of the Carolina Low Country* (Charleston: Carolina Art Association, 1964), pp. 53-54.

[14] Gregorie, *Christ Church*, pp. 21, 52-53.

[15] Samuel Gaillard Stoney, *Colonial Church Architecture in South Carolina* (Charleston: Dalcho Historical Society, 1953), p. 2; Stoney, *Plantations of the Carolina Low Country*, pp. 53-54.

(Top) A View in St. Thomas' Parish, Pompion Hill Chapel, *watercolor by Charles Fraser, painted from Jonathon Lucas's rice mill at Middleburg Plantation.*
(Bottom) The chapel looks out on the Cooper River.

ST. THOMAS' AND ST. DENIS' PARISH

POMPION HILL and CHAPEL OF EASE

Shall we gather at the river, where bright angel feet have trod;
With its crystal tide forever flowing by the throne of God?
On the margin of the river washing up its silver spray
We will walk and worship ever, all the happy golden day.

Revelation 22: 1-5
R. Lowry, 1864

For nearly three centuries, worshipers have gathered on a picturesque bluff overlooking the east branch of the Cooper River. One might imagine Peter St. Julien de Malacare, a wealthy Huguenot of noble background, as he made his way up the east branch of the Cooper River in a periagua rowed by Indian slaves to select a site for a plantation. He chose the bluff called Ponkin Hill, where his daughter, Charlotte St. Julien, married Rene Ravenel in 1687. Wealthy and influential colonists such as Sir Nathaniel Johnson, governor of the province, and John Ashby, a cassique, or member of the nobility created by the Lords Proprietors, claimed large tracts in the vicinity. The settlers chose the river bluff as the site for a church. Although the first wooden structure did not survive, the brick church built in the 1760s under the leadership of the rector, Alexander Garden, with craftsmen Zachariah Villepontoux and William Axson would secure for the parish a place in architectural history. It would become a place for family and community gatherings and would be a revered place of worship from the colonial period to the modern era.[1]

"The first Church that (I find) was built here for ye Church of England Worship was my Chappel of Eease, commonly called Pompkinhill Church, being Built upon a Riseing Ground that goes by that name and runs along ye River Side." So wrote missionary Thomas Hasell to his sponsors, the Society for the Propagation of the Gospel. The first missionary sent by the Society, Samuel Thomas, had preached at Pompion Hill, although his base was at Goose Creek. Hasell further noted that the church, of cypress timber thirty feet square, was built about 1703 with contributions from neighbors and the special assistance of Sir Nathaniel Johnson, governor from 1703 to 1709. Johnson owned a plantation in the vicinity called Silk Hope, where he directed experiments with silk production in hopes that it would prove economically feasible for South Carolina.[2]

Johnson's plantation as well as Pompion Hill were included in the parish of St. Thomas', established on the neck of land to the northwest of Wando River and southeast of Cooper River by the Church Act of 1706. Within the boundaries of St. Thomas', the act also established the parish of St. Denis'.[3] This unusual arrangement arose because French Huguenots who had settled in what was known as the Orange Quarter had requested parish status in order to have financial help with paying a minister. As early as 1696, a French congregation of about a hundred persons was in existence. Many did not understand English, and they were willing to have an ordained Anglican minister if he could preach to them in French. Thus, the Assembly created a parish named for St. Denis, the patron saint of France, with the stipulation that once the people could understand English, the church would become incorporated into St. Thomas'.[4]

John LaPierre was the first Anglican minister assigned to the parish of St. Denis'. A college graduate, he was ordained in 1708 by the Bishop of London, who recommended him to Commissary Gideon Johnston. The commissary was the representative of the bishop in South Carolina. LaPierre was fluent in both French and English, so he sometimes assisted Thomas Hasell, who had two churches in his charge.

The Beresford family vault in the St. Thomas' Parish churchyard.

The vestry house dates from the eighteenth century.

In asking for a minister, the French of Orange Quarter insisted that they must be permitted to receive the communion in Calvinistic form. LaPierre had a difficult time satisfying his parishioners and maintaining Anglican standards demanded by Commissary Johnston. He also struggled to support five children and a wife who had lost her eyesight before their departure from England. Nevertheless, LaPierre served St. Denis' Church for about twenty years before moving to Cape Fear, North Carolina, in 1728. John James Tissot, his replacement, arrived in 1730.[5]

Thomas Hasell was the first minister of St. Thomas' Parish. He had served briefly in Charleston as a catechist before the Society appointed him to St. Thomas'. The foundation of the brick church was laid in 1707, and the building was completed the following year with funds provided by the tax on skins and furs.

One of the primary purposes of the SPG was to bring the gospel to those who had never before heard it. Hasell wrote to the Society in 1712 that between twenty and thirty African men and women regularly attended services at Pompion Hill. One of the Africans was free, and two were baptized. He closed his letter, "...begging the continuance of their good prayers that God would make me an Instrument of doing him further and greater Service in this Wilderness...." In a letter the next year, Hasell noted that there were many impediments to instructing African and Indian slaves. One problem was the language barrier. He said that "those that are brought hither from their own Country Except a few that come very young seldom or never Speak good English." He thought that the only solution was to instruct the young, and he proposed to set aside one day in the week to do so.[6]

Hasell reported to the Society in 1716 that the parish owned more than six hundred acres of glebe land, two hundred adjoining the parish church and four hundred twenty near Pompion Hill about ten miles away. No parsonage existed, although the vestry had started a fund and put the money at interest for the purpose. Hasell did not object, for he said, "I comply'd with this Proposal, haveing in ye mean time a Small Settlement of my own, adjoyning to ye Glebe Land of ye Chappel upon which I am Settled."[7]

Hasell must have faced some hardships, but his problems were nothing like those of the missionaries who went to wilderness areas. The east branch of the Cooper River was well settled and boasted some large and prosperous plantations by the time Hasell arrived. On January 21, 1715, he married Elizabeth Ashby, daughter of Cassique John Ashby, Jr. "Cassique" was a hereditary title of nobility provided for by the Fundamental Constitutions of Carolina which technically entitled the bearer to two baronies of 12,000 acres each. Ashby's wife was Constantia Broughton, daughter of Thomas Broughton and Anne Johnson, whose father was Governor Sir Nathaniel Johnson. Thomas Broughton, owner of Mulberry Castle, became acting governor when Sir Nathaniel died. Elizabeth Ashby Hasell's sister, Anne, married Gabriel Manigault. Through his wife's family, Hasell had very important kinship connections which probably worked to benefit his parish.[8]

Thomas Broughton, the grandfather of Hasell's wife, was executor of the estate of Richard Beresford, a community leader who made provision in his will for educating the poor children of the parish. Beresford died in a freak accident when, as Hasell reported to the SPG, "a Limb from an High Tree fell upon him and Struck him dead without speaking a word." A problem arose because since the time that Beresford wrote his will, his wife had died, he had remarried, and he had a second son for whom he had made no provision in the will. A lawsuit ensued, but the outcome was that the parish would receive the income from the estate until the sons came of age. The vestry invested the money, which amounted to a substantial sum and became known as the "Beresford Bounty." By 1771, it was worth more than £16000. Richard Harris, for many years senior warden, left an additional £500 to be put at interest until it reached £1000, then to be used for educational purposes. Thus, St. Thomas' Parish was able to establish a school. In 1736, the vestry found it necessary to incorporate in order to manage the Beresford and Harris trusts.[9]

In 1742, the vestry applied to the Bishop of London for an assistant to the rector, Thomas Hasell, who was not in good health. They requested someone who could also teach more advanced classes at the school, instruction having previously been limited to reading, writing, and arithmetic. The Reverend Alexander Garden, nephew to Commissary Alexander Garden, arrived in 1743, and Hasell died early in 1745. An inventory of his estate listed fifty-six slaves by name. On Hasell's 1540-acre Pompion Hill plantation, he had owned a flock of sheep, a herd of cattle, five horses, twenty oxen, and twenty-six hogs. Produce on hand included 120 bushels of rough rice and 100 bushels of corn. Among his luxury items were silver plate, pewter dishes, table linen, feather beds, bed curtains, and a library worth £150. The appraisers valued his personal possessions (other than land) at £13,197. Hasell, the gentle parson, the able and dedicated rector, managed to acquire a fortune as well.[10]

After Hasell's death, the vestry requested that the Society appoint Garden as his successor. The parish flourished under Garden's leadership. In 1750, the Assembly authorized £400 for enlarging the parish church.[11] Twelve years later, the parish again felt the need to expand. Alexander Garden wrote to the Society that Pompion Hill chapel, having stood some sixty years, had "become ruinous" and was "too small to accommodate the congregation conveniently." Therefore the parishioners had decided to build a new chapel of brick near the site of the old one, to be 48 feet by 35 feet.[12]

The chapel was nearly complete in 1765, when Garden reported that it was "almost finished in a very neat commodious and decent manner." He said that the vestry intended not only to adorn the inside of the church, but also "to build a new and genteel Pulpit of Cedar, for which they have already contracted with a workman."[13]

The workman mentioned by Garden was William Axson, Jr., a master carpenter who left his mark in a brick near the north door which displays WAXSON 1763 and a crossed square and compass, a standard mark of a Freemason. Axson was in business with Stephen Townsend on the northeast corner of Tradd and Church Streets in Charleston, where they had a carpentry shop.[14]

Axson's extraordinary pulpit stands in the center of the western wall and visually dominates the interior of the chapel. Steps with turned balusters and a newel post lead to the hexagonal pulpit. In each face of the pulpit box, Axson placed egg-and-dart molding. The central panel of the pulpit exhibits an inlaid IHS[15] in a sunburst pattern. The base of the box is trimmed with elegantly detailed leaf designs, and a graceful stem supports the whole. Fluted columns with Corinthian capitals support the canopy, which also bears an inlaid sunburst surrounding a triangle, symbol of the trinity. The top of the pulpit is graced by a dove in flight, representing the Holy Spirit. The pulpit design bears great resemblance to a pattern in Batty Langley's *City and Country Builder's and Workman's Treasury of Designs*.[16]

Opposite the pulpit at the east end is a slightly projecting chancel which adds liturgical space for minimal square footage. A Venetian, or Palladian, window illuminates the chancel area. Although the exterior is square, the interior of the chancel is rounded, and an arch relieves the pressure on the columns, producing a very pleasing architectural effect.[17]

Zachariah Villepontoux also left his initials engraved in brick near the doors. A Back River

The parish church of St. Thomas and St. Denis (photos before and after renovations) dates from about 1819.

planter, he manufactured brick at his Parnassus Plantation. The finely tooled Flemish bond of Pompion Hill exhibits the quality of his product. He had supplied brick for St. Michael's in Charleston some years earlier, and it is likely that he had a part in the actual building and possibly the design of Pompion Hill.[18]

Four arched windows and a centrally located double door penetrate the north and south elevations. Although a nineteenth-century addition of a vestry room blocks the western end, it originally had two small doors flanked by windows on either side.[19] The doors probably served as separate accesses for the rector and the clerk. These doors contribute to the unique quality of the Pompion Hill design. Other rural Anglican churches of the period had a central entrance on each of the western, northern, and southern walls, a free standing pulpit, and an interior chancel. The placement of the pulpit along the western wall between the entrances for clergy and clerk created a liturgical center for Anglican worship for the reading of scripture and prayers and delivery of the sermon. The projecting chancel where the priest celebrated the Eucharist further added to the liturgical orientation of the building.[20]

Other features which contributed to the total design were the coved tray ceiling with elaborate moldings, the defined rectangular plane of the ceiling's center, and the floor tiles laid in a neat pattern. The convergence of tiles at the very center of the plan lends credence to the idea that this may have been the original location of the baptismal font. The tiles, 960 in number, were the gift of Gabriel Manigault, Charleston merchant and by that time owner of Silk Hope plantation.[21]

The simple elegance of Pompion Hill as well as the unique liturgical design speak to the theological training of the rector, Alexander Garden; the affluence of the Cooper River planters who supported the building program; and the excellence of the builders such as Zachariah Villepontoux and William Axson, as well as to unnamed and unremembered slaves who undoubtedly worked on the building.

The completion of the beautiful new chapel at Pompion Hill was probably an incentive to both those of French and English descent to renew their allegiance to the established church. With the death of the French minister, the Reverend John James

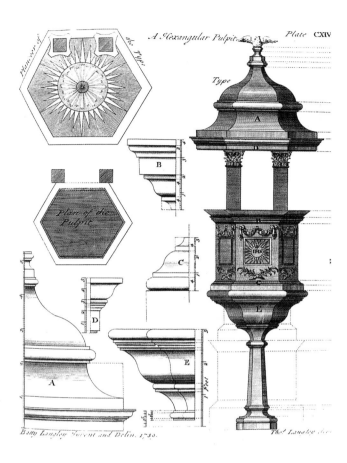

A design by Batty Langley, published in London in 1750, served as a pattern for the pulpit at Pompion Hill.

Tissot, in 1768, the South Carolina Assembly disestablished the French congregation in Orange Quarter and gave its assets to the vestry of St. Thomas' for the benefit of the poor. The official name later became the Parish of St. Thomas' and St. Denis'. Since about 1755, the language barrier had virtually disappeared, and many of the French had joined the Anglican congregations. Alexander Garden served with distinction for thirty-nine years until his death in 1783.[22]

The parish church of St. Thomas' burned in a woods fire in 1815, but the vestry house survived. The current church building dates from about 1819. In the modern day, both the parish church and Pompion Hill chapel are used on special occasions, but neither has a regular congregation. The old cemeteries have felt the ravages of time. At one point some enterprising moonshiners set up a distilling apparatus within the Beresford vault—giving new meaning to the term "Beresford Bounty." Under the watchful eye of John Slayton, in charge of the property in 1999, depredations have ceased and many broken tombstones have been repaired.[23]

In the Parish of St. Thomas' and St. Denis', many of the old plantations remain intact. Pompion Hill is only a short distance from Middleburg and Silk Hope. The view of the Cooper River from "punkin" hill is still breathtaking, and the architecture of the chapel draws national attention. The names of Villepontoux and Axson are permanently preserved in marked bricks as well as in the overall design of the building.

In the churchyard, tombstones record the names of others who worshiped at this spot throughout the centuries. There is a strong sense of continuity of religious belief and the importance of the bluff as a place of reverence and history.

Through the years, the recurring tides wore away the banks of the Cooper River. Unfortunately, Thomas Hasell's grave eventually disappeared. The shining river may be a metaphor of the path to eternal life (Revelation 22:1), and in this sense it seems somehow appropriate that the good minister's earthly remains slid away into the water.

As the descendants of the early settlers meet to worship and remember their ancestors, perhaps they will sing:

Yes we'll gather at the river, the beautiful, the beautiful river,
Gather with the saints at the river that flows by the throne of God.

[1]John B. Irving, *A Day on the Cooper River*, ed. Louisa Cheves Stoney and Samuel Gaillard Stoney (Columbia: R. L. Bryan, 1969), p. 160; Henry A. M. Smith, *The Historical Writings of Henry A. M. Smith*, Vol. 1, *Rivers and Regions of Early South Carolina* (Spartanburg, SC: Reprint Company, 1988), p. 13; Smith, "The Baronies of South Carolina," *South Carolina Historical Magazine*, Vol. 18, pp. 18-19. For information on St. Julien, see

Pompion Hill is unusual in design. The pulpit is against the western wall opposite the chancel located at the eastern end. Benches face the aisle.

[1] Arthur Henry Hirsch, *The Huguenots of Colonial South Carolina* (Hamden, CN: Archon Books, 1962), pp. 237-238.

[2] Thomas Hasell to the Society, December 27, 1716, SPG MS, B4-1 #88; Irving and Stoney, *Day on the Cooper River*, pp. 168-169. "Pompion" was an early English name for pumpkin. *A Dictionary of American English on Historical Principles* refers to John Smith [1607], "He sowes his wheat, tobacco, pompions, etc." See *Names in South Carolina*, IX: 5, p.100.

[3] Thomas Cooper, ed., *Statutes at Large of South Carolina* (Columbia: A. S. Johnston, 1838), II, 282-283.

[4] Hasell to SPG, December 27, 1716; Arthur Henry Hirsch, *The Huguenots of Colonial South Carolina* (Durham, NC: Duke University Press, 1928; rpt. London: Archon Books, 1962), pp. 73-75. Some disagreement exists as to why the parish was named St. Denis'. The author finds the argument of H. A. M. Smith to be most convincing. See *Rivers and Regions*, p. 22. Smith noted that Huguenots did not generally choose saints' names for their churches, and rather than being in honor of some obscure battlefield called St. Denis, the Assembly probably chose the name because St. Denis was the patron saint of France.

[5] Hirsch, *The Huguenots*, p. 135; Robert Clute, ed., *The Annals and Parish Register of St. Thomas and St. Denis Parish, in South Carolina, from 1680 to 1884* (Charleston: Walker, Evans, and Cogswell, 1884), p. 13.

[6] Thomas Hasell to the Society, SPG MS, August 18, 1712, A7 #26; March 12, 1712/13, A7 #11.

[7] Thomas Hasell to the Society, December 27, 1716, SPG MS, B4-1, #88; Clute, *The Annals*, p. 11.

[8] Walter B. Edgar and N. Louise Bailey, *Biographical Directory of the South Carolina House of Representatives* (Columbia: University of South Carolina Press, 1977), pp. 41-42, 103-105.

[9] Clute, *The Annals*, pp.12-14; Thomas Hasell to the Society, October 13, 1722, SPG MS, B4-1 #122; Church Wardens and Vestry of St. Thomas, n.d. [received August 20, 1722], to David Humphrys, Secretary of the SPG, SPG MS, B4-1 #121; Thomas Hasell to the Society, March 20, 1721/22, SPG MS, B4-1 #103.

[10] Clute, *The Annals*, p. 14; Inventories of Estates, March 8, 1745, Vol. 1732-1746 [B], pp. 161-164; Smith, *Baronies*, p. 19.

[11] R. Nicholas Olsberg, ed., *The Journal of the Commons House of Assembly, 1750-1751* (Columbia: University of South Carolina Press, 1974), May 1, 1750, p. 58.

[12] Alexander Garden to the Society, April 22, 1762, SPG MS, B5 #216.

[13] Alexander Garden to the Society, May 6, 1765, SPG MS, B5 #220.

[14] *South Carolina Gazette*, February 12, 1763, as cited in E. Milby Burton, *Charleston Furniture 1700-1825* (Columbia: University of South Carolina Press, 1997), pp. 69-70.

[15] A transliteration of the Greek abbreviation or monogram for Jesus.

[16] Louis Nelson, "South Carolina Anglican: the architecture of the Lowcountry plantation parishes," Draft of November 17, 1997, Diocese of South Carolina, pp. 87-88. Nelson noted a difference in quality of carving, indicating that at least two persons worked on the pulpit. He said, "The varying quality of carving might reveal the work of both a master carver and an apprentice in Axson's shop or the possibility that Axson hired the carved elements out to a number of independent craftsmen." Batty Langley, *The City and Country Builder's and Workman's Treasury of Designs* (London: S. Harding, 1750; rpt., New York: Benjamin Blom, 1967), plate CXIV.

[17] Samuel Gaillard Stoney, *Colonial Church Architecture in South Carolina* (Charleston: Dalcho Historical Society, 1953), p. 7. Stoney believed that ideas for Pompion Hill were taken from St. Michael's in Charleston.

[18] *Ibid*. See also I. Heyward Peck, "The Villepontoux Family of South Carolina," *South Carolina Historical Magazine*, Vol. 50, pp. 34-36.

[19] The two doors are clearly shown in a watercolor by Charles Fraser painted before the addition of the vestry room. See Charles Fraser, *A Charleston Sketchbook, 1796-1806*, ed. Alice R. Huger Smith (Rutland, Vermont: Charles Tuttle for Carolina Art Association, 1959), #28.

[20] Nelson, *South Carolina Anglican*, p. 90.

[21] *Ibid.*, pp. 89-90; Clute, *The Annals*, p. 15. See also St. Michael's note 3. Manigault had employed Acadian laborers to cut Purbeck stones for St. Michael's.

[22] Clute, *The Annals*, pp. 14-17; *Statutes*, IX, 225; IV, 584.

[23] John Slayton, interview with the author, May 1, 1998.

Pon Pon Chapel of Ease, St. Bartholomew's Parish, is called the "Burnt Church" because it burned in the Revolution, was rebuilt, and burned again about 1819. Charles Fraser painted this watercolor about 1796.

ST. BARTHOLOMEW'S PARISH

PON PON CHAPEL

Thanksgivings for the Natural Order
For the Beauty of the Earth
We give you thanks, most gracious God, for the beauty of earth and sky and sea;
For the richness of mountains, plains, and rivers; for the songs of birds and the loveliness of flowers.
We praise you for these good gifts, and pray that we may safeguard them for our posterity.
Grant that we may continue to grow in our grateful enjoyment of your abundant creation,
To the honor and glory of your Name, now and for ever. Amen.

The Book of Common Prayer

The region that formed St. Bartholomew's Parish is a land of marsh and forest, of slow, meandering rivers where the mighty power of the tide—unimpeded by hills or rocks—pushes the water into marsh and creeks, then turns and rushes back towards the sea. It is a land of extremes, of unrelenting summer sun that beats down and turns the pluff mud to sticky black dust, of winter winds that chill the early morning hunter to the bone.

Today the tidal zone is known as the ACE Basin, the land of three rivers, the Ashepoo, the Combahee, and the Edisto, with a multitude of creeks and marshes that transect the land and limit transportation by highway. Mankind's limits have proven beneficial to nature, leaving the area sparsely settled and making the ACE a haven for wildlife and waterfowl as well as a paradise for canoe and kayak enthusiasts. Vistas of marsh extend as far as the eye can see, the horizon unmarred by any sign of civilization, graced by gentle egrets and majestic bald eagles. In the creeks and old rice canals, alligators and cottonmouth moccasins add an element of danger to the scene.[1]

To the first Anglican missionaries, the land was dangerous indeed. The few settlers were widely dispersed, and although St. Bartholomew's was one of the parishes established by the church act of 1706, no minister resided there until Nathaniel Osborne arrived in 1713. He described the parish as "being very large and Scattered much about," an area about thirty miles north to south and forty miles east to west. The one hundred and twenty families lived so far apart that Osborne found it necessary to officiate at four or five places, some about twenty miles from his residence. He makes no mention of a parsonage, but documentary evidence shows that a glebe of 500 acres was purchased by the commissioners of the parish church on May 10, 1713. The glebe was on the Townsend Tract on the Chehaw River, a smaller stream between the Combahee and the Ashepoo. Although there was no church building in 1713, the missionary reported that he had baptized more than seventy persons, six of whom were adults. Among the children were five of mixed blood "being those of our Indian Traders, by Indian Women during their abode amongst them."[2]

It is likely that one of those children was Cousaponakeesa, the niece of old Brim, a Creek chieftain. Her father is unknown, but in later life she said that he had brought her to St. Bartholomew's to be educated in the Christian religion. She later became famous as Mary Musgrove, wife of John Musgrove, when she acted as interpreter for James Oglethorpe, founder of Georgia.[3]

The Indian traders' children that Osborne baptized may have been those who had been receiving instruction from schoolmaster Ross Reynolds of St. Bartholomew's parish. A local planter, John Norris, wrote to the SPG that "there lives near me a Schoolmaster, that hath for a Year past or more encouraged and undertaken to teach gratis reading and writing in the English Tongue such Young Indians as wou'd frequent his School...." Norris believed that the Indians were very receptive to learning. He said, "I find they seem generally well pleased & Admire that We make Paper speak (as they term it) and are very sensible and apprehensive of what they are Instructed in." Ross Reynolds insisted to Commissary Gideon Johnston that the Indian traders paid him for teaching their children. Reynolds said that "Mr. Norris owed him Seven Months Schooling for his Son & that if ever he taught anyone gratis it was him. And the Reason was because he could not help it."[4]

The efforts of Reynolds and Osborne were tragically interrupted by the Yamassee War, which broke out in April 1715. Osborne wrote to the Society, "I Escaped very narrowly with the Loss of almost all that I had, which was very Considerable, the Indians being within 3 Miles of my house, when I left it was forced to run away with nothing but the very Cloaths upon my back." The first day that war broke out, about ninety to a hundred colonists fell to the attackers, who killed some immediately and tortured others to death. Osborne continued, "My Parish is intirely deserted, Except a small Garrison,[5] and most of the houses either burnt or spoiled by the Enemy." Osborne felt forced to go to Charleston for security. Most of the women and children also went to Charleston, for the men were with the army or manning various garrisons. The Indians were so numerous and "all so skulking about in the Night in partyes to do Mischief, and by day hid in swamps, that they do a world of damage and when least Suspected...." Eventually some 400 colonists would die in the war.[6]

Osborne died before St. Bartholomew's could be resettled.[7] The next record is from Robert Gowie in April 1734, although Gowie spoke of "my Predecessor Mr. Thompson." Possibly Thompson only preached there occasionally. In 1725, the Assembly had authorized a chapel of ease at Pon Pon, a neighborhood near where the road to Charleston crossed the Edisto River.[8] Pon Pon is also another name for the Edisto below that point. Gowie reported that Pon Pon Chapel was small, but the congregation, which included some dissenters, was numerous. He intended to preach at Combahee every five or six weeks. Plans were in the works to build a parsonage at Pon Pon that would be 29 feet by 17 feet with a Dutch roof. Gowie did not live to enjoy it, for he was dead of "intermittent fever," probably malaria, by November 1734.[9]

Gowie's replacement, Thomas Thompson, was in St. Bartholomew's by August 1735. He reported that there were 120 families of white people and 1200 Negroes. Thompson lived at Pon Pon and preached mainly at the chapel there, but he officiated once a month at Chehaw. An undated plat in the state archives shows the Pon Pon Chapel located on the road from Parker's Ferry to Ashepoo and the parsonage land at the intersection of the Parker's Ferry road with the road to Jacksonborough, adjoining the plantation of Major William Smith.[10]

On April 22, 1737, Thompson attended a meeting of all the Anglican clergymen in South Carolina at the home of Commissary Alexander Garden. John Wesley, an Anglican minister from Savannah, Georgia, who would later found the Methodist denomination, was a guest at the meeting. Wesley recorded in his journal that all the ministers attended church together and met again in the afternoon "where was such a conversation for several hours, on Christ our Righteousness...as I never heard in England...."[11]

Wesley mentioned to Thompson that he had been disappointed in getting a passage by boat back to Savannah, and Thompson offered to lend one of his horses. Thompson rode part way with Wesley, then sent his servant to guide him the rest of the way to Pon Pon. Wesley had a conversation with "Nanny," a slave girl who worked for Thompson. He explained that the body would turn to dust. "But there is something in you that will not turn to dust, and this is what they call your soul. Indeed you cannot see your soul though it is within you; as you cannot see the wind, though it is all about you." After a lengthy conversation, Wesley thought that Nanny understood.

The Savannah minister preached twice at Pon Pon Chapel, once on the thirteenth chapter of First Corinthians, which begins "Though I speak with

The ruins of Pon Pon Chapel.

the tongues of men and of angels and have not love, I am become as sounding brass, or a tinkling cymbal." At the request of his host, Wesley prayed extemporaneously rather than from the Prayer Book in deference to the many dissenters in the congregation. Wesley was impressed that many people came eight to twelve miles to hear the gospel.[12]

By 1743, Thomas Thompson had lasted longer than any other minister in St. Bartholomew's, but he was becoming discouraged. He reported that the parsonage which was begun eight years previously never was half completed. "I have lived two years in it without a chimney, and it is now so ruinous that I am obliged to leave it," he said. In addition, bad neighbors had robbed him and shot his horse. The lack of support by his parishioners was especially hard to bear because "there is no parish in the Province That has produced a greater, and few (if any) so great a quantity of rice." The rice production along with three or four thousand slaves, in addition to the value of the land, made St. Bartholomew's, according to Thompson, richer than some parishes in England itself.[13]

Alexander Garden, the bishop's representative in South Carolina, was not very sympathetic to Thompson because the vestry of St. Bartholomew's had complained that their minister was chaplain of a British ship and spent too much time away from his duties as pastor. Thompson, however, had developed a friendship with Philip Bearcroft, Secretary of the SPG. On his last visit to England, Thompson left a slave boy with Bearcroft. Thompson wrote, "I hope the black boy turns out to Your satisfaction. His mother made a great noise about him on my return here, but seems now to be well satisfied." Thompson reported that he had made several attempts without success to raise a young mockingbird in a cage to send to Mrs. Bearcroft. Neither Thompson nor Bearcroft apparently sensed any contradiction with Thompson's next letter, in which he stated that "there is Nothing in the World I desire more than the advancement of our blessed Lord's Kingdom, and to be in any degree serviceable to the increase of well-being of the Subjects thereof." Even without Garden's cooperation, Thompson got his transfer to St. George's Dorchester.[14]

Thompson's successor, Charles Boschi, who arrived in 1745, was also unhappy with the parsonage. He said, "I came to a house that there was not a stool to sit down nor one nail in the walls, neither a place to keep the library, and was obliged to keep them upon the ground." He preached at Pon Pon Chapel and every fortnight at Ashepoo, where a chapel had been authorized by the Assembly but not yet built. Boschi was unhappy with the congregation at Ashepoo for their lack of reverence. He said, "It seems the best people used there to go throng and fro' continualy out of chapel, and made punch in time of sermon or Prayer...." In addition, the minister was very concerned that with only two or three exceptions, every woman who came to be married was pregnant. "I was oblige sometimes to call for a chair to make the woman to sit down in the time of Marriage because they were fainting away," he exclaimed. Boschi reported that the building at Chehaw had fallen into ruins.[15] The congregation could not agree on a place to build a parish church, so they resolved not to have one and to utilize chapels instead. The vestry sold the glebe land at Chehaw in January 1762 and purchased slaves for the use of the rector and his successors.[16]

A plan for the town of Edmundsbury was on record by 1742. Located at the intersection of the Ashepoo River and the road from Charleston to Port Royal, the village was on land that had been part of Landgrave Edmund Bellinger's barony. A large lot labeled "The Church Land" was in a prominent spot near the high road. Although church services continued until the Civil War, the town saw little development beyond the church, a ferry landing, and possibly a store.[17]

The population of the parish had increased substantially by 1752, when the missionary William Langhorne reported to the Society that the number of inhabitants was 1280, of whom 820 professed membership in the Church of England. In addition, he considered 5200 residents [slaves] "Heathens and Infidels." He also optimistically reported, "Number of Converts from a profane, disorderly, and unchristian Course, to a Life of Christian Purity, Meekness and Charity...I hope Many."[18]

The 1750s were a time of prosperity for rice and indigo planters in South Carolina. The British offered a bounty on indigo beginning in 1748, and by growing both rice and indigo, planters on the Ashepoo, Combahee, and Edisto could become very wealthy.[19] St. Bartholomew's chapels reflected this prosperity. In 1753, the vestry determined to build two chapels of brick, one to replace the wooden structure at Pon Pon and the other at Edmundsbury

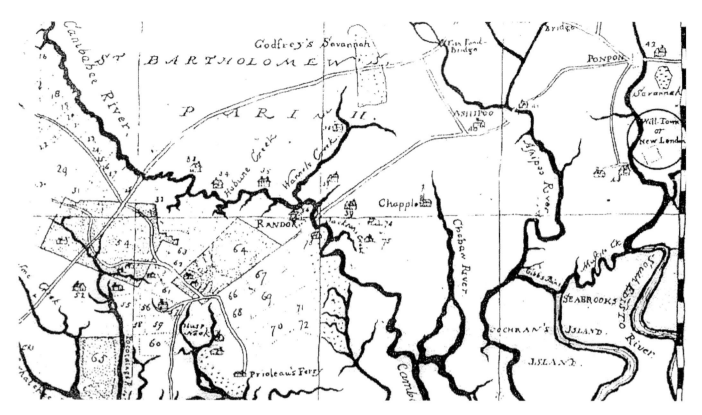
Detail of the Boss-Brailsford Map of 1775 shows the location of the earliest St. Bartholomew's chapel on Chehaw River.

on the Ashepoo River. The dimensions were to be 52 feet by 36 feet and the walls about 18 feet high. Legislative acts of April 12, 1755, and April 7, 1759, authorized the selling of pews in the two chapels. Robert Baron, minister since 1753, reported in 1760 that the chapels had for two years been finished enough to be used for worship. He asked the SPG for Bibles and prayer books suitable for the reading desks.[20]

Other than the ruin of the foundation, no visual evidence survives for the Edmundsbury Chapel. Pon Pon Chapel is in ruins, but a Charles Fraser watercolor of 1796 shows the chapel and what appears to be a vestry house to the side.[21] The modified baroque gable west end exhibits two round "bull's-eye" windows which may have provided light for a gallery in the western end of the chapel. The east end had a similar gable as outlined in the watercolor. Uniformity or regularity as defined by the Book of Common Prayer was an essential characteristic of Anglican worship. Pon Pon Chapel manifests this regularity in its arched windows and the handsome arched entrances on the west, north, and south elevations, indicating a lengthwise and a crosswise aisle.[22]

According to the plaque erected at the site, the chapel burned sometime between 1796 and 1804. It has since been known as "The Burnt Church."[23] The churchyard shelters the grave of O'Brien Smith of Duharra plantation, who represented St. Bartholomew's Parish in the state convention that ratified the United States Constitution and later served in the House of Representatives. Smith entertained George Washington on his trip through South Carolina in 1791.[24] Near Smith's is the grave of his friend and fellow native of Ireland, Aedanus Burke, who also served in the House of Representatives but was better known for his services as a South Carolina judge.[25] Even in ruins, Pon Pon Chapel has a quiet dignity and grace. Located in the woods, far from any major thoroughfare, the ruins evoke a solitude that is reminiscent of the isolation of the early settlers of St. Bartholomew's Parish, separated from each other by marshes and waterways and by their large landholdings which limited the number of settlers. Among the ruins, wildflowers flourish in the filtered sunlight, and bird songs sound clearly in the quiet forest. Along with nature, the crumbling walls honor the Creator and recall the faith of the early settlers who worshiped there.

[1] The author spent extended amounts of time in the ACE Basin in preparation for writing the *Historical Atlas of the Rice Plantations of the ACE River Basin—1860* (Columbia: South Carolina Department of Archives and History, 1995).

[2] Nathaniel Osborne to the Secretary of the SPG, March 1, 1714/15, SPG MS, A10 #15, Library of Congress, Transcripts of Documents of the Society for the Propagation of the Gospel pertaining to South Carolina, microfilm in the South Carolina Department of Archives and History, hereinafter cited as SPG MS. Existing letters of the missionaries to St. Bartholomew's have been published. See Florence Gambrill Geiger, "St. Bartholomew's Parish as Seen By Its Rectors, 1713-1761," *South Carolina Historical Magazine*, 50: 173-203. Documentation for the glebe land comes from McCrady Plat 6326, SCDAH. The Townsend Tract is now part of Cheeha Combahee Plantation.

[3] Mary later married Jacob Matthews, and then Thomas Bosomworth, an Anglican minister. E. Merton Coulter, "Mary Musgrove, 'Queen of the Creeks,': A Chapter of Early Georgia Troubles," *The Georgia Historical Quarterly*, XI (March 1927), pp. 2-5.

[4] John Norris to John Chamberlayne, March 20, 1711, SPG MS, A6 #39, cited in Frank Klingberg, "Early Attempts at Indian Education in South Carolina, A Documentary," *South Carolina Historical Magazine*, 61: 5-6; Gideon Johnston, *Carolina Chronicle: The Papers of Commissary Gideon Johnston, 1707-1716* (Berkeley: University of California Press, 1946), pp. 107-108.

[5] A fortification was located at John Woodward's plantation on the west side of the head of the Ashepoo River. It guarded the major southern trail leading from Charleston to Palachacola on the Savannah River. See Larry E. Ivers, *Colonial Forts of South Carolina 1670-1775* (Columbia: University of South Carolina Press, 1970), p. 76.

[6] Osborne to the Secretary, May 28, 1715, SPG MS, A10 # 18; David D. Wallace, *South Carolina: A Short History* (Columbia: University of South Carolina Press, 1951), p. 90.

[7] S. Charles Bolton, *Southern Anglicanism: The Church of England in Colonial South Carolina* (Westport, Connecticut: Greenwood Press, 1982), p. 167.

[8] Thomas Cooper, *Statutes at Large of South Carolina* (Columbia: A. S. Johnston, 1838), III, 253-254. Francis Varnod, missionary at St. George's Dorchester, wrote to the SPG in January 1727 that the St. Bartholomew's Chapel was finished, and he preached there when he could. January 4, 1726/7, SPG MS, B4 #2.

[9] Robert Gowie to the Secretary, April 25, 1734, SPG MS, A25 #8. Alexander Garden reported Gowie's death to Bishop Edmund Gibson in London in a letter of November 12, 1734. See William Manross, *The Fulham Papers in the Lambeth Palace Library* (Oxford: Clarendon Press, 1965), Vol. 9 #314, p. 146.

[10] Thomas Thompson to the Secretary, August 14, 1735, May 1, 1736, SPG MS, A26 #11; B II, Part 4 #266. McCrady Plat 6315, SCDAH.

[11] John Wesley, *The Journal of the Rev. John Wesley, A.M.*, ed. Nehemiah Curnock (London: Epworth Press, 1938), I, 349-350. Courtesy of The World Methodist Council Museum, Lake Junaluska, North Carolina.

[12] John Wesley, *Journal*, pp. 350-351.

[13] Thompson to the Secretary, April 23, 1743; August 16, 1743; January 30, 1744; SPG MS, B10 #166, B11 #214, B12 #112. Part of Thompson's problem seemed to be that he was also serving as chaplain of a man-of-war, necessitating his absence from the parish from time to time, and displeasing the vestry. See Bolton, *Southern Anglicanism*, pp. 57-58.

[14] *Ibid.*, and Thompson to Bearcroft, June 1, 1743, SPG MS, B11 #211.

[15] Charles Boschi to the SPG, October 30, 1745, SPG MS, B12 #112; April 7, 1746, B14 #235. The Assembly passed an act May 25, 1745, "for founding and establishing a Parochial Chapel of Ease at the Town of Edmundsbury...." Henry Hyrne, David Godin, and Barnaby Bull were appointed commissioners. Thomas Cooper, ed., *Statutes at Large of South Carolina* (Columbia: A. S. Johnston, 1838), III, 652. The chapel at Chehaw appears on the Boss-Brailsford map of 1775, which was based on DeBrahm's 1757 map. Original in the Library of Congress, copy in the South Caroliniana Library at the University of South Carolina. No description of the building or further documentary evidence about this chapel has been found.

[16] Thomas Thompson to the SPG, April 23, 1743, SPG MS, B10, #166; Dalcho, *The Protestant Episcopal Church*, pp. 371-372; *Statutes*, IV, 152-153.

[17] Charleston Deeds AA: 45; Henry A. M. Smith, *The Historical Writings of Henry A. M. Smith*, Volume II, *Cities and Towns of Early South Carolina* (Spartanburg, SC: Reprint Company, 1988), 154-156.

[18] William Langhorne to the SPG, August 22, 1752, SPG MS, B20 #140.

[19] Lawrence S. Rowland, Alexander Moore, and George C. Rogers, Jr., *The History of Beaufort County, South Carolina* (Columbia: University of South Carolina Press, 1996), I, 161-162. Although the authors are discussing Beaufort County, the background information on South Carolina would also apply to St. Bartholomew's Parish, just across the Combahee from Beaufort County. Isaac Hayne, mentioned as an indigo planter on p. 161, owned a plantation adjacent to Pon Pon Chapel. See McCrady plat #6315, n.d., South Carolina Department of Archives and History.

[20] Frederick Dalcho, *An Historical Account of the Protestant Episcopal Church in South Carolina* (Charleston: E. Thayer, 1820; rpt. New York: Arno Press, 1970), pp. 369-371; Robert Baron to the SPG, June 20, 1760; B5 #213; and n.d., B5 #214; *Statutes*, IV, 15-16; 94-95.

[21] "The Church in St. Bartholomew's Parish," by Charles Fraser, courtesy of the Gibbes Museum, Charleston, South Carolina.

[22] Louis P. Nelson, "South Carolina Anglican: the architecture of the Lowcountry plantation parishes," MS, November 17, 1997, on file at the offices of the Diocese of South Carolina, pp. 82-83; Samuel G. Stoney, "Colonial Architecture in South Carolina," Dalcho Historical Society, Diocese of South Carolina, pp. 5-6.

[23] Plaque erected at the site by the National Society of Colonial Dames of America in the State of South Carolina.

[24] Terry W. Lipscomb, *South Carolina in 1791: George Washington's Southern Tour* (Columbia: South Carolina Department of Archives and History, l993), pp. 51-52.

[25] N. Louise Bailey and Elizabeth Ivey Cooper, *Biographical Directory of the South Carolina House of Representatives* (Columbia: University of South Carolina Press, 1981), III, 667-668, 105-107.

Monument commemorating the church of St. Paul's Parish at Stono.

ST. PAUL'S PARISH

I like that ancient Saxon phrase, which calls
The burial-ground God's-Acre! It is just;
It consecrates each grave within its walls,
And breathes a benison o'er the sleeping dust.

From "God's Acre"
Henry Wadsworth Longfellow

In a sunlit clearing in the woods on Dixie Plantation, a few beautifully carved tombstones and a marble monument mark the spot as "Church flats," the location of the old St. Paul's Parish Church. It is truly "God's Acre," set aside in memory of the first Anglican church in the community. Only a mound and some old bricks give a suggestion of the outline of the building. A mulberry tree presides over the site of the altar, and singing birds provide the choir.

One of the ten original parishes established by the Church Act of 1706, St. Paul's was southeast of the Stono River, north of the South Edisto River, and bounded to the east by the Atlantic Ocean. It originally included Wadmalaw, Edisto, and Johns Islands, but these and other small sea islands became the parish of St. John's Colleton in 1734.[1]

Landgrave Edmund Bellinger (d. 1739), owner of Ashepoo Barony and various other lands, donated thirty acres on the south branch of Stono River on a bluff near the cut which connects the Stono and Wadmalaw Rivers. Here, in 1707, parishioners built a brick church thirty-five feet long by twenty-five feet wide. They also secured a glebe of seventy-one acres and built a small brick parsonage with convenient outbuildings.[2]

The first missionary to St. Paul's, William Dunn, was in the province by December 1706, after a very dangerous and tedious voyage of five months. He began preaching in a house and found that his congregation of between seventy and ninety people included Presbyterians, Anabaptists, and independents in addition to Anglicans. Dunn explained to the Society that because there had never been a minister settled in the community, very few of his parishioners had ever received the sacrament. Nevertheless, under Dunn's leadership the church was under construction by April of 1707.[3]

The Society had instructed the missionary to convert "heathens and infidels," and he wrote, "There is in the said Parish a great Number of Negro and Indian Slaves but tis extreme difficult to perswade their Masters to have them taught in the Christian Religion…." He found that the masters believed that if the slaves were baptized they would be free. Nevertheless, Dunn convinced them to allow their slaves to come to hear the sermon every Sunday and encouraged them to teach the slave children to read. The minister thought that the masters themselves were "generally grossly ignorant of the principles of Christianity."

Although Dunn received a salary from the provincial government, he also got a supplement from the SPG. He must have been an enterprising man, for he asked that he be paid in merchandise rather than cash. He wanted such things as six dozen glazed lamb gloves for women, some fashionable ribbons, a ream of best writing paper, weirs for head dresses, leather clogs for women, Holland (linen), and two dozen women's masks. "I am told," he wrote, "that I may make of these goods after the rate of 100 per cent."[4]

With Dunn's leadership, the church was finished by November 1707. It included a cushion, a pulpit, and a communion table with a linen cloth. Dunn expected to have a silver chalice and plate before Christmas, when he planned to celebrate communion. Although Dunn's letter was very optimistic about the new building, he expressed difficulty due to transportation. The lack of bridges was a major problem in visiting parishioners and getting back and forth to Charleston on business. He said, "I am settled in a place where I can see but very few of them without going by water and it is very chargeable to keep a boat and slave to row me...."[5]

In September 1708, Dunn reported about 150 families in the parish or 300 adults, of whom about 80 professed to be Anglican. Others included 150 Presbyterians, 8 independents, 40 Anabaptists, 10 Quakers, and 12 others who professed to believe in Christ but did not participate in any organized religion. He estimated the Negro and Indian slaves at about 1000 and the free natives at 400. This was Dunn's final report, for he expressed his intention to resign due to business in Europe.[6]

Dunn's successor, John Maitland, was popular at first, particularly among the Presbyterians, who liked his extemporaneous preaching. Maitland, however, got carried away with his exhortations and started pointing his finger and railing at people from the pulpit. Commissary Gideon Johnston, the bishop's representative, found that the congregation was down to three persons, and "sometimes he has nothing but the bare Walls to preach to." Johnston tried to work with Maitland and reconcile him with the vestry, but it was to no avail. Finally Johnston worked out a deal in which the vestry would pay Maitland £70 to resign and leave the province. Johnston had the power to suspend a minister, but not to take away his salary due to "a defect in the Church Act." The controversy was a prime example of why the Anglican vestries hesitated to elect a minister, for once elected he had tenure. The problem was resolved when Maitland died in April 1711.[7]

William Tredwell Bull arrived in 1712 and served St. Paul's in an exemplary manner for the next eleven years. After Gideon Johnston's death in 1716, Bull served as commissary. He led the parish through the devastating Yamassee War in 1715, when the Indians burned the parsonage and the homes of many of the parishioners. Bull had to take refuge in Charleston for about four months, where prices were exorbitant. He said, "The Burning of my House, the Loss of a considerable Part of my Goods & cloaths, all ye Provisions & most of ye Little stock of cattle I was possessed of proves a yet greater burthen to me." Because the danger was not completely over, his parishioners kept to their little garrisons, and Bull preached there rather than in the church. These impromptu services offended his Anglican sense of regularity, and he said it would be a great comfort to return to the church, "to have ye happiness of Performing ye Service of God in ye Same good Order of Decency we were before this Unhappy Warr."[8]

When he resumed services in the church, Bull found that nearly seventy white people and numerous slaves had died since the beginning of the war a year before. He continued sadly, "There have not many Children been born this year & most that were are already deceased." Since he had recently married twenty couples he had hopes that "ye succeeding year may prove fruitfull."[9]

The vestry of St. Paul's appreciated their dedicated and able minister. Members of the vestry were outstanding and prosperous citizens: Thomas Farr, Abraham Waight, Abraham Eve, Arthur Hall, Joseph Morton, and John Fenwicke. They wrote to the Society in December 1716 of William Tredwell Bull that "his Life & conversation hath been amongst us unblameable, his Doctrine & Labours greatly Edifying & his Affection & Zeall for ye Present happy Establishment in Church & State Unquestionable."[10]

Under Bull's leadership the congregation grew, and by 1721, the church was too small. The vestry petitioned the Assembly, saying "for want of room, some were forced to stand without the door, and others hang at the windows." After securing a plan, the vestry estimated that the building would cost more than £1000, "to compleat the Same with such Decency as becometh the House of God." The legislature obliged by contributing £500. Bull said that the building would be "a neat & regular Building & large enough commodiously to hold upwards of two hundred People." The emphasis on neatness and regularity was consistent with the image of the established church.[11] A survey of the ruins appears to indicate that the brick church was in the shape of a Latin cross with a protruding chancel for the celebration of the Eucharist. The church was located at "Church Flats" on the south branch of the Stono River.[12]

In the letter in which he reported the new church, Bull said, "At midsummer last I finished the tenth year of my mission with some satisfaction...that my Labours here by the Blessing of God have done some Good." He then asked permission to return to England. The next year his request was granted and he was promoted to a benefice, an endowed position.[13]

The church continued to grow, and in 1725, parishioners enlarged the church again. In 1727, they purchased a glebe of 400 acres of land adjoining the church and pleasantly situated on the river.[14] The lower part of the parish was growing rapidly, and in 1725 the Assembly authorized a parochial chapel of ease at Willtown, a village on the Edisto River. Willtown had been the location of a fort during the Yamassee War, and since that time, scout boats for patrolling the inland passage as lookouts for Spaniards or Indians operated out of Willtown. The village included a Presbyterian church, a school, a court of law, and at least one general store. Willtown was a logical place for a chapel except for the fact that it was a stronghold of the Presbyterians. The Reverend Archibald Stobo, pastor of the Willtown church, was a strong and outspoken advocate for the Presbyterian faith. Probably because of lack of local support, the Anglican chapel of ease was never built at Willtown.[15]

After the sea islands formed a separate parish in 1734, the location of the parish church at Stono was no longer central. The Assembly authorized a parochial chapel at Beech Hill in 1737. Jeremiah Miles, who represented St. Paul's in the Assembly at that time, donated two acres on the northwest side of the high road from Thomas Elliott's plantation to Parker's Ferry at the intersection of the high road from Dorchester. Parishioners removed the frame of the Beech Hill Chapel to the glebe in 1756 because the parish church was in bad condition.[16]

St. Paul's Parish never again achieved the vigor it had enjoyed under the leadership of William Tredwell Bull. Population shifts caused a gradual decline. In the nineteenth century, an Episcopal church was built at Willtown. Summerville, the summer resort of planters of St. Paul's Parish, grew in importance, and the church of St. Paul's Summerville inherited the communion silver. In the twentieth century, most of the land was sold and the proceeds given to St. Paul's Meggett. The trustees of the diocese reserved four and a half acres, the site of the old Stono church and the cemetery. It is appropriate to remember the pioneers who founded that church in spite of the hardships of clearing land and building a civilization in a daunting wilderness. The site of their church remains "God's Acre" in memory of them.[17]

[1] Frederick Dalcho, *An Historical Account of the Protestant Episcopal Church in South Carolina* (Charleston: E. Thayer, 1820; rpt., New York: Arno Press, 1970), p. 351.

[2] Dalcho, p. 351; Henry A. M. Smith, "Historical Notes," South Carolina Historical Magazine, Vol. 11, 72-73.

[3] William Dunn to the SPG, December 6, 1706, SPG MS, A3 #53; April 21, 1707, A3 #99.

[4] *Ibid.*, April 21, 1707.

[5] *Ibid.*, Nov. 24, 1707, A3 #154.

[6] Dunn to the Society, September 20, 1708, SPG MS, A4 #111.

[7] Gideon Johnston, *Carolina Chronicle: The Papers of Commissary Gideon Johnston 1707-1716* (Berkeley: University of California Press, 1946; rpt. Millwood, New York: Kraus Reprint Company, 1974), pp. 49-51, 80-81, 93.

[8] William Tredwell Bull to the Society, February 6, 1716, SPG MS, B4-1 #45.

[9] Bull to the Society, May 16, 1716, SPG MS, B4-1 #70.

[10] Vestry to the Society, December 24, 1716, SPG MS, B4-1 #82.

[11] Dalcho, *Protestant Episcopal Church*, p. 352; Petition enclosed with letter of William T. Bull to the Society, October 10, 1722, SPG MS, B4-1 #124.

[12] Louis P. Nelson, "South Carolina Anglican: the architecture of the Lowcountry plantation parishes," Draft of November 17, 1997, Diocese of South Carolina; Dalcho, p. 51.

[13] Dalcho, p. 352.

[14] Dalcho, p. 355.

[15] Suzanne Linder, "Willtown, Colonial Village on the Edisto," study on file at the Charleston Museum, pp. 26-28.

[16] Dalcho, pp. 355, 357; Thomas Cooper, ed., *Statutes at Large of South Carolina* (Columbia: A. S. Johnston, 1838), III, 453-454; Walter B. Edgar and N. Louise Bailey, *Biographical Directory of the South Carolina House of Representatives* (Columbia: University of South Carolina Press, 1977), pp. 463-464; Albert Sidney Thomas, *A Historical Account of the Protestant Episcopal Church in South Carolina, 1820-1957* (Columbia: R. L. Bryan, 1957), p. 410.

[17] Thomas, pp. 410-412.

A beautifully carved gravestone, St. Paul's Parish.

St. James' Parish, Santee, built in 1768 and known as "The Brick Church." The body of each column of the portico is of brick, especially cast in a curve, while the capitals and bases appear to be of ground brick.

ST. JAMES' PARISH, SANTEE

"THE BRICK CHURCH"

What language shall I borrow to thank thee, dearest friend,
For this thy dying sorrow, thy pity without end?
O make me thine forever; And should I fainting be,
Lord, let me never, never, Outlive my love to thee.

From "O Sacred Head Now Wounded"
Anonymous Latin, Trans. Paul Gerhardt (1607-1676)

One of the most significant problems experienced by the parishioners of St. James' Santee was agreeing on the language to be used in worship. Communicating with Indians for trading purposes and with slaves newly arrived from Africa also posed a problem. French and English were the predominant languages, but Indians and Africans contributed numerous dialects to the microcosm of the American melting pot on the Santee.[1]

French Protestants known as Huguenots left their native country to escape religious persecution. Their exodus intensified in 1685 after the French monarch, Louis XIV, repealed the Edict of Nantes granting protection to Protestants. By 1690, about eighty families of French refugees lived along the Santee and its various tributaries from Mazyck's Ferry, South Santee, two miles below Wambaw Creek, to within a few miles of Lenud's Ferry just above the French settlement called Jamestown, a village on the Santee laid out in 1706. By that date, about one hundred French families and sixty English families lived in the vicinity.[2]

The French organized the first church, which boasted 111 members by 1699. The Reverend Pierre Robert, a native of Basle, Switzerland, came to South Carolina in 1686 and settled on the Santee. A tradition states that Robert was the first among the local settlers to own a horse. He was thus able to visit the homes of his congregation and hold services in various locations. Documentation is unavailable to show when settlers built their first church building, but it must have been standing by 1700 when John Lawson, deputy surveyor for the British government, visited the region. Lawson noted that he met several Frenchmen coming from their church and that they helped him cross creeks with their dories (rowboats).[3]

John Lawson said that the French were "a temperate and industrious People," very clean and decent looking. Many carried on a successful trade with the Indians. He admired their plantations and attributed their success, at least in part, to the fact that they lived as a kindred tribe, "every one making it his Business to be assistant to the Wants of his Country-man, ...as he does his own; all seeming to share in the Misfortunes, and rejoyce at the Advance, and Rise, of their Brethren." They were also very kind and hospitable to him. Lawson mentioned gentlemen named Huger, Gendron, LeGrand, Gaillard, and the "French doctor," names which are still associated with St. James' Santee.[4]

After dining with the settlers, Lawson commented on the joys of hunting wild game. In England, hunting was a privilege reserved for nobility or wealthy people who owned hunting preserves. The English visitor was impressed that in South Carolina deer and other game were not preserved within boundaries "to satisfy the Appetite of the Rich alone." A poor laborer with a gun had as good a chance at "Coarses of Delicacies crouded upon his Table, as he that is Master of a greater Purse."[5]

In response to an application by the French settlers, the Assembly passed an act on April 9, 1706, declaring that the church "which is now built in Jamestown" be declared to be a parish church of St. James' on Santee River. The act further provided that the minister should be paid £50 per year from the funds derived from the tax on furs, and that it would be lawful for the services to be in French so long as the minister used the French translation of the Prayer Book by Dr. John Durel, which had been commissioned by Charles II. The act establishing St. James' Santee was superseded by the much more comprehensive "Church Act" of November 1706, which added many provisions but did not substantially change the act establishing the parish.[6]

Pierre Robert continued as rector until 1710, when James Gignillat, another Swiss native who was an SPG missionary, arrived. In his first letter to society headquarters, Gignillat described a situation that he found "very strange and of a very ill attendancy." His apprehension had to do with the fact that the parishioners had the authority to elect their rectors. He feared that he would not be elected and asked the society to provide for his support. Furthermore, he considered it "hard Labour" to preach in two churches, in French in the morning and in English in the evening. The most difficult thing was that the people had never used the Anglican Book of Common Prayer, and there was so much resistance to the Anglican liturgy that he was hesitant to enforce its use. Furthermore, Pierre Robert continued to christen children and minister to his former parishioners.[7]

Gignillat soon found a way to guarantee his subsistence. He married Marie Postell, widow of John Boisseau. Francis LeJau, rector of St. James' Goose Creek, wrote in January 1712 to John Chamberlayne, secretary of the Society, that Gignillat "marryed an Ancient Woman in my parish, the world had spoken much of the unworthy manner of his useing her, but I could not creditt the whole till she came to me and complained." Mrs. Boisseau was said to have a fortune of £4000, of which Gignillat had gained control. According to LeJau, he denied her even necessary food and clothing, and "he forced the poor old woman out of doors, and makes a meer jest of his promises.…" By September 1711, Gignillat had left his wife and parish and returned to Switzerland, leaving no descendants in America.[8]

The language dilemma in St. James' Santee was significant enough to command the attention of Governor Nicholas Trott, who wrote to the Society of his concern that five parishes in South Carolina were vacant. He pointed out that the "Minister for Saint James Santee must be a Frenchman but with all must understand English too, that so he may Preach to the French in French and to ye English in English."[9]

In 1712, the Reverend Claude Phillippe de Richebourg moved to St. James' Santee from Manakintown, Virginia. The move proved advantageous, for the church had made arrangements to purchase the 1000-acre plantation of Alexander Chastaigner as a glebe for the use of the minister. The plantation also included buildings suitable for a church and a parsonage.[10]

Evidence of church growth under Richebourg occurred in 1714, when the Assembly authorized a chapel of ease to be built on the southeast side of Echaw Creek, a tributary of the Santee.[11] Prosperity was short-lived because the parish suffered severely in the Yamassee War, which began in April 1715. The settlers initially fled from their plantations, but a week later they returned and made a fortress of Richebourg's house, which served as a militia center and army garrison until March 1716.[12]

Richebourg applied to the Society to become a missionary so that he could receive financial aid. He explained that "the army hath destroyed all my provisions not onely for the year past, butt for this very year also." The fact that he had five small children amplified the problem. His orchard, garden, and outbuildings were destroyed, and as Gideon Johnston, the Bishop's representative, said, "…where every thing must be Suppos'd to be in common in Such places, it is natural to believe, that great losses must be sustain'd within doors, as well as without." Johnston explained that the two Frenchmen, John LaPierre of St. Denis' Parish and Richebourg of St. James' Santee, were in so desperate need that one or both were considering leaving the province. A gift from the SPG of thirty pounds each helped them to survive although they were not official missionaries.[13]

Richebourg had a controversial career. Although he had been a Roman Catholic before he converted to the Anglican faith, he sympathized with the Huguenots and conducted services in the form of French Protestant liturgy. He baptized without the sign of the cross and without godfathers or godmothers. His parishioners could receive communion kneeling, sitting, or standing. At one point, his practices became so contentious that gentlemen drew swords at the church door. The issue was resolved without blows, but Commissary Johnston

Arched doors and windows give an inspiring sense of light at St. James' Santee.

threatened to curtail Richebourg's salary and remove him from the province unless he conformed to Anglican worship practices. Richebourg submitted, at least temporarily. He died in 1717 widely mourned by his predominantly Huguenot parish.[14]

The hostility between the French and the English settlers was possibly exacerbated by Queen Anne's War (1702-1713). Great Britain was at war with Spain and France. In America the war was primarily concerned with control of the lucrative Indian trade. South Carolina traders were penetrating as far as the Mississippi and were coming in conflict with the Spanish at St. Augustine and their French allies at Mobile.[15]

A division of the large parish may have helped to separate diverse groups. An act of the provincial Assembly created Prince George's Parish, Winyah, from that portion of St. James' Santee north of the Santee River on March 10, 1721. The part of St. James' located upriver on the south side of the Santee was separated to form St. Stephen's Parish on May 11, 1754. St. Stephen's became known as English Santee as opposed to St. James', which was French Santee.[16]

Albert Pouderous, a Frenchman, was minister at St. James' from 1720 to 1730. His hardships included a seven-month voyage to America during which he was shipwrecked. Once he settled on the Santee, a flood destroyed his plantation crops and reached a depth of six feet inside his house. Because he lived on a major thoroughfare, he was obliged to offer aid to weary travelers at great expense to himself. He also kept medicine to minister to those who were ill. In April 1724, he wrote to the Bishop of London seeking financial aid. Somehow he was able to hold out until his death in 1730.[17]

The old frame church at Jamestown was no longer convenient due to a shift of the population away from the village as inhabitants developed their own plantations. The Assembly authorized two new chapels in 1731. One was to be in the upper part of the parish and one in the lower, and the law required the minister to officiate in English. Parishioners completed a new brick chapel in 1748 near the site of the old chapel at Echaw. A brick parsonage was near the church. When St. Stephen's Parish was established in 1754, the chapel of ease at Echaw became the parish church of St. James'. It remained such until 1768, when parishioners built a new brick church near Wambaw Bridge and relegated the building at Echaw to chapel of ease status once more.[18]

The lovely new brick church reflected the increasing wealth of the Santee planters, who were making fortunes growing rice and indigo.[19] One of the workmen, probably the man in charge, recorded the date 1768 in a brick about shoulder height on the right side of the south door.[20] The design of the building is balanced and pleasing to the eye. Originally, the chancel was beneath the Palladian window at the east end. Identical four-columned porticoes adorned the north and south sides. A long aisle from the west entrance to the chancel bisected a cross aisle between the north and south doors. Tradition states that the French parishioners entered from the north door, while the English used the south entrance. In later years the north portico was made into a vestry room opening on the chancel, and the pulpit was moved to the east end. Architectural historian Samuel Gaillard Stoney expressed regret at the changes. He still considered the south portico as outstanding. He said, "There are no more gracefully proportioned columns in brick that I know of anywhere around this country." The columns are unusual in several ways. The body of each column is of brick especially cast in a curve, while the capitals and bases appear to be made of ground brick. Most classic columns have an abacus, a flat square tablet, at the top. Stoney continued, "Having no stone and not being able to make big square members that projected, the architect of this good church contrived these little delicate capitals with moulded brick or ground brick, and did it so successfully that you're not at all troubled by the loss of the regular scheme of design." Stoney further explained that the abacus was so called because before the days of calculators, a workman might carry around a square plank on which he could spread fine sand and do calculations by writing with his finger.[21]

By the time the Wambaw Church was completed, the controversy over the language to be used in worship had largely disappeared. After about 1736, intermarriages between French and English families along with the gradual demise of the older generation of original French immigrants meant that the majority of inhabitants understood English.[22]

The Reverend Samuel Fenner Warren, a missionary of the SPG, served the church from 1758 until shortly before his death in 1789. A man of remarkable energy and high esteem, Warren was meticulous in keeping parish records. The church prospered under his leadership. Although Warren had strong family ties in England, he supported the patriot cause in the American Revolution. During Warren's tenure, Thomas Lynch, signer of the Declaration of Independence, presented a silver communion service to the church. Rebecca Brewton Motte, widow of Jacob Motte, donated an elegant folio Bible and two Prayer Books. She later gained fame in the Revolution when she encouraged American officers to set fire to her home to rout a British garrison in residence there. British soldiers stole the Motte Bible from St. James' Santee, but after the war, an acquaintance of Mrs. Motte noticed the Bible with her name inscribed on it at a bookstore in London and restored it to the church.[23]

The fact that the La Mottes anglicized the name to Motte illustrates the acculturation of the French Huguenots. Through the years, the community which began with serious ethnic divisions became almost like one huge extended family. Santee families developed cultural and kinship ties which remain important to the present day. Although St. James' is no longer a parish church, once a year descendants of the original settlers gather for a worship service and picnic on the grounds. They are now united by a special language of kinship and shared heritage.

[1]For a discussion of Indian and African languages in Carolina, see Peter Wood, *Black Majority* (New York: Alfred A. Knopf, 1974), pp. 178-180.

[2]Arthur Henry Hirsch, *The Huguenots of Colonial South Carolina* (Durham: Duke University Press, 1928), pp. 14-15; Henry A. M. Smith, "French James Town," *South Carolina Historical Magazine*, 9, pp. 222-223. Lenud's Ferry was near the spot where the present-day Georgetown-Williamsburg County line

meets the Santee River.

[3] *Ibid.*, 60-61; John Lawson, *A New Voyage to Carolina*, ed. Hugh T. Lefler (Chapel Hill: University of North Carolina, 1967), pp. 19-20. Henry Martyn Robert (1837-1923), a descendant of Pierre Robert, became famous for his *Rules of Order*. See Anne Baker Leland Bridges and Roy Williams, III, *St. James Santee, Plantation Parish* (Spartanburg, SC: The Reprint Company, 1997), p. 28.

[4] *Lawson*, pp. 19-21. Agnes Leland Baldwin identified the "French doctor" as Isaac DeJohn or DeJean from Colonial Grants, Vol. 38, p. 377, South Carolina Department of Archives and History. See also Anne Baker Leland Bridges and Roy Williams, III, *St. James Santee: Plantation Parish* (Spartanburg, SC: The Reprint Company, 1997), pp. 16-17.

[5] *Lawson*, p.20.

[6] Thomas Cooper, ed., *Statutes at Large of South Carolina* (Columbia: A. S. Johnston, 1838), II, pp. 268-269, 282-294; hereinafter cited as *Statutes*.

[7] James Gignillat to the Society, May 28, 1710, Library of Congress Transcripts of the Society for the Propagation of the Gospel, documents pertaining to South Carolina, microfilm, South Carolina Department of Archives and History, Vol. A5, #119; hereinafter cited as SPG MS.

[8] Francis LeJau to John Chamberlayne, January 10, 1711/12, SPG MS, Vol. A7, #8; Bridges and Williams, *St. James Santee*, p. 31. Governor Nicholas Trott to John Chamberlayne, Secretary of the SPG, September 19, 1711, SPG MS, Volume A7, #5.

[9] Trott to the Society, *op.cit.*, September 19, 1711, SPG MS, A7, #5.

[10] Frederick Dalcho, *An Historical Account of the Protestant Episcopal Church in South Carolina* (Charleston: E. Thayer, 1820; rpt. New York: Arno Press, 1970), p. 296; Bridges and Williams, *St. James Santee*, pp. 32-33.

[11] *Statutes*, II, 618-620.

[12] Bridges and Williams, *St. James Santee*, pp. 33-34.

[13] Claudius Philippe De Richebourg to the Society, February 12, 1715/16, SPG MS, B4-I #48. Gideon Johnston to the SPG, January 27, 1716, in Frank J. Klingberg, ed., *Carolina Chronicle: The Papers of Commissary Gideon Johnston, 1707-1716* (Berkeley: University of California Press, 1946), pp. 154-155.

[14] Hirsch, *The Huguenots of Colonial South Carolina*, pp. 133-134; Bridges and Williams, *St. James Santee*, p. 35. Bridges and Williams note that one of the descendants of Claude Philipe de Richebourg was Senator Sam Ervin, chairman of the Senate Watergate hearings. See p. 32.

[15] For a thorough discussion of Queen Anne's War in the southeast, see Verner W. Crane, *The Southern Frontier, 1670-1732* (Ann Arbor: University of Michigan Press, 1956), pp. 71-107, passim.

[16] *Statutes*, III, 171; IV-2, 8-12.

[17] Albert Pouderous to Bishop of London, April 15, 1724, quoted in full in Hirsch, *The Huguenots of Colonial South Carolina*, pp. 320-321.

[18] Dalcho, *An Historical Account of the Protestant Episcopal Church*, pp. 297-299. The Echaw church was abandoned by 1826. The site became "lost" until rediscovered by a hunter. Bridges and Williams, *St. James Santee*, pp. 158, 325-326.

[19] Bridges and Williams, *St. James Santee*, pp. 45-49; Hirsch, *The Huguenots of Colonial South Carolina*, p. 214.

[20] Oran Baldwin, interview with the author, September 11, 1998.

[21] Samuel Gaillard Stoney, "Colonial Church Architecture," [booklet] (Charleston: The Dalcho Historical Society, 1954), p. 8; See also Stoney, *Plantations of the Carolina Low Country* (New York: Dover and Carolina Art Association, 1989), p. 69; Harold Wickliffe Rose, *The Colonial Houses of Worship in America* (New York: Hastings House, 1963), pp. 434-435.

[22] Bridges and Williams, *St. James Santee*, pp. 41-42.

[23] Dalcho, *The Protestant Episcopal Church*, pp. 300-301; Rebecca Brewton inherited her wealth from her father, Robert Brewton, and her brother, Miles Brewton. She married Jacob Motte in 1758. He served in the Assembly and owned 244 slaves at his death in 1780. Walter B. Edgar and N. Louise Bailey, *Biographical Dictionary of the House of Representatives* (Columbia: University of South Carolina Press, 1977), pp. 480-481; see also Bridges and Williams, *St. James Santee*, pp. 55-58.

Heavy brick walls with quoins and rusticated openings attest to the massive stability of the original "Biggin Church" at St. John's Parish, Berkeley.

ST. JOHN'S PARISH, BERKELEY

BIGGIN CHURCH AND STRAWBERRY CHAPEL

*In sylvan silence stands our shrine No worshipers are near,
No thankful heart pours forth its praise Nor troubled soul a prayer.*

*Its doors are closed and all is still Nor can a sound be heard
Save but the whisper of the wind, Or note of forest bird.*

*Soft sunlight streaming through the trees, Sheds beauty all around,
A sense of Peace pervades the scene One feels 'tis hallowed ground.*

Excerpt from "Strawberry Chapel"
Isaac Ball, 1913

St. John's Berkeley was one of the larger parishes established by the Church Act of 1706. It was roughly thirty-four miles long and twelve miles wide, or 408 square miles. The lower part of the parish encompassing the western branch of the Cooper River was accessible by ocean-going vessels as far as Strawberry Landing and the town of Childsbury, and by smaller boats to Stoney Landing near Monck's Corner. Peter Colleton, the first son of the original Proprietor Sir John Colleton, received a grant to Fairlawn Barony in 1685. By 1688, the Colleton family owned 74,216 acres of land in what would later become St. John's. The parish was sparsely settled with an estimated population of 315 whites and 180 blacks in 1705, which increased to 437 whites and 1439 blacks in 1720.[1]

The tremendous increase in the number of slaves shows the growth in the plantation economy during that fifteen-year period. The growth of the plantation elite also contributed to building a church on Biggin Hill about 1715 and a chapel at Childsbury Town prior to 1725. In the 1760s, residents of the upper part of the parish built a log house at a location later known as Chapel Hill, where the parish minister held services once in two months. In 1770, the Assembly authorized a chapel of ease near Markley's Old Field in the upper part of the parish, but no evidence has surfaced to indicate that parishioners built a church there before the Revolution. Anglican worship in the colonial period in St. John's Berkeley centered around the parish church, called Biggin, and Strawberry Chapel at Childsbury.[2]

No church building existed when Robert Maule, the first SPG missionary, became a resident. Maule possessed a true missionary spirit. He arrived in Charleston in 1707 after a passage of nearly five months—three months "wind-bound" in the English harbors and between ten and eleven weeks in passage. The governor and council assigned him to St. John's Berkeley Parish on the western branch of the Cooper River, in the vicinity of present day Monck's Corner. The authorities assured Maule that the location was in a pleasant and healthy part of the province and the planters there were generally good, sober, teachable people. With no Anglican church building, Maule arranged to cooperate with Florente Philippe Trouillard, a Huguenot who had allied with the Anglican Church after the establishment of St. John's Parish by the Church Act of 1706. At the invitation of the French settlers, Maule preached to the English colonists in their building.[3]

The English clergyman suffered from the heat as he rode long distances to visit parishioners scattered about the parish. In March 1709, he wrote the Society that he had been sick with fever and ague, "which at length concluded in a most Violent Belly Ache; so violent indeed that I verily believed it would have ended my days," he said. His trials had just begun, for in October of 1709, his house caught fire and burned to the ground. He thought that a spark from the chimney "which was raised but a little from the roof" started the fire. Maule said, "Had I continued sleeping but a quarter of an hour longer, I should have perished." He lost everything he had—books, clothes, linens brought from England, and household goods purchased in South Carolina.[4] For nearly three years he lived in a small outbuilding which, he said, was insufficient to defend him from the violence of the heat in summer or from the extreme sharpness of cold in winter. He reported, "Tis true the Inhabitants of my parish are Generally but poor—And which is the greatest hindrance have not one leading man among them by whose Influence & authority this or any other Charitable work might be promoted." Maule asked the Society to consider a transfer.[5]

Fortunately, his lot improved considerably by 1712, after Colonel Thomas Broughton moved into the parish. Broughton, son-in-law of Sir Nathaniel Johnson, governor from 1703 to 1708, was developing Mulberry Plantation on the western branch of the Cooper River. Maule, with high hopes of getting a parsonage, said, "This Pious Gentleman has not only subscribed very generously himself, but being a Person Universally Esteamed both by his Interest and Influence...prevailed with Several others of them also to Subscribe for the Purchase of the house and settlement." The parish purchased a glebe from Sir John Colleton, owner of Fairlawn Barony, on December 5, 1712. In addition to the sale of land for the parsonage, Colleton donated three acres for the site of the parish church.[6] After the building was completed, Thomas Broughton "very generously adorned the Church, made a Communion Table, railed in the Chancel, made a Pulpit, Reading Desk, and some Pews, all of Cedar, and at his own expense."[7]

No record of the plan or footprint of the church has been found. Notes about repairs scattered through the minutes of the vestry (which survive from 1731 to 1768) provide some intriguing clues. Orders to glaze (insert glass in) the west door, another to glaze the church doors, and a note to put a sill to the north door indicate that the traditional plan of a chancel at the east end with doors on the west, north, and south, and cross aisles would be a possibility. Compass-headed or arched windows over the entrances at various colonial churches such as St. Andrew's, St. James' Santee, Pompion Hill, and others suggest what the vestry meant by glazing the doors. Another mention of repairs noted that due to the ruinous condition of the chancel floor, it was resolved to have the same floored with "glaz'd dutch Tile of two collours."[8]

The sale of a pew "in the middle isle" to Abraham Sanders raises the question of a possible central aisle, but it is also possible that the middle aisle referred to the north-south orientation which would be roughly in the middle of a rectangular building. The window arrangement is also puzzling. The vestry agreed to pay John Vaughan "for cutting the gable end window to the church." Later the vestry "ordered the church wardens to get the bull's eyes [small round windows] on the gallery of the church taken down and the vacancys to be filled up by shingling and to get two windows broke out in the wall of the west end of the Church, one on each side of the window in the Gallery and the Bulls Eye Windows to be fix'd therein."[9]

Although exact information about the appearance of the church is unavailable, enough evidence survives to support a statement by William Tredwell Bull, commissary (bishop's representative) in 1723, when he called St. John's "a large populous parish in which is a decent brick Church lately beautified at ye charge of the parish." Bull also mentioned a very convenient brick house for the minister pleasantly situated on a glebe of 300 acres of land. Church historian Frederick Dalcho states that the church was begun in 1710. It certainly was not finished at that date. Robert Maule's letters indicate that the impetus to build a church and parsonage occurred after 1712, when Thomas Broughton became active in the parish. It was not unusual for colonial churches to take several years to complete. Beautification of the interior may even have occurred after the Yamassee War caused a major upheaval in the parish in 1715.[10]

A letter from Maule to the Society written in August 1711 described the situation that led up to the war. Maule conversed with some of the local Indians and reported, "They are for the most part great Lovers of Justice and Equity in their dealings and can't endure either to Cheat or be Cheated." In talking with some of the old men, Maule found that they believed in God and in future rewards or punishments. When he approached them about accepting the white man's religion, they rejected his efforts and explained, "Backarara [white men] no good; Backarara Cheat, Backarara Lye, Backarara Drink Grandy; me no Lovy that." Maule concluded that the best way to reach the Indians was to persuade the white men "to live a more moral and regular life than the generality of them have hitherto done."[11]

Mistreatment of the Indians led to bloody war in 1715. Colonists in St. John's Parish took refuge in the fortified house of Thomas Broughton. With cannon emplacements and probably a stockade wall, the residence known as Mulberry Castle served as a garrison.[12] Robert Maule stayed there about four months, where he baptized children, visited the sick and wounded, and buried the dead. He read prayers every day and preached on Sundays. Maule found it difficult to remain in a numerous crowd penned up in a small enclosure in the heat of summer, but he said, "That having hitherto Resided amongst them in their prosperity, I could not, in conscience, disert them in Times of Danger & distress."[13]

After Maule returned home, he suffered from dysentery. He died December 23, 1716, "after 3 years Sickness which brought him to a Consumption and Lingering feaver," according to his friend Francis LeJau, pastor of St. James Goose Creek. LeJau further commented, "I believe the retird life he led, with his hard Studying, & the great cold he got in Serving the town Parish...brought the distemper upon him." Maule was the fourth missionary to die within eighteen months. His death was "lamented by this whole Province which have been witnesses of the Excellent and Christian Qualityes that adornd the Life and conversation of our late deceasd Brother. His Piety, modesty, charity and Sweet temper renderd him the Object of our Love, & the Clergy lost in him one of their brightest ornaments."[14]

St. John's Church was without a minister until 1721. The vestry wrote to the Society, "In May last arrived here the Reverend Mr. Moses Clarke, who discharged his mission in said parish till the month of September and then it pleased God to afflict him with a feavour of which he dyed." The vestry begged the Society to send another missionary soon. They were not particularly pleased with the next candidate.[15]

The Reverend Brian Hunt served St. John's for about five years. Despite the fact that the parish supplied him with the services of five slaves, he constantly had financial problems. The vestry claimed that he began with "lesser Indecencies and transcient levities & follies" and progressed to gross repeated vices including drunkenness, quarreling, defaming, lying, and abusive language. The precipitating factor which forced his resignation was that sometime in May 1727, Hunt performed a marriage ceremony for Gibbon Cawood and Robert Wright. Gibbon, the sixteen-year-old daughter of John Cawood, deceased, was the ward of two Charleston merchants, Andrew Allen and Charles Hill. Despite the fact that her guardians had filed a caveat against issuing a marriage license, the wedding took place at midnight at the home of the bride's mother in Charleston. Mrs. Cawood was not at home at the time. Hunt was out of his jurisdiction, but he had the couple rent rooms in his parish, which established his right to marry them.[16]

A public outcry resulted when the marriage became known. The bride's guardians appealed to Governor Arthur Middleton, who referred the matter to the Society. Allen and Hill explained that they had lost hope of securing a marriage settlement (prenuptial agreement), and they feared Gibbon's substantial estate would soon be lost. In the eighteenth century, a married woman could not own property. Whatever she owned automatically became her husband's when they married. To protect a woman's fortune, it was customary to put the property in trust with guardians or family members as trustees and to have the groom sign a marriage settlement agreeing to the procedure. There was usually a clause stating that the woman could use the income from the trust, but it could not be used to pay the husband's debts. Without this protection, Gibbon could quickly lose her inheritance.[17]

The SPG immediately suspended its supplement to Hunt's salary and informed the guardians that a new commissary would soon come to the province who would prosecute Hunt if possible. Hunt found himself confined to the Charleston jail, where he wrote letters expressing his outrage and some element of surprise at his predicament. Surely, there had been other elopements or marriages of questionable legality.

The difference in this case went to the heart of what the Church of England was and what the people expected of church officials. A large sum of money was at stake, and in addition to the legacy to his daughter Gibbon, John Cawood had been a member of the SPG and had left £3000 "towards the repairing and adorning of the new Brick Church [St. Philip's] in Charles Town."[18] South Carolina residents expected the established church to promote respectable, orderly behavior and to support the mores of the upper class. Wealthy contributors counted on the clergy to maintain the rules of society. Otherwise, what was the purpose of a tax-supported established church? Hunt wrote to the SPG enclosing a "certificate of the mother of Mr. Wright

...which fully shows it was neither a sudden, nor injurious marriage." After all, the Wrights were a very respectable family, and Robert Wright, Sr., father of the groom, later served as chief justice of the province. Nevertheless, Hunt was soon on his way back to England. The swift reaction to Brian Hunt's indiscretion affirmed Anglican advocacy of upper-class interests.[19]

For the period of Hunt's tenure, minutes of the vestry of St. John's Berkeley do not survive. Minutes of meetings from 1731 to 1768 indicate that most of the business of the parish was concerned with repairs to the church or parsonage or provision for the poor. When a "poor vagabond boy" whose parents were either dead or had run away appeared at Northhampton Plantation, the vestry arranged for blacksmith David Geddy to employ him as an apprentice. Michael Butcher's detailed apprentice bond provided that he would faithfully serve his master, his secrets keep, his lawful commands gladly obey; that he should not waste his master's goods nor lend them to others; he should not commit fornication or contract matrimony, should not play at cards, dice, or haunt ale houses, taverns or play houses, but in all things behave himself. In return, Geddy was to teach him the whole art and mystery, trade, and occupation of a blacksmith; teach him to read and write; and supply food, lodging, apparel, washing, and all other necessaries.[20]

The vestry minutes of February 2, 1755, state casually, "The Parish Church being accidentally Burnt on Monday...a letter was wrote to Emanuel Giggerman...to survey the walls in order to repair it." Apparently, after consultation, the vestry members decided that a new church was necessary. In June 1755, they agreed on a plan for a new church and sent it about the parish to see who would subscribe. On March 19, 1756, the Assembly passed an act for building a new church on any part of the three acres previously given for a church and churchyard. The location was near Biggin Swamp, which was probably named for Biggin Hill in Kent, near London, and St. John's Church was often called Biggin Church.[21]

Construction progressed slowly, for in 1767, the vestry advertised for workmen and described the building as "60 by 40 feet in the clear, three bricks thick in the Foundation, and two and a half in the well, and 17 Feet high above Ground." Architectural details included English bond brickwork with quoined corners, rusticated openings, and a brick watertable capped by three courses of molded bricks.[22]

From the ruins that remain, one can discern the three standard doorways and openings for large arched windows. Evidence in the brickwork suggests a gallery in the west end. An advertisement in the Charleston *Gazette* April 28, 1777, requested that "any tradesman who is capable of executing a genteel Altar piece for this Church, and is willing to undertake the same immediately; or to glaze the Windows, and plaister and whitewash the inside, is desired to apply to Captain John Cordes."[23]

If the church remained unfinished more than twenty years after the old church burned, it is highly questionable whether it reached completion during the Revolution. Patriots had repulsed the attack on Charleston in June of 1776, but the British managed to capture the port city in 1780. In July 1781, British Lieutenant Colonel James Coates took a position at Biggin Church. When patriots Wade Hampton, Henry Lee, and Thomas Sumter pursued Coates there, the British officer set fire to his baggage and stores in the church and retreated. The patriots noticed the flames about three o'clock in the morning of July 17. They overtook Coates and defeated him at Quinby Bridge later in the day.[24] Parishioners repaired the church after the Revolution, but it burned again in a forest fire in the late nineteenth century.[25]

STRAWBERRY CHAPEL

The dignified and substantial building known as Strawberry Chapel seems firmly settled—almost *planted*—amid the live oaks and weathered grave stones of its churchyard. A brick enclosure sets apart the Ball family section of the cemetery and makes a subtle statement that although designated as a publicly established chapel of ease in the colonial period, it was, and remains to the present, more of a family chapel. This is particularly true when one considers the elaborate kinship network among Cooper River planters, so that many people with other surnames are considered to be a part of the extended Ball family. Although the chapel is no longer in regular use, it is customary to have services several times a year.[26]

Construction of the chapel took place after 1718, when James Child bequeathed an acre and a

Strawberry Chapel was in the village of Childsbury at the location of the ferry across the Cooper River.

half "for to build a Church or Chapel upon it, and for a burying place for the inhabitants…," and before December 9, 1725, when the Assembly passed an act establishing a parochial chapel of ease at that site. The statute recited that James Child and others had built a chapel at their own expense which would become part of the Anglican Church. The Reverend Brian Hunt, rector of St. John's Berkeley, took credit for establishing the chapel. In August 1726, he wrote to the Society, "I formerly wrote you of a village in this Parish well situated on Cooper River at which a Ferry attends which causes a concourse of people. A Chappel having been formerly built but never used I…petitioned the house of Assembly, …and obtained a law." Hunt reported that divine service was established once a month besides which he performed it every second Sunday afternoon "to encourage the people to a more frequent devotion." The minister pointed out the hardship of riding twenty miles in the summer, "which is the hottest ever been known in these parts."[27]

James Child, who donated land for the church, had surveyed and sold lots to establish a village which he called Childsbury Town. Child was in the province by 1698, when he obtained a grant for land on the western branch of the Cooper River later known as Strawberry, an excellent location for an entrepreneur.[28] This location was near the intersection of two Indian trading paths. "The path to Virginia by way of Cape Fear" ran through Strawberry and intersected with the Cherokee Path which ran parallel with the entire length of the western branch of the Cooper River.[29] James Child was heavily involved in the Indian trade, and Thomas Nairne, later Indian Agent of the colony, accused him of setting a band of Cherokees against some friendly Indians to obtain slaves. As a result, the Assembly asked the governor to ban Child from the Indian trade in 1706.[30] The next year, Child laid out the plan for the town of Childsbury on his Strawberry property. The site was at the highest point on the western branch of the Cooper to which ocean-going vessels could travel. It was also the location of a ferry established by the government in 1705 with Child as one of the commissioners.[31]

In 1723/24, the Assembly authorized a fair and markets at Childsbury. Markets would be held on Tuesdays and Saturdays. Fairs took place in May and October for four days as a time "for exposing to sale horses, cattle and merchandize" such as grain, victuals, provisions, and all sorts of items. No one could be arrested for minor crimes such as previous debts while at the fair, and for disputes arising on site, a "Court of Pipowders" had authority. "Pipowders" comes from the French *pied poudre*, or dusty foot. An offender did not have to wait for a regular court date, but could receive justice as he was, dusty feet and all. Any time a problem arose, the Court of Pipowders could hear the case and make a ruling on the spot.[32]

In addition to the chapel, James Child had made provision for a school in the village. Before 1750, three carpenters, two tailors, two butchers, a tanner, a shoemaker, and a doctor operated in the town at various times. In the 1740s, there was even an attorney in the neighborhood, which also boasted a general store, a tavern, and a track for horse races. Travelers awaiting the ferry or crews from boats in the river patronized local businesses.[33]

If the walls of the old chapel could talk, what tales they might relate of peddlers at the fair selling ribbons and trinkets, of sailors finding refreshment in the tavern, of planters loading produce for export, or of ladies and gentlemen arriving by boat to attend church on Sunday. The shadow side of the picture would be the stories of the Indians and Africans who served as slaves. Although there were no official population statistics, Africans probably outnumbered whites by more than five to one by the beginning of the Revolution.[34] The population ratio is one indication of the wealth of the elite which enabled them to support both the parish church and Strawberry Chapel.

The chapel plan is similar to that of St. James' Goose Creek, completed in 1719, less than thirty miles away. It is the typical plan for Anglican churches in colonial South Carolina: rectangular with entrances on the north, south, and west sides. Single windows flank the doorways, and the roof, like that of St. James', is in the jerkin-head style with beveled-off gables. Bull's-eye windows with tripartite keystones on four sides ornament both gable ends and provide additional illumination. The building is now stuccoed, but the under bricks are laid in Flemish bond with a tooled mortar joint, suggesting that the brickwork was at first exposed. An old newspaper clipping from the *Charleston*

Strawberry Chapel has an arched ceiling with a bull's eye window over the altar.

The Ball family vault at Strawberry Chapel. Before modern embalming, bodies were sometimes placed in this vault to await burial so that family members could gather for the funeral.

News and Courier of 1929 indicates that the original high pulpit was torn down in renovations between 1854 and 1858. The gallery at the west end met a similar fate after the earthquake of 1886.[35]

During the period when the Biggin Church was not operational, the parish silver was moved to Strawberry. It includes a silver gilt chalice presented to St. John's in 1748 by Madam Damaris Ravenel. The Minutes of the Vestry record that it was brought to America by the Reverend Francis LeJau, "and the said cup was formerly used by the Protestants in France before the Persecution."[36] During the Civil War, Keating Simons Ball had the silver buried for safe keeping beneath a barn at Comingtee Plantation. The location was lost, and the silver remained hidden until 1947, when a mine detector was employed to find it. It is currently used on special occasions at Strawberry Chapel.[37]

No essay on Strawberry would be complete without mention of "Little Mistress Chicken." The great-granddaughter of James Child, founder of Childsbury, Catherine Chicken was the subject of a serialized story written for *The Youth's Companion* in the late nineteenth century by Jennie Haskell Rose. The story related that Monsieur Dutarque, the schoolmaster at Childsbury, tied eight-year-old Catherine to a tombstone in Strawberry churchyard as punishment for running away. Having forgotten about her, he left her there until she was found cold and unconscious. In outrage, the villagers drummed him out of town, tied backwards on his mount. Whether from exposure or lack of circulation, the experience left Catherine with a slight facial deformity, which appears in a portrait painted after she married Benjamin Simons, III, of Middleburg Plantation. Mrs. Rose ended Catherine's story by saying, "You will not find Childbury town upon your map, and should you visit to-day,...you will see...Strawberry chapel, old and quaint and tree-begirt, where on winter Sundays you may still find assembled many direct descendants of the determined men who on that bright May-day, so long ago, drummed Monsieur Dutarque out of Childbury town."[38]

[1]George Terry, "'Champaign Country': A Social History of an Eighteenth Century Lowcountry Parish in South Carolina, St. Johns Berkeley County," Ph.D. Dissertation, University of South Carolina, 1981, pp. 17, 20, 45.

[2]Frederick Dalcho, *An Historical Account of the Protestant Episcopal Church in South Carolina* (Charleston: E. Thayer, 1820; rpt. New York: Arno Press, 1970), pp. 271-272.

[3]Robert Maule to the SPG, November 25, 1707, SPG MS, A3 #185; Dalcho, *Protestant Episcopal Church,* pp. 264-265; Arthur Henry Hirsch, *The Huguenots of Colonial South Carolina* (Hamden, CN: Archon Books, 1962), pp. 79-81.

[4] Robert Maule to the Society, SPG MS, July 21, 1708, A4 #141; March 6, 1709, A4 p. 387; February 18, 1710; A5 #101.

[5] Robert Maule to the Society, SPG MS, April 4, 1711, A6 #127.

[6] Robert Maule to the Society, SPG MS, August 2, 1712, A7, #24; Walter B. Edgar and N. Louise Bailey, *Biographical Directory of the South Carolina House of Representatives* (Columbia: University of South Carolina Press, 1977), pp. 103-105; Dalcho, *Protestant Episcopal Church*, p. 265.

[7] Dalcho, *Protestant Episcopal Church*, p. 265.

[8] St. John's Berkeley, Minutes of the Vestry, 1732-1813, Mf., January 2, 1732/33; July 25, 1753; South Carolina Department of Archives and History, hereinafter cited as Minutes of the Vestry and SCDAH.

[9] Minutes of the Vestry, January 2, 1732/33; August 14, 1749.

[10] "Memorial of ye Revd. Mr. Bull to ye Society," SPG MS, August 16, 1723, A17 #45; Dalcho, *Protestant Episcopal Church*, p. 265.

[11] Robert Maule to the Society, SPG MS, August 2, 1711, A7 #1.

[12] Larry E. Ivers, *Colonial Forts of South Carolina, 1670-1775* (Columbia: University of South Carolina Press, 1970), pp. 25-27, 63.

[13] Robert Maule to the Society, SPG MS, February 18, 1716, B4-1 #55; Samuel Gaillard Stoney, *Plantations of the Carolina Low Country* (Charleston: Carolina Art Association, 1964), p. 51.

[14] Francis LeJau, *The Carolina Chronicle of Dr. Francis LeJau, 1706-1717,* ed. Frank Klingberg (Millwood, New York: Kraus Reprint, 1980), p. 191.

[15] St. John's Vestry to the Society, February 6, 1721/22, SPG MS, B4-1 #107.

[16] S. Charles Bolton, *Southern Anglicanism: The Church of England in Colonial South Carolina* (Westport, CN: Greenwood Press, 1982), pp. 136-137; The Clergy of South Carolina to Bishop Gibson, May 9, 1727, abstract in William W. Manross, *The Fulham Papers in the Lambeth Palace Library* (London: Oxford University Press, 1965), IX, 192-193, p. 140.

[17] Walter B. Edgar, *South Carolina* (Columbia: University of South Carolina Press, 1998), p. 168.

[18] Will of John Cawood, Charleston Wills, 2 (1724-25), 105-106, South Carolina Department of Archives and History; SPG to John Cawood, October 16, 1725, SPG MS, A19 #110.

[19] Bolton, *Southern Anglicanism,* pp. 136-139. See Manross, *The Fulham Papers,* p. 141, IX, 218-219, "Alexander Garden and wardens and vestry of St. Philip's, Charleston, to Bishop Gibson, June 26, 1728. John Cawood, Gibbon's father left…£428 to repair or adorn their new brick church and they have decided to spend it on an organ." The will clearly states the amount as £3000. Perhaps the vestry converted colonial currency into pounds sterling when writing to England. (The exchange rate was about 7 to 1.) Hunt's letter of May 6, 1729: SPG MS, B4-2 #224. Reference to chief justice comes from Baptismal notice: Robert Wright born to Gibbon C. Wright and Robert Wright (son of Robt. Wright, Chief Justice), baptized October 5, 1731, St. Andrews Parish, Berkeley, in *South Carolina Historical Magazine,* XIII, 105. For biographical information on Robert Wright, Jr., see Walter B. Edgar and N. Louise Bailey, *Biographical Directory of the South Carolina House of Representatives* (Columbia: University of South Carolina Press, 1977), p. 726.

[20] Minutes of the Vestry, October 3, 1750.

[21] Minutes of the Vestry, February 2, 1755; June 12, 1755; Dalcho, *Protestant Episcopal Church,* p. 270; Stoney, *Plantations of the Carolina Lowcountry,* p. 66.

[22] Nelson, "South Carolina Anglican," p. 95. See glossary for definition of terms.

[23] Nelson, "South Carolina Anglican," p. 96.

[24] Henry Lumpkin, *From Savannah to Yorktown: The American Revolution in the South* (Columbia: University of South Carolina Press, 1981), pp. 10, 41, 207-209.

[25] Stoney, *Plantations of the Carolina Lowcountry,* p. 66.

[26] For the number and extent of the Ball family plantations on the Cooper River see Anne Simons Deas, *Recollections of the Ball Family* (Privately printed, 1909; rpt. Charleston: South Carolina Historical Society, 1978); and Edward Ball, *Slaves in the Family* (New York: Farrar, Straus, and Giroux, 1998), passim.

[27] Probate Court, Charleston, Book 1671-1727, pp. 137-142; *Statutes*, III, 252; Brian Hunt to the SPG, August 11, 1726, SPG MS B4 #205.

[28] Colonial Grants, 38, p. 364, SCDAH.

[29] George Terry, "'Champaign Country': A Social History of an Eighteenth Century Lowcountry Parish in South Carolina, St. Johns Berkeley County," Ph.D. Dissertation, University of South Carolina, 1981, pp.177-178.

[30] When Child offered thirty of these slaves for sale in Charleston, the Assembly set them free. Child was reputed to be in collusion with Governor Nathaniel Johnson and Johnson's son-in-law, Thomas Broughton, patron of the St. John's Parish Church. See Verner W. Crane, *The Southern Frontier, 1670-1732* (Ann Arbor: University of Michigan Press, 1956), p. 147.

[31] Terry, "Champaign Country," p. 209; *Statutes*, IX, 6-7, as cited in Terry, p. 189.

[32] *Statutes*, III, 204-206; Samuel G. Stoney, *Colonial Church Architecture in South Carolina* (Charleston: Dalcho Historical Society, 1953), p. 2.

[33] Terry, "Champaign Country," p. 209.

[34] For an analysis of population data, much of which is based on reports by missionaries to the SPG, see Terry, pp. 116, 144-145.

[35] Clipping in files of South Carolina Historical Society, Charleston, and communication with Mr. Rip Bennett, Master Mason in charge of restoration of Strawberry Chapel, as cited by Louis Nelson, "South Carolina Anglican," p. 61.

[36] Minutes of the Vestry, May 7, 1748.

[37] Stoney, *Plantations of the Carolina Lowcountry,* p. 54.

[38] Mrs. Arthur Gordon Rose, *Little Mistress Chicken* (n.p.: The National Society of the Colonial Dames of America in the State of South Carolina, l993), p. 61; Christie Fant, Margaret Hollis, and Virginia Meynard, eds., *South Carolina Portraits* (Columbia: National Society of the Colonial Dames of America in the State of South Carolina), p. 345.

(Top) The chapel plan is similar to that of St. James' Goose Creek.
(Bottom) Many communicants arrived by boat to attend services at Strawberry Chapel.

St. Helena's Parish Church in Beaufort, South Carolina.

ST. HELENA'S PARISH

O God, our help in ages past, our hope for years to come,
Our shelter from the stormy blast, and our eternal home!
Under the shadow of thy throne, still may we dwell secure;
Sufficient is thine arm alone, and our defense is sure.

Isaac Watts, 1719

During the early colonial period, the region around Port Royal Sound seemed to be constantly in danger of attack. The Spanish destroyed Stuart Town, a Scots settlement, in 1686. The Yamassee War devastated and depopulated the entire region in 1715, and intermittent raids continued until 1728. Because Port Royal Harbor was the most accessible harbor on the southern coast and was capable of receiving large warships, it was vulnerable to attacks by Spanish and French privateers which effectively prevented maritime commerce from thriving. In the face of danger that persisted from both land and sea, the founders of St. Helena's Parish had to be both courageous and determined.[1]

One of the motivating factors in forming the parish of St. Helena's was the creation of the port of Beaufort. On June 6, 1711, the Lords Proprietors of Carolina authorized Governor Charles Craven to issue warrants to eight persons, four from Colleton and four from Granville County, "to sound the River of Port Royal & to examine which is the fittest place to fix a Town upon." They named the new town in honor of Henry, duke of Beaufort. A year later, June 7, 1712, the Assembly of South Carolina established St. Helena's Parish to contain land from the Combahee River and St. Helena Sound to the Savannah River and to a line drawn from the head of the Combahee to the Savannah.[2]

The inhabitants of the parish pledged to build a church and a rectory with no charge to the provincial government provided that a salary for the minister would be available. Members of the congregation invited William Guy, assistant to Commissary Gideon Johnston at St. Philip's in Charleston, to serve the new parish at Beaufort. A graduate of Cambridge University in 1695, Guy had acquired some experience in teaching and had served as an usher in the London workhouse, an institution which provided work for the unemployed poor. He took deacon's orders in the Anglican Church and secured an appointment as a teaching missionary to South Carolina for the Society for the Propagation of the Gospel. When he arrived, the position of schoolmaster had already been filled, so he became assistant at St. Philip's.[3]

Francis LeJau, rector of St. James' Goose Creek, wrote to the Society, "That Young Gentleman has behaved himself with So much Discretion and his Life and Conversation have been so Edifying as to induce the Governour & Chief Persons of this Province to recommend him to...St. Helens." When Guy received the call from St. Helena's, it was necessary to go back to England for ordination since there was no bishop in America who could perform the rite. Had he known what adventures awaited him as an Anglican clergyman in colonial America, he might have thought twice about his decision. On his return voyage to South Carolina, he warned the captain about some moral lapse, and in the words of LeJau, "Mr. Guy has been used very rudely by the Master of the Ship that brought him here, so as to be beaten of him, for no other provocacon [*sic*] from that Inoffensive young Gentleman but because he gave him a Just and Seasonable reproof."[4]

Guy survived the unpleasant encounter and proceeded to St. Helena's Parish, an outpost community with a blockhouse and a small garrison for protection from the Spaniards at St. Augustine and hostile Native Americans. Britain had concluded Queen Anne's War against the Spanish and French in 1713, but the garrison at Port Royal was maintained to monitor the harbor and the traffic on the inland passage between the Savannah River and Charleston.[5]

William Guy was concerned about his responsibility as a missionary to bring Christianity to Native Americans. St. Helena's Parish included "Indian Land," an area set aside as reserved for the Yamassees. In January 1715, he reported to the Society that Indian Agent Thomas Nairne had told him there were 270 "heathen" within his parish, but he had no idea how many were outside it. Guy also approached his parishioners about converting both their Indian and Negro slaves, and he said that "they are very willing to forward and promote so pious a design." He also reported that the Yamassee "emperor" was visiting Captain [John] Cochran, who was instructing the chief in the Creed, the Lord's Prayer, and the Ten Commandments.[6]

On Good Friday, April 15, 1715, the Yamassee Indians attacked the traders who had come to negotiate with them and then proceeded to raid settlements and plantations. Indian Commissioner Captain Thomas Nairne, one of the founders of Beaufort, was brutally tortured to death by having slivers of resinous fat pine wood stuck into his flesh and set afire. Seymour Burroughs, a trader, managed to escape the village massacre and, despite severe wounds, made his way to John Barnwell's plantation and gave warning to the settlers at Beaufort. Some escaped in a ship that was anchored in the harbor.[7] William Guy wrote to the SPG, "I very miraculously escap's their Cruelty, being forced to venture out to Sea in a very small canoe with one white man and three slaves, in which with no small hazard I got safe to Charlestown...."[8]

The Yamassee War was the most dangerous and decisive Indian war in South Carolina history. It was a far-reaching conspiracy involving most of the Indian nations on the southern frontier. South Carolinians managed to survive with help from other colonies and from the Cherokee. In addition to the evacuation of the settlers, the war brought destruction of large herds of cattle which provided the principal means of support on the frontier. The war also removed Beaufort from the prevailing Indian trade routes. Intermittent skirmishes, which continued to 1728, seriously impaired the development of St. Helena's Parish.[9]

Settlers gradually returned, but it was nine long years before regular Anglican services resumed. In 1724, parishioners built a church of brick, forty by thirty feet with a chancel ten feet square. The roof timbers of the church apparently remained exposed, for in 1757, the vestry provided "orders to secure the X beams at the West end of the Church, by proper Pillars as supports." Although not conclusive evidence, the vestry minutes seem to indicate that the ceiling was not arched and plastered, as those in several other contemporary sanctuaries were. However, St. Helena's met the programmatic designs for Anglican worship by providing a distinct chancel separate from the nave. By 1737, the building included a steeple and a bell, and by 1757, a weathercock painted yellow stood on the steeple.[10] The cock, a fowl that crows in the early morning, indicates vigilance or watchfulness. It is also reminiscent of Jesus' prophecy that the cock would not crow before Peter had denied him three times (John 13: 38).[11]

Improvements to the church in the 1730s reflected the increasing prosperity of the region that accompanied the growing of rice. Removal of the Native Americans opened inland swamps to rice cultivation, and as a result, some of South Carolina's wealthiest and most prominent planter families moved into St. Helena's Parish.[12]

Parishioners applied for a missionary, and the Society for the Propagation of the Gospel sent the Reverend Lewis Jones in 1726. A Welshman and a recent graduate of Oxford University, Jones faced many hardships as minister to a frontier society. He had to travel long distances to remote islands of the parish, often thirty miles each way, to hold services. After many years of ministry, there was still no rectory, although an entry in the vestry minutes for April 4, 1743, stated that the vestry would attempt to raise the money by subscription for Jones's rent. In 1742, Jones and his family took shelter in a barn for sixteen days in fear of an attack by the Spanish. Despite hardships, Jones turned down a chance to move closer to Charleston because there was no other Anglican clergyman within eighty miles of St. Helena's, and he said that "the small congregation which I have collected here, and have been at some pains to Cultivate, would soon be dispersed."[13]

It was during Jones's tenure that the Great Awakening proved a challenge to Anglicanism in the

The interior of St. Helena's church has survived use as a stable in the Revolution and a Union hospital in the Civil War.

Beaufort area. John Wesley visited St. Helena's as a guest of Jones on December 7, 1737. Community leader Nathaniel Barnwell gave Wesley "a lively idea of old English hospitality." Romantic difficulties he had encountered in Georgia limited the impact of Wesley's South Carolina ministry, but he returned to England to gain prominence as the founder of Methodism.[14]

In August 1740, Jones and Barnwell accompanied William Tilly, a Baptist minister, along with Hugh and Jonathan Bryan, Presbyterians, on a trip to Savannah to hear the evangelist George Whitefield. Barnwell had a very moving religious experience in which he "dropped down as though shot with a gun" while Whitefield was praying. Tilly perpetuated Whitefield's teachings at the Euhaws Baptist Church, while the Bryans were influential in establishing the Stoney Creek Presbyterian congregation.[15]

Whitefield criticized the Anglican ministers for not preaching justification by faith alone. According to the evangelist, the standard handbook of popular piety, *The Whole Duty of Man* by Richard Allestree, was "calculated to *civilize*, but…it never was a Means of *converting* one single soul." Whitefield's personal charisma, "enchanting" voice, and evangelical message of a salvation experience drew large crowds to his sermons. Lewis Jones found himself in an awkward position when Commissary Alexander Garden reprimanded Whitefield, but Jones claimed that he would have alienated his congregation had he refused Whitefield the use of his church.[16]

At Lewis Jones's death in 1745, the church officers praised him to the SPG by saying that in his nineteen years of service he had gained the esteem of all who knew him. "He won the respect of his people by his untiring work and infeigned [*sic*] piety and unselfishness." Jones left one hundred pounds sterling to found a free school in Beaufort which was established in 1749. The minister's will specified that orphan children who were left poor and destitute should have preference.[17]

The vestry also took an active part in providing for the poor. In 1754, the wardens assessed the parish poor tax at the rate of two shillings six pence for every pound paid to the general tax. Among other things, they used the money to pay Sarah Mathews to care for an orphan child, to pay Richard Dale on account of a poor lame woman, and to pay for burial expenses for the poor. It was not unusual for the vestry to provide ingredients for a stiff drink to bolster the spirits of the parishioners at a funeral.[18]

The vestry minutes do not record expenditures for building a chapel on St. Helena Island, so it is likely that residents of the island built their place of worship independently about 1748. Lewis Jones had preached on the island on a regular basis as early as 1734.[19] As the ruins stand today, the bare walls measure approximately thirty feet by fifty feet with a seven-by-seventeen-foot projecting chancel. Construction is of tapia, or "tabby," a type of masonry made of oyster shells cemented with oyster shell lime. Window arches are supported by water-rubbed brick. Columns supporting the covered portico are rounded tabby. Following standard design, a central door flanked by single windows opens through the western elevation. There is a round window over the central door. Single doors with one window to the west and two windows to the east appear on the side elevations, while a large window opening lights the chancel.[20]

Frederick Dalcho, writing in 1820, said that the building had been enlarged. Without the final ten feet of the eastern end and the portico on the west, St. Helena's Chapel differs little from Strawberry Chapel. The ruins of St. Helena's seem to indicate that it had a jerkin head roof as did Strawberry. Both measure about thirty by forty feet with centrally located doors on the north, south, and west elevations, and bull's-eye windows on the gable ends. The placement of a cross-aisle in the second instead of the third of four openings (counting west to east) seems to support the theory of a ten-foot addition on the chancel end.[21]

In 1762, St. Helena Island residents petitioned the South Carolina Common House for permission to become a separate parish since they had to cross two islands and take two ferries to reach Beaufort. The Assembly refused their request because the tax base of the island was not sufficient to support a minister.[22]

Difficulties in keeping a minister at the Beaufort church may have contributed to the discontent of

The chapel of ease on St. Helena Island is of tapia or "tabby" construction.

the island residents. The SPG sent the Reverend William Peasley to St. Helena's in 1751. By 1756, the vestry had dismissed him. They reported that Peasley (who was married) made "too frequent and ill timed Visits to a Woman who then lived in this Town," and that a witness had accused the couple of "indecent familiarities."[23] A succession of ministers followed Peasley, but none who came before the Revolution served more than three years. Four died while serving St. Helena's.[24]

The American Revolution brought war again to St. Helena's Parish. The British advance through the southern parishes of South Carolina was especially destructive because a group of bandits and horse thieves accompanied the British regulars. The officers soon lost control of the motley auxiliaries.[25]

In the summer of 1779, nine hundred British and Hessian troops occupied Port Royal Island. Tradition states that the British stabled their horses in the back pews of the church. All of the pews were missing by war's end, possibly having been used as firewood. Two British soldiers lie buried in the churchyard. American troops conducted a funeral service for them in which the speaker said, "We have now shown our enemies that we have not only the courage to face and best them in the field, but that we have the humanity to give their dead a decent, and Christian burial."[26]

In the Civil War, Beaufort bore the brunt of Union occupation of South Carolina. Old St. Helena's Church became a hospital for Union soldiers, and the entire community suffered a long occupation by the Union army.[27]

Through wars and rumors of wars, St. Helena's Church has stood for nearly three centuries as a symbol of faith in the presence of danger. It remains today an active parish and also a memorial. Each year, thousands of visitors from many states and foreign countries come to reverently explore the sanctuary and the churchyard. In the age of ephemeral cyberspace, the stress of the hurried world, and a myriad of disposable products, perhaps the solid walls of the church with its steeple reaching towards heaven stand as a tribute to spiritual stability and the defense of a faith which has endured.

[1] Lawrence S. Roland, Alexander Moore, and George C. Rogers, *History of Beaufort County, South Carolina, I, 1514-1861* (Columbia: University of South Carolina Press, 1996), 80, 139; hereinafter cited as *History of Beaufort County*.

[2] British Public Record Office Transcripts, 6: 1, 3, 10-12, 43-47; John Drayton, *A View of South Carolina, As Respects Her Natural and Civil Concerns* (1802; Spartanburg, S. C.: Reprint Co., 1972), pp. 208-209, as cited in *The History of Beaufort County*, 88-91.

[3] History Committee, *The History of the Parish Church of St. Helena* (Columbia: R. L. Bryan, 1990), pp. 3, 69; *Journal of the SPG* (L. C. Trans.), II, Jan. 25, 1711/12, No. 6, pp. 161-162, SPG MSS A7: #2, p. 28, as cited in Frank J. Klingberg, ed., *Carolina Chronicle: The Papers of Commissary Gideon Johnston* (Berkeley: University of California Press, 1946), p. 106.

[4] Frank J. Klingberg, ed., *The Carolina Chronicle of Dr. Francis LeJau, 1706-1717* (Berkeley: University of California Press, 1956), pp. 131, 142.

[5] *History of Beaufort County*, pp. 88-89.

[6] SPG A-10 #13, Jan. 10, 1714/15.

[7] *History of Beaufort County*, pp. 95-96.

[8] SPG B-4 #23 as cited in Edgar Legare Pennington, "The South Carolina Indian War of 1715, As Seen by the Clergymen," SCHM, 32: 255.

[9] *History of Beaufort County*, 107-108.

[10] Frederick Dalcho, *An Historical Account of the Protestant Episcopal Church in South Carolina* (Charleston: E. Thayer, 1820; rpt. Protestant Episcopal Society for the Advancement of Christianity, 1970), p. 378; A. S. Salley, Jr., *Minutes of the Vestry of St. Helena's Parish, South Carolina, 1726-1812* (Columbia: The State, 1919), pp. 26, 91; Louis P. Nelson, "South Carolina Anglican: the architecture of the Lowcountry plantation parishes," Ph.D. Dissertation, University of Delaware, in progress, MS in possession of the author, p. 51.

[11] George Ferguson, *Signs and Symbols in Christian Art* (New York: Oxford University Press, 1955), p. 9.

[12] *History of Beaufort County*, pp. 111-115.

[13] S. Charles Bolton, *Southern Anglicanism: The Church of England in Colonial South Carolina* (Westport, Connecticut: Greenwood Press, 1982), p. 92.

[14] *History of Beaufort County*, p. 133.

[15] *Ibid.*, p. 134.

[16] Bolton, *Southern Anglicanism*, pp. 52-53.

[17] *History of the Parish Church of St. Helena*, pp. 73-74; Salley, *Minutes of the Vestry*, p. 43.

[18] Salley, *Minutes of the Vestry*, pp. 62, 66, 91, 108, 118.

[19] In 1734, the vestry instructed Jones to preach at St. Helena Island once every six weeks for a six-month period. *Ibid.*, p. 22.

[20] Nelson, *South Carolina Anglican*, pp. 63-64; Dalcho, *Historical Account of the Protestant Episcopal Church*, pp. 395-396; Harold Wickliffe Rose, *The Colonial Houses of Worship in America* (New York: Hastings House, 1963), p. 439.

[21] *Ibid.*

[22] South Carolina Commons House Journals, no. 35 (February 6-September 12, 1762), p. 68, as cited in *History of Beaufort County*, p.176. The church burned in a forest fire in 1865, and has remained a ruin since that time. Rose, *Colonial Houses of Worship*, p. 439.

[23] Salley, *Minutes of the Vestry*, p. 83.

[24] *History of the Parish Church of St. Helena*, pp. 74-76.

[25] *History of Beaufort County*, p. 222.

[26] *Ibid.*, p. 227; *History of the Parish Church of St. Helena*, pp. 24, 22.

[27] For an in-depth discussion of the Union occupation of Beaufort, see Willie Lee Rose, *Rehearsal for Reconstruction: The Port Royal Experiment* (New York: Oxford University Press, 1964).

The tower is all that remains of the church of St. George's Parish, Dorchester, located in Dorchester State Park, Summerville, South Carolina.

ST. GEORGE'S PARISH, DORCHESTER

*The Lord is my rock, and my fortress, and my deliverer; my God, my strength, in whom
I will trust; my buckler, and the horn of my salvation, and my high tower.*

Psalm 18: 2

All that remains of the once proud parish church of St. George's Dorchester is a crumbling tower. Nevertheless, after nearly two hundred and fifty years, the ruin still makes a statement of strength, stability, and permanence. By 1753, the parishioners had added the tower to their sanctuary and had opened a subscription for a ring of bells. At that time, the village of Dorchester had been in existence more than half a century.[1]

A group of Congregationalists from New England under the leadership of Elder William Pratt came to South Carolina in 1695. They chose to settle on the upper Ashley River near the plantation of Lady Rebecca Axtell, widow of Landgrave Daniel Axtell. Along with Benjamin Blake and Joseph Morton, Axtell had been a leader in encouraging dissenters to settle in the province. By 1697, the New Englanders had laid out a town and drawn lots for first choice of land in the village.[2]

By an act of December 11, 1717, the provincial Assembly separated the parish of St. George's from St. Andrew's. Alexander Skene, Walter Izard, John Cantey, Thomas Disto, Samuel Wragg, Thomas Waring, and Jacob Satur were commissioners authorized to supervise the building of the church. They zealously promoted a subscription and received additional funds from the Assembly. By 1720, the outer work on the brick church, thirty feet wide by fifty feet long with an additional chancel, was complete. The church officers purchased 145 acres for a glebe and an additional five acres with a brick dwelling for a parsonage.[3]

The first minister, Peter Tustian, stayed only a short time and moved on to Maryland. His successor, Francis Varnod, arrived in 1723 and met with such success that the church was soon too small for the congregation. The village was apparently thriving at this time, for in 1723, an act was passed establishing a fair and markets in the town of Dorchester, " being a frontier in that part of the Country." In 1722, Jacob Satur of London, along with Eleazer Allen and William Rhett, Jr., of Charleston formed a partnership to carry on trade at Dorchester. By 1724, Gillson Clapp was a merchant "on the Bay" (fronting the river).[4]

Varnod wrote to the Society, "I have the misfortune to be in a place that was 20 years ago all settled by ~~Presbyterians~~ Dissenters, & where they have a very considerable meeting house together with being supplied with a Teacher...." In hopes that some dissenters might attend services at St. George's, Varnod had a large pew speedily built for strangers. He also prevailed upon the vestry to set up a public register so that vital statistics might be kept for all denominations. By 1725, Varnod was able to send the Society a virtual census of his parish, including the heads of families; numbers of men, women, and children in each family; and numbers of slaves divided into men, women, and children. He also indicated whether the family was Anglican or dissenter.[5]

In July 1725, David Humphreys, secretary of the SPG, sent a letter to all the missionaries in which he said, "It hath been intimated to the Society that proper care hath not been taken to instruct in the Christian Religion and baptize the Negroes in the Plantations in America." He went on to say that if any missionaries owned slaves, they should be particularly diligent in instructing and baptizing them.6

Varnod was diligent in including slaves. Soon after his arrival he reported forty or fifty whites and about thirty blacks attended his services. His success was due at least in part to the fact that Alexander Skene and his family instructed their servants and encouraged them to participate in worship. Skene was a member of the local church commission, and he had attended services at St. Andrew's before the creation of St. George's. Most, if not all, of the slaves who participated belonged to the Skene family. In 1726, Varnod reported at Easter forty-seven communicants, only twenty-five of whom were white. At Whitsuntide (Pentecost), he actually had twenty-four blacks and twenty-two whites.7

Early in his ministry, Varnod took a particular interest in Indians. He reported to the Society that the Cherokees gave their first ears of corn as an offering and celebrated several festivals. He sent a copy of a prayer used by an Indian king before the baking of his morning meal which, Varnod said, deserved "to be printed in Gold letters." The king prayed, "Thou chief King of all things let this thy day be a prosperous one to me, & favour me with the continuance of my being, for I thank thee who regardest me."8

Once the missionary came upon a "Winiaw" Indian in the woods and perceived that he was very melancholy. The Indian explained that he had pawned his gun for two gallons of rum. He and his best friend drank the rum, and both got a fever. The friend, "not being able to support the pains...which he had got by drinking also too much," shot himself. Varnod accompanied the Indian to the woods to the body of his friend. When four comrades who had been hunting arrived, Varnod prevailed upon them to bury the dead man. He reported, "The dead Indian being about 6 foot tall, they digged a grave hardly 4 foot long, & 6 deep, laid a few boards at the bottom of it, then the deceased was carry'd upon a Deer Skin, being covered with another, & having his knees pressed as close as cou'd be to his body, was in that posture put in the grave." A few planks were placed over him, and he was buried with his head turned toward the east according to their custom. A small pine tree with the bark bitten away in three places marked the grave, and one of the Indians threw a handful of shot on the ground to indicate that the deceased had killed himself.9

Varnod enclosed along with the report a list of fifty-three Cherokee towns with the numbers of men, women, and children who lived in each. The following year he sent a list of the Creek villages, which he had persuaded the Indian trader and entrepreneur Charlesworth Glover to compile. Glover compared the accounts of various traders and listed thirty-one Creek villages. He also noted, "The Savana Indians on Savana river are 8 men 12 women & 10 children. The Chikasaws nobody can give an acct. Being they are distributed among all other Nations."10

In July 1724, Varnod was absent for two Sundays from St. George's when he made a trip into Indian country about 150 miles beyond the settlements. He wrote, "The woods under the noble canopy of Heaven was the place where I lay most nights, being supplied sufficiently with Deers & Tigers flesh & now & then with wild Turkeys. Being disturbed in the nights only with the woolfs when we were apprehensive of the Yamesees Indians." He preached at Savannah Garrison (opposite present day Augusta, Georgia, on the Savannah River), where, he said, "no minister had been seen before." Two of the chief warriors of the Creeks stayed during the whole service and assured Varnod through an interpreter that they were well pleased. The missionary stated, "I got from hence among the Savern [Savannah] Indians & others the name of a conjuror, rainmaker, & of knowing the things in heaven."11

Varnod conversed with the Creek warriors about the ceremony of the busk, one of their principal festivals, when they extinguished the old fire and made a new one by rubbing two sticks together. Preparations for the ceremony included washing, vomiting, and purging for three days, and no talk of war was allowed during the festival. When the new fire appeared, the participants threw some new corn on the fire "which is thought by some to be an offering to the fire, & by others to the Sun, but I take it to be to the alone supreme being." The men could not eat any new corn until the completion of the ceremony at which their priests were "adorned with feathers of divers colours." Varnod understood that the white feathers represented the flood and the red ones, the world's destruction by fire. In further conversation Varnod learned, "They give out that they come from the west & have a tradition among them that some people, with grey eyes & beards (things uncommon among the Indians) shall make men of them: hence it is that their Old King has often prevented them to disturb the Europeans."[12]

In the summer of 1726, Varnod went back to the Savannah Garrison, and in 1729 he visited Palachacola town on the west bank of the Savannah River, about thirty-five miles north-northwest of present Savannah, Georgia. Again he reported to the Society that no clergyman had ever been there. He visited the Uchee Indians and baptized a mulatto child of an Indian trader. In 1731, Varnod again visited Savannah Town and baptized seven children. He said that he undertook the voyage "at the request of Col. Peter Purry to this Government to see with him for a proper place for a Township and Settlement for 300 Swiss Familys." They chose the Great Yamassee Bluff, which Varnod said was about thirty miles from the mouth of the River. This settlement became St. Peter's Parish.[13]

Varnod not only preached at St. George's and traveled to the Indian country but also supplied other parishes when they were without a minister. At various times he preached at St. Bartholomew's, St. Paul's, St. James' Goose Creek, English Santee, and at chapels on Edisto Island and at Wassamasaw, where he was required to preach in French.[14]

In 1734, the Assembly authorized repairing, enlarging, and re-pewing St. George's parish church.[15] Francis Varnod wrote to the Society in June 1736 that the repairs and additions were progressing slowly for lack of funds, but the doors and windows were finished and the floor would soon be laid.[16]

The Assembly also provided for a free school at Dorchester in 1734.[17] The commissioners of the school were Alexander Skene, President, Thomas Waring, Joseph Blake, Arthur Middleton, Ralph Izard, Robert Wright, Paul Jenys, Walter Izard, Benjamin Waring, William Cattell, John Williams, and the Reverend Francis Varnod. It is not known if a school was established at that time, but in 1757 a new act was passed for more effectually putting in force the provisions of the act of 1734. With Henry Middleton, afterwards president of the First Continental Congress, as chairman, two brick houses twenty-three feet wide and thirty-six feet long were built, one for a schoolhouse and one for a residence for the schoolmaster. The school continued in active existence for many years, and the funds composed of donations beginning in 1734 were still in existence and available for the Summerville schools in the twentieth century.[18]

Francis Varnod died in 1736 and was succeeded by a number of ministers, none of whom stayed more than a few years. Varnod had been the real moving force in the founding of St. George's Dorchester. During the pastorate of William Cotes (1748-1752), the parishioners added the tower, which is all that remains of the church. In 1752, William Langhorne transferred from St. Bartholomew's. During his pastorate, parishioners enlarged the parsonage and purchased two servants for his use. Between 1752 and 1756, a general exodus of the Congregationalists to Georgia took place. Despite this migration, at the outbreak of the Revolution Dorchester was the third largest village in South Carolina, exceeded only by Georgetown and Charleston.[19]

In 1767, the Assembly passed an act for erecting a chapel of ease on the north side of Four Hole Swamp. The minister of St. George's parish church was required to perform services there every sixth Sunday except for church holy days. There is no evidence to show whether the chapel was ever built.[20]

The church suffered at the hands of the British in the Revolutionary War. After the Revolution, sources for funds for repairing the church were no longer available from the SPG or the British government, and the growing settlement of Summerville soon made the old parish church obsolete. Today, the ruined tower stands in Old Dorchester State Park at Summerville, a monument to a once vital and alive South Carolina parish.

---

[1]Frederick Dalcho, *An Historical Account of the Protestant Episcopal Church in South Carolina* (Charleston: E. Thayer, 1820; rpt. New York: Arno Press, 1970), p. 349; Henry A. M. Smith, "The Town of Dorchester, in South Carolina—A Sketch of Its History," *South Carolina Historical Magazine*, VI: 71.

[2]Smith, "Town of Dorchester," pp. 67-71; David D. Wallace, *South Carolina, A Short History, 1520-1948* (Columbia: University of South Carolina Press, 1951), pp. 37-38.

[3]Dalcho, *Protestant Episcopal Church*, pp. 345-346.

[4]Dalcho, p. 346; Smith, "Town of Dorchester," pp. 79-80; Thomas Cooper, ed., *Statutes at Large of South Carolina* (Columbia: A. S. Johnston, 1838), III, 214-216.

[5]Francis Varnod to the Society, January 13, 1723/4, copy in a letter of April 1, 1724, SPG MS, B4-2 #173; "Names & Number—of the Inhabitants of St. George's parish So. Carolina—Inclosed in Mr. Varnods Ltre dated 21 January 1725," SPG MS, A19 #5. Letter not included at this location.

[6]David Humphreys, "To All the Missionaries," July 30, 1725, SPG MS, A19-2 #2.

[7] Francis Varnod to the SPG, April 1, 1724, SPG MS, B4-2 #173.

[8] *Ibid.*

[9] *Ibid.*

[10] *Ibid.*, Varnod to SPG, SPG MS, March 21, 1724/5, A-19 #2, pp. 117-119.

[11] Varnod to Society, July 21, 1724, SPG MS, B4-2 #183.

[12] *Ibid.*

[13] Varnod to the Society, August 9, 1731 [1731 (?)—year not given], SPG MS, B4-2 #149.

[14] SPG MS, January 13, 1723/4, B4-2 #173; July 21, 1724, B4-2 #183; June 14, 1726, B4-2 #203; January 4, 1726/7, B4-2 #194.

[15] Thomas Cooper, ed., *Statutes at Large of South Carolina* (Columbia: A. S. Johnston, 1838), III, 376-377.

[16] Dalcho, *Protestant Episcopal Church*, p. 348.

[17] The first act for establishing a school was in 1724, but there is no evidence that it was implemented. See Smith, "Town of Dorchester," p. 93.

[18] Smith, "Town of Dorchester," pp. 93-95.

[19] Smith, "Town of Dorchester," pp. 81-83; Legaré Walker, *Dorchester County* (Charleston: privately printed, 1979), p. 64d.

[20] Dalcho, *Protestant Episcopal Church*, p. 350; Thomas Cooper, ed., *The Statutes at Large of South Carolina* (Columbia: A. S. Johnston, 1838), pp. 255-256.

The tower of St. George's Parish, Dorchester.

Prince George's Parish, Winyah, built in 1745 in Georgetown, South Carolina, attested to the eighteenth century prosperity of the seaport.

PRINCE GEORGE'S PARISH, WINYAH

*They that go down to the sea in ships, that do business in great waters,
These see the works of the Lord, and his wonders in the deep.*

Psalm 107: 23-24

The settlers who lived north of the Santee River at Winyah petitioned the Assembly in 1720 to have a parish established. "An act for erecting the settlement at Winyaw, in Craven County, into a distinct parish from St. James Santee..." was passed on March 10, 1721/22. The name of the new parish honored George, Prince of Wales, who later reigned as King George II. The boundaries extended from the Santee northward to the Cape Fear River and westward "as far as it shall be inhabited by his Majesty's subjects."[1] The first church building was scarcely completed when Prince Frederick's Parish was formed in 1734. Because the location of the first building fell within the boundaries of the new parish, it became the parish church of Prince Frederick's.[2]

The most outstanding physical feature of the region encompassed by Prince George's Parish was the harbor. The great Yadkin-Pee Dee River with its major tributaries—the Uwharrie, Rocky River, Lynches River, Little Pee Dee, Black, and Waccamaw—enters the Atlantic Ocean at Winyah Bay. From its headwaters near Blowing Rock, North Carolina, the Yadkin flows northeast for about a hundred miles, then turns almost due south and joins the Uwharrie to form the Great Pee Dee. The Yadkin-Pee Dee Basin covers over 18,000 square miles in the Carolinas and a small portion of Virginia. Thirty North Carolina counties and fourteen South Carolina counties are entirely or partially included in the area, which is second only to the Susquehanna River Basin in drainage area on the Atlantic coast. In addition to the Pee Dee, the Sampit River also empties into Winyah Bay.[3]

The potential for trade through a port at the confluence of the rivers was tremendous. The people of Winyah had petitioned for a port of entry as early as 1723. An official port could ship produce directly to a foreign destination, and the shippers could avoid freight charges to Charleston. The production of naval stores reached a peak in 1725 and further stimulated the desire for a port at Winyah. In 1727, a large group of citizens marched on Charleston and demanded action. By 1732, the village of Georgetown had become an official port of the British Empire.[4]

The naval lists are a tribute to the meticulous record keeping of the British bureaucracy. In artistic script, the officer recorded the date of entry, the vessel's name and home port, the master's name, type of ship, number of tons, guns, and men, when and where the ship was built and registered, and the owner's name. Additional information listed what the ship carried, its proposed destination, and date of departure.

Schooners, brigantines, snows, and sloops with names like "Amelia" of Providence, "Success" of Bermuda, or "Dolphin" of New London brought manufactured goods from Europe, fruit and rum from the West Indies, and bricks and earthenware from New England. Exports included rice, pitch, tar, turpentine, logwood (used to make dye), skins, sassafras, pork, corn, and peas.[5]

The extent of trade and the growth of the community encouraged residents of Georgetown to contribute towards building a truly impressive parish church. In 1736, John Cleland, principal landholder in the town, and his agents Daniel La Roche and

Company offered £200 each to the building fund. Cleland offered a choice of cash or 100 acres of land for a glebe. Anthony White, who raised cattle on Black Mingo Creek and owned fourteen lots in the town, gave £100. The old Indian trader William Waties and his comrade George Pawley, for whose family Pawley's Island was named, donated £50 each. They were two of the leaders of the group that had marched to Charleston to demand designation as a port. Promoters of the port and those who owned extensive real estate in the town were prominent contributors. Those who gave lesser sums included William Allston, Joseph LaBruce, James Lesesne, and Thomas Paget. The Reverend Thomas Morritt, who was criticized for spending too much time on planting and trade, shared some of his material success by donating the communion silver. The cash subscriptions totaled £1050 in addition to some gifts of materials. As historian George Rogers said, "The motives of those who contributed were undoubtedly mixed, some desiring an edifice worthy of their own expectations in this world, others desiring to glorify the Lord."[6]

A legacy from the estate of Meredith Hughes, an Indian trader and planter who had served on the first church commission to establish the parish of Prince George's, added £100 to the contributions. In addition, the 1742 Church Act provided that the income from import duties collected at Georgetown for five years would apply to construction costs. The *Gazette* reported that church commissioners George Pawley, Daniel LaRoche, and William Whiteside along with the vestry attended the ceremony to lay the cornerstone on October 30, 1745.[7]

The Reverend Alexander Keith arrived in 1746 and began services before the new church was complete. On Sunday, August 16, 1747, Keith preached in the sanctuary, which still lacked interior amenities but was nonetheless impressive.[8] Features of the building such as exterior pilasters and curvilineal gables appear more frequently in Anglican architecture after 1750. Pilasters appear to be columns imbedded in the wall. According to church historian Frederick Dalcho, at St. Philip's church in Charleston (built in 1723), "Pilasters of the same Order with the Columns, are continued round the Body of the Church...." James Gibbs, an English architect who published his *Book of Architecture containing Designs of Buildings and Ornaments* in 1728, featured exterior pilasters in many of his designs. At Prince George's large windows capped with roman arches and glass fanlights opened between the pilasters. Curvilinear gables, which also appear at Pon Pon Chapel and St. Stephen's, beautifully terminate the roof framing, but their aesthetic origins remain uncertain. The gables were more prominent before the addition of the tower in the 1820s. The building was large and rectangular with entrances in the western, northern, and southern elevations.[9]

The interior of Prince George's remained unfinished for several years. On April 21, 1753, the Assembly authorized the selling of pews to raise money for completing and adorning the church.[10] George Pawley, Thomas Mitchell, and Thomas Hasell, commissioners for finishing the church, authorized an advertisement in the *South Carolina Gazette* of April 24, 1755, asking for bids on joinery, carpentry, plastering, tiling, glazing, and painting.[11]

Charles Woodmason, who later became an Anglican minister, wrote a report on the churches in the Carolinas, Georgia, and Florida which appears in the records of the Bishop of London dated 1766. In it he noted, "This Church is in the Town of Georgetown—is 80 feet by 50 has 3 Isles, but no Galleries as yet—The Pulpit and Pews are well Executed, but the Altar Piece is not yet up."[12]

The great width of the interior necessitated internal support, which was provided by columns which divide the interior into the nave-aisle plan utilized previously at St. Philip's and St. James', Goose Creek. The fact that St. David's Church in Cheraw wanted to duplicate the pulpit at Prince George's attests to its beauty and quality. The St. David's vestry minutes specify the following: "The Pulpit and Sounding Board of polished black walnut To be built together with the Clerks Desk staircase and Bannister After the model of George Town Pulpit as near as possible." The altarpiece that Woodmason anticipated would probably have included framed inscriptions of the Ten Commandments and the Creed, but there is no evidence to show whether or not it was ever constructed. Prince George's Church burned in the Revolution and suffered extensive damage in the Civil War, so original details of adornment have been lost.[13]

The first rector, Alexander Keith, recorded quotations, notes, and prayers in his "Common Place Book." At least two handwriting styles appear, and

The interior of Prince George Winyah.

it is not clear if the material is original or quoted, but the language and the thoughts which he expressed give some insight into his character. A prayer, "In a Long Sickness," gives Keith's attitude toward a condition that afflicted many in the mid-eighteenth century:

> But why is it that thou dost consume Me with Pain and even as it were undo Me
> Is it not that I may henceforth dye to Myself, and live in and for Thee only!
> My God I would be willing to do so in some Measure but my Nature is false and repineth.
> O that Thou shouldst hallow and exalt my Nature, and fill my whole Soul with thy Presence: That so, if I live, I may live unto Thee, and if I dye I may dye unto Thee.[14]

Keith served the parish until late in 1749, when he resigned to become assistant at St. Philip's in Charleston. He later moved on to St. Stephen's Parish.[15]

The story has often been told that when Peter Manigault learned that his cousin Betsy was keeping company with Alexander Keith, he said, "If she likes him I can have no Objection to the Match, but I would have her consider, that Gentlemen of his Cloth wear their Clothes longer than other Sort of People, & that there is no great diversion in sewing a Horsehair Button on a greasy black Waistcoat." Peter Manigault, heir to a large fortune, had become the richest man in America by 1774, so perhaps his idea of what constituted a pleasant living was somewhat prejudiced, but it was true that ministers did not become wealthy on the scale of the Manigaults. Elizabeth Banbury (Cousin Betsy) never married, but Keith had a long and fruitful career. An inventory of his estate in 1772 showed that he held bonds and notes worth slightly more than £17,345 (estimated at nearly $207,000 in 1996 dollars). In his will, he freed his "Negro Wench Bess to whom I Give her freedom and Liberty with one hundred pounds currency for her care Industry and Fidelity...."[16]

After Keith's departure, Prince George's was without a rector for about eight years. In 1757, the Reverend Samuel Fayerweather of Massachusetts, a graduate of Oxford and former Presbyterian, arrived. He stayed less than three years because he thought Georgetown was the "worst of all places on this Terraquasus globe." As soon as he could he moved to Narragansett, Rhode Island, where he found the climate much more agreeable.

The third rector of Prince George's, Offspring Pearce, was a graduate of Cambridge University. He served from 1763 to 1767, then moved on to St. George's Dorchester and eventually to St. Helena's in Beaufort. The Reverend James Stuart came from Maryland to be the last rector of Prince George's before the Revolution. Stuart supported the Crown and thus found it necessary to leave the province in 1777.[17]

The stately building begun in 1745 continues to serve as the parish church in the modern era. Some parishioners are descendants of the people who worshiped between those same strong brick walls some two hundred and fifty years ago. In addition, more than 4000 visitors come to the church each year, and volunteer docents tell the story of Prince George's Winyah.[18]

Georgetown harbor still sees some commercial shipping, but it has also developed into a major attraction for travelers who come to enjoy the view as well as the cuisine in the waterfront restaurants. Attractive shops, the Rice Museum, and other historic buildings add to the ambiance. Whether they be merchant marines, commercial fishermen, pleasure boaters, or visitors who stand on the dock, all are drawn to a view of the sea and a chance to glimpse the wonders in the deep.

---

[1]Thomas Cooper, ed., *Statutes at Large of South Carolina* (Columbia: A. S. Johnston, 1838), III, 171-172; hereinafter cited as *Statutes*. For explanation of date, see glossary.

[2]See essay on Prince Frederick's Parish in this volume. For an excellent detailed study of the history of Prince George's, see Sarah Parker Lumpkin, *Heritage Passed On* (Columbia: R. L. Bryan, 1992).

[3]United States Water Resources Council, *Comprehensive Water Resources Study, Level B, Yadkin-Pee Dee River Basin Plan of Study* (Columbia: South Carolina Water Resources Commission, 1979), pp. 1, 4; Suzanne Linder, "A River in Time: A Cultural Study of the Yadkin/Pee Dee River System to 1825," Ph.D. Dissertation, University of South Carolina, 1993.

[4]George C. Rogers, Jr., *The History of Georgetown County, South Carolina* (Columbia: University of South Carolina Press, 1970), pp. 30-32.

[5]British Public Records Office, Naval Office Shipping Returns, MS, MF Reel 89, South Carolina Department of Archives and History, passim.

[6]Rogers, *History of Georgetown County*, p. 81; Frederick Dalcho, *An Historical Account of the Protestant Episcopal Church in South Carolina* (Charleston: E. Thayer, 1820; rpt. New York: Arno Press, 1970), p. 305. See also the essay on Prince Frederick's Parish

in this volume.

[7] Rogers, *History of Georgetown County*, p. 82; *South Carolina Gazette*, November 11, 1745.

[8] *Ibid.*

[9] Dalcho, *The Protestant Episcopal Church*, p. 121; Louis P. Nelson, "South Carolina Anglican: the architecture of the Lowcountry plantation parishes," Draft of Nov. 17, 1997, Diocese of South Carolina, pp. 75-77; Rogers, p. 82.

[10] *Statutes*, IV, 3-4.

[11] Rogers, *History of Georgetown County*, p. 82.

[12] "Mr. Woodmason's Account of South Carolina, North Carolina, Georgia &c 1766" quoted in Charles Woodmason, *The Carolina Backcountry on the Eve of the Revolution*, ed. Richard J. Hooker (Chapel Hill: University of North Carolina Press, 1953), p. 72.

[13] Nelson, "South Carolina Anglican," p. 76; Dalcho, p. 308; Brent Holcomb, ed., *Saint David's Parish, South Carolina Minutes of the Vestry 1768-1832, Parish Register 1819-1924* (Easley, SC: Southern Historical Press, 1979), p. 13.

[14] Alexander Keith, "Common Place Book," MS, South Caroliniana Library, University of South Carolina, p. 120.

[15] Rogers, *History of Georgetown County*, p. 83.

[16] *South Carolina Historical Magazine*, Vol. 32, p. 179; Vol. 7, p. 49; as cited in Lumpkin, *Heritage Passed On*, p. 26. Inventory of Alexander Keith, Book &, pp. 205-206; Will Book 15 [WPA Transcript], pp. 349-50. Peter Manigault's net worth was £32,737.8, or more than $2,721,185 converted into 1996 dollars. Walter Edgar, *South Carolina, A History* (Columbia: University of South Carolina Press, 1998), p. 153.

[17] Lumpkin, *Heritage Passed On*, pp. 33-34.

[18] Church staff telephone interview with the author, July 21, 1998.

The ornate gothic style of Prince Frederick's Parish Church reflected the expensive tastes of the Pee Dee and Black River planters in the antebellum period. It is known locally as the "Gunn" church because a workman by that name fell to his death from the scaffolding during construction.

PRINCE FREDERICK'S PARISH

Time like an ever rolling stream,
Bears all its sons away;
They fly forgotten, as a dream
Dies at the opening day.

From "O God, Our Help in Ages Past"
Isaac Watts (1674-1748)

In the summer of 1716, William Waties loaded a periagua with Indian trade goods and secured some stout Indian slaves to man the oars. He set out from Charleston bound for Black River, where the Indian Commission of South Carolina had authorized him to establish a trading post, or "factory," at "the old Casekey's House on Black River at Wineau." John Vourmerl'n, probably an indentured servant, accompanied him. The high bluff overlooking the Black River was a strategic point, and the location of the trading post later became the site of Prince Frederick's Parish Church. The log houses of the settlement have long since crumbled to oblivion, and all that remains is the lovely churchyard with its weathered tombstones overlooking the Black River.[1]

The periagua was a versatile and functional vessel for river transportation which was useful not only for trading purposes, but also as family transportation to church. It was a large cypress canoe which the builder had split and inserted boards in the middle for added width. Various models included a rudder, oars, sails, a tarpaulin, or even an awning to shade passengers. A large periagua could carry as many as one hundred barrels of pitch or tar or even horses and cattle. Although there was no set number, the standard crew for the factors of the Indian trade seemed to be four to six oarsmen.[2]

One reason for sending William Waties to Black River was that the Yamassee War, which began in 1715, had disrupted trade south of Charleston. Waties's instructions authorized him to trade for deerskins, furs, Indian slaves, or other vendable commodities. The Indian Commission set prices in deerskins; for instance, fifty bullets were worth one deerskin, while a "Duffield Blanket" was worth fourteen skins. A yard of "Strouds" sold for seven skins. Exports of deerskins had reached a high of 121,355 in 1707, but due to the war the number had dropped to 4,702 by 1716, causing a major blow to the colonial economy.[3] Some 400 colonists had died in the war, including a large number of Indian traders. With skirmishes continuing until 1728, to open a new trading post in 1716 must have required considerable courage.[4]

William Waties also established a trading post at Uauenee, later called Yauhannah, on the Pee Dee River. He did not continue as factor for very long, for by February 1717 he had resigned, and his assistant, Meredith Hughes, took over the post. Hughes preferred the Black River trading post, for it was not as exposed to attack. He notified the Indian Commission that there might be trouble at the Pee Dee location, particularly with the Cheraws. In fact, one of the Cheraws had tried to shoot him. The tribe paid a fine of thirty deerskins, but the Commission instructed Hughes that the skins were "adjudged to be the Publick's Due," and not for his personal use.[5]

When additional hostilities broke out in 1720 as a part of continuing Indian warfare, it was not the Cheraws but the Waccamaw warriors who fought against the settlers. Of the one hundred braves who participated, sixty were killed or captured and sent to the West Indies as slaves. This encounter marked the virtual end of the tribe as well as the end of the profitable Indian trade in the immediate vicinity. The colonists would find other means of livelihood, but nothing could replace the

Native American cultures which were gradually being destroyed by the pressure of settlement.[6]

Meredith Hughes stayed at Black River and became a planter. In later years, he held many public offices, including representative in the provincial assembly. When the parish of Prince George's Winyah was created in March 1722, Hughes served with John Lane and John Hayes on the commission to establish the church. The commissioners chose Wineau on Black River, the site of the Indian trading post, as the site for the parish church. The name "Wineau," spelled in a variety of ways, became "Winyah" in the statute. Lane and Hughes maintained an interest in the church, and both served on the vestry with regularity until they died in 1739.[7]

A population shift occurred in the 1730s, when the cultivation of rice surpassed the Indian trade and the production of naval stores in the local economy. Georgetown became an official port in 1731, and the need for a church in the port became apparent. The Assembly divided the parish on April 9, 1734, and named the new parish Prince Frederick after the son of King George II, for whom Prince George's Winyah had been named. Prince Frederick died before his father and thus never became king, but his son reigned as George III.[8]

Because the parish church of Prince George's Winyah was located on Black River, it fell within the bounds of the new parish and therefore became the parish church of Prince Frederick's. Begun in 1726 and completed by 1734, the wooden church was 45 feet by 25 feet. According to the first minister, Thomas Morritt, it was "decently raised," and conveniently situated on Black River "where it branches and makes it convenient for about 120 families which are not above 12 or 14 miles at the farthest distance from the church most of whom can and do come by water."[9]

The vestry minutes provide further information about the church building. The rectangular plan included compass-headed windows (semi-circular at the top) and three doors on the north, south, and west, providing for cross aisles. In 1733, the vestry hired Thomas Landon to build a pulpit, pews, and a

Rice planters took summer refuge in the pineland village of Plantersville where they built this small chapel.

gallery. The pulpit, located to the left of the north entrance, and the communion table, located in the east-end chancel, were of natural wood. A neat rail enclosed the chancel area. In 1734, the vestry hired Peter Secare to plaster the interior and agreed to supply him with lime, hair, and boards for scaffolding.[10]

At a vestry meeting on November 24, 1740, the vestry and wardens agreed with Alexander Davidson to make new doors and window shutters for the church and to paint inside and out—including "the cornishes, corner-facings, front of the Gallary, the Pillars and the Rails about the Alter." The pulpit and table were to be polished and the pews numbered for the sum of £180.

The finer material of the two liturgical fittings, the altar table and the pulpit, along with the compass-headed windows, cross aisle arrangement, and neatly plastered walls, contributed a sense of order and reverence which set the Anglican church of Prince Frederick's apart from the profane world in which it existed. The rectangular proportions and east-end chancel distinguished Prince Frederick's from the dissenter meeting houses, which were often square. The plan of the church, though atypical for the period, would, after 1750, become the predominant arrangement for Anglican church buildings.[11]

The allocation of the pews illustrates the social hierarchy within the church. The vestry set a value on each pew, which ranged from £12 for pew number 13 in the rear to £22 for numbers 1, 5-9, and 18, large pews located near the pulpit and the chancel. Those who subscribed the highest sums toward building the church had first choice of pews. Visitors and those unable to purchase pews could worship from the gallery, or possibly from pew 13, for whom no buyer was listed.[12]

Although the church was established as the parish church of Prince George's Winyah, the vestry sold the pews after the creation of Prince Frederick's Parish. The purchasers were John Brown, John Lane, John Thompson, Jr., Daniel Shaw, Francis Avant, John Walliss, Edward Hendlin, Meredith Hughes, Anthony White, Anthony Atkinson, John White, Daniel and Thomas Laroche, William Swinton, John Bonnell, Josias Dupre, and Caleb Avant. Considering that the amount allocated by the Assembly to pay the minister for a year was £100, the price of pews represented a considerable sum. The vestry collected a total of £330.[13]

The Reverend Thomas Morritt, who had been sent by the SPG to be a schoolmaster in Charleston, became minister of Prince George's Winyah in 1728. His parishioners welcomed him by refurbishing the parsonage and its kitchen and donating fourteen cows and their calves with the provision that the cattle would remain with the parsonage if Morritt left the parish. When Prince Frederick's Parish was established in 1734, Morritt declared that he would preach in Georgetown only one Sunday in the month and that he would "take care of this parish untill the Society's pleasure is known."[14]

A problem arose in 1735 when the parishioners complained that their minister was spending too much time in trade and planting to the neglect of his duties. A plat recorded in 1739 shows that he owned a 440-acre tract with two structures, probably a house and a barn, at the intersection of the Sampit River and Deep Gulley Creek. Morritt was apparently a successful planter, and he resigned from the ministry.[15]

John Fordyce, another SPG missionary, arrived in 1736 and served Prince Frederick's longer than any other minister until his death in 1751. He was successful both as a pastor and as a planter, for the vestry recorded no complaints against him. The inventory of his estate shows that with the help of fifteen slaves, he grew corn, rice, and potatoes. He owned three horses, sixteen head of cattle, a flat, a boat, a canoe, and a pair of "neat silver mounted pistols." In addition to his Prayer Book, he possessed a stack of manuscript sermons weighing about twenty pounds, but valued by his appraisers at only one pound currency. His luxury items included shoe buckles, a watch, and a snuffbox, all made of silver. When he went out, he might put on his "new grizzle bob wig," wear his riding coat, and carry his cane as he mounted Beauhicket, or hitched his white horse "Singletary" to his horse chair.[16]

Fordyce's successor, Michael Smith, was not as successful either in agricultural or theological pursuits. He scandalized his parishioners by neglecting his children and his sick wife, who died, and traveling about with a woman supposedly his nurse. Smith even "affix'd up at Blk River Church" a scandalous and libertine paper, allegedly from scripture, in justification of fornication. The vestry wrote to

Ruins of the church stand today.

the Society that they tried to pass over Smith's irregulatities, "being inclined from Charity and regard to his function to impute his faults, rather to Levity, Indiscretion, and Human Infirmity, than to a bad, or a corrupt Heart." Smith's offenses became too flagrant, and in a letter to the Bishop of London, the vestry declared that Smith had rendered himself infamous and obnoxious, and in his three years of bad conduct he had done more injury to the cause of virtue, religion, and the church than his successors could repair in many. They urgently requested a new minister because they said "that there is not a Clergyman from Santee River to Cape Fear, to perform any Ecclesiastical Office, or administer the Sacraments on any Emergency."[17]

In the absence of a regular minister, the vestry requested that Charles Woodmason, a churchwarden, should "read Prayers and a Sermon every Sunday, with which proposal he complied." Woodmason also visited various parts of the parish to collect the poor tax. He later traveled to England, was ordained, and returned as an itinerant Anglican minister to the backcountry.[18]

The search for a regular minister was in vain until 1762, when George Skeene contacted the vestry about the position. He came "well recommended both for Ability Life and Conversation," and was duly hired. He served only four years and died in 1766.[19]

During this period, the parish was active in making provision for the poor. The vestry paid individuals to care for adults who were sick or unable to work. For instance, it paid Mary Williams "for ye Bord of Michal Cary & Margaret Spencer for one year, £110." Thomas Scott received £14 for nursing Rachel Downing and her child. "Likewise Six Pounds Ten Shillings Payable to Doct. Andrew Burnett for attendance to Rachel Downing." Homeless orphans were usually apprenticed to learn a trade and contribute to their own upkeep. In 1757, the church wardens apprenticed Shadrack MacCormack, a poor boy about seven years old, to John Simpson, a cooper or barrel maker, on Jeffrey's Creek, till the boy came of age.[20]

A group of parishioners requested a place of worship nearer their homes, and the provincial Assembly authorized building a chapel of ease at Murray's Old Field, near Murray's Ferry on the Santee River. The vestry forwarded £500 from the public treasury to Theodore Gourdin and William Michau, commissioners for the chapel.[21]

After the death of George Skene, there was only one incumbent minister. John Villette served less than a year in 1772. Prince Frederick's Parish flourished after the British placed a bounty on indigo in 1748. Some considered Black River indigo the finest in the province. After the Revolution, indigo production declined, and population shifted to the tidal rice lands nearer the coast. The old church fell into disrepair, and by 1790, Prince Frederick's no longer existed as an election district. In the nineteenth century, parishioners built nearer the coast, first a small wooden chapel, followed by an impressive gothic brick church authorized in 1857, but due to the Civil War, not completed until 1878. This structure, called the "Gunn" church, is now a ruin.[22]

The Black River, that "ever rolling stream," continues its course by the bluff where the first church stood. Each year volunteers from Prince George's Winyah respectfully clean the underbrush from the old churchyard, which now boasts huge azalea and camellia bushes. Elizabeth Allston Pringle, the woman rice planter who wrote several books about the Lowcountry and edited the parish register of Prince Frederick's, visited the site in the early nineteenth century. She said, "Nothing could have been more beautiful and peaceful than this God's Acre, lying high above the fast-flowing river, shaded by stately water-oaks, rejoicing in their glistening new foliage...." All that remained of the first settlers who built a church at the site of an Indian trading post were "white marble monuments, peeping through a tangle of wild azalea, dogwood, and honeysuckle, with wild violets, purple and white, and tiny perfect blossoms of wild for-get-me-nots."[23]

[1] W. L. McDowell, ed., *Journals of the Commissioners of the Indian Trade* (Columbia: South Carolina Archives Department, 1955), pp. 74, 96; hereinafter cited as JCIT; Sarah Parker Lumpkin, *Heritage Passed On: History of Prince George, Winyah, Parish* (Columbia: R. L. Bryan, 1992), p. 14.

[2] Suzanne Linder, "A River in Time: A Cultural Study of the Yadkin/Pee Dee River System to 1825," Ph.D. Dissertation, University of South Carolina, 1993, pp. 61-62. See also the essay on St. Peter's Parish in this volume. The derivation of the word "periagua" is from Carib via Spanish, piragua, a dug-out. The word is variously spelled periauger, pettiauger, periago, etc. See Jess Stein, ed., *The Random House Dictionary of the English Language* (New York: Random House, 1966), p. 1071.

[3] Converse D. Clowse, *Economic Beginnings in Colonial South Carolina* (Columbia: University of South Carolina Press, 1971), p. 207. For a chart of exports from Charleston see Clowse, Appendix, Table III; JCIT, p. 104. For other rate schedules see pp. 210, 269, 281. "Strouds" referred to a coarse woolen cloth named after Stroud in Gloucestershire, England, where woolens were made. Likewise, the town of Duffel near Antwerp gave its name to a coarse woolen cloth having a thick nap. *Random House Dictionary*, pp. 1409, 440.

[4] David Duncan Wallace, *South Carolina: A Short History, 1520-1948* (Columbia: University of South Carolina Press, 1951), p. 90. For a comprehensive treatment of the Indian trade and the Yamassee War, see Verner Crane, *The Southern Frontier* (Ann Arbor: University of Michigan Press, 1956), Chapter V, "The Charles Town Indian Trade," and Chapter VII, "The Yamassee War, 1715-1716." See also the Introduction to this volume.

[5] JCIT, pp. 202, 206, 254, 297. George C. Rogers, Jr., *The History of Georgetown County, South Carolina* (Columbia: University of South Carolina Press, 1970), pp. 16-19.

[6] John R. Swanton, *The Indians of the Southeastern United States* (Washington: Smithsonian Institution Bureau of American Ethnology, Bulletin 137, Government Printing Office, 1946), p. 203.

[7] Thomas Cooper, ed., *Statutes at Large of South Carolina* (Columbia: A. S. Johnston, 1838), III, 171. The usual date given for establishing Prince George's is March 10, 1721, because this is the date given in the statute. Actually, it was 1722, because before 1752 [old style calendar], the new year began March 25. The new year was changed to January 1 in 1752. Rogers, *Georgetown County*, p. 3. Walter B. Edgar and N. Louise Bailey, *Biographical Directory of the South Carolina House of Representatives* (Columbia: University of South Carolina Press, 1977), pp. 345-346; Elizabeth W. Allston Pringle, ed., *The Register Book for the Parish Prince Frederick Winyaw* (Baltimore: Williams & Wilkins, 1916), pp. 63-86, passim., hereinafter cited as *Register Book*.

[8] Rogers, *Georgetown County*, pp. 29, 32-33.

[9] Thomas Morritt to the SPG, September 1, 1729, SPG MS, B-4, II #234.

[10] *The Register Book for the Parish Prince Frederick Winyaw*, ed. Elizabeth W. Allston Pringle (Baltimore: Williams and Wilkins for The National Society of The Colonial Dames of America, 1916), pp. 76, 79, 80, 110; hereinafter cited as *Register Book*.

[11] Louis P. Nelson, "South Carolina Anglican: the architecture of the Lowcountry plantation parishes," Draft of November 17, 1997, Diocese of South Carolina, pp. 52-54.

[12] *Register Book*, pp. 78-81; Nelson, "South Carolina Anglican," p. 53.

[13] *Register Book*, p. 78.

[14] Rogers, *Georgetown County*, p. 80; *Register Book*, pp. 64, 78.

[15] William W. Manross, ed., *The Fulham Papers in the Lambeth Palace Library* (Oxford: Clarendon Press, 1965), Vol. 10, #7-10, p. 147; Surveyor General's Office, Colonial Plats, Vol. 2, p. 436, South Carolina Department of Archives and History; Frederick Dalcho, *An Historical Account of the Protestant Episcopal Church in South Carolina* (Charleston: E. Thayer, 1820; rpt. New York: Arno Press, 1970), p. 319.

[16] Inventory of John Fordyce, July 17, 1751, Inventories, R-1 (1751-1753), pp. 314-322, SCDAH.

[17] *Register Book*, pp. 131-136, 161-162.

[18] *Register Book*, p. 130; Charles Woodmason, *The Carolina Backcountry on the Eve of the Revolution: The Journal and Other Writings of Charles Woodmason*, ed. Richard J. Hooker (Chapel Hill: University of North Carolina Press, 1953), pp. xv, xxi. See also the essay on St. Mark's Parish in this volume.

[19] *Register Book*, pp. 176, 189.

[20] *Register Book*, pp. 145, 181, 187.

[21] *Statutes*, IV, 268; *Register Book*, p. 194.

[22] *Register Book*, pp. vii-viii; Rogers, *Georgetown County*, pp. 52, 279. The origin of the name "Gunn Church" is unknown. The architect was Louis Barbot, and the contractor, who died before the building was finished, was named Glen, according to the introduction to the Register. Another source says the contractors were Philip and Edward Green. Albert Sidney Thomas, *A Historical Account of the Protestant Episcopal Church in South Carolina 1820-1957* (Columbia: R. L. Bryan, 1957), p. 398. See Map 3, *South Carolina Election Districts, 1790*; N. Louise Bailey and Elizabeth Ivey Cooper, *Biographical Directory of the South Carolina House of Representatives* (Columbia: University of South Carolina Press, 1981), III, Map 3.

[23] *Register Book*, pp. vi, vii.

This watercolor, painted by Charles Fraser about 1797, shows the church of St. John's Parish, Colleton, on John's Island.

ST. JOHN'S PARISH, COLLETON

I speak as to wise men: judge ye what I say. - I Corinthians 10:15

- Text for Samuel Quincy's sermon,
"Christianity a Rational Religion"

Samuel Quincy, the first rector of St. John's Parish, Colleton, was a well-educated, articulate minister who spoke out in favor of a rational approach to religion. He never stooped to sneering or sarcasm, but spoke his mind in intelligent and carefully outlined sermons. His approach was pleasing to the leaders of the parish, gentlemen of wealth and intelligence who were leaders in the province. They wanted a very regular church, in both religious matters and architecture, that would reflect their support for the status quo and their affluent life style. For example, vestryman Edward Fenwicke owned some 13,000 acres, which included the impressive mansion Fenwicke Hall on Johns Island. He served on the council, and to enhance his interest in horse racing, he imported thoroughbred horses and operated a stud farm.[1]

An act of Assembly on April 9, 1734, established St. John's Parish, Colleton by a division of St. Paul's. St. John's would include Edisto, Johns, and Wadmalaw Islands and "other adjacent islands to the seaward." Commissioners to organize the new parish were Colonel John Fenwicke, Colonel John Gibbes, John Stanyarne, Samuel Underwood, and John Jenkins. On June 18, 1734, parishioners met on Johns Island and decided to build the church on land to be acquired from Abraham Waight.[2]

At the beginning of the vestry book, the register recorded the various oaths required of church officers. The oath of loyalty to the monarch stated that the candidate did swear that he would be faithful and bear true allegiance to His Majesty King George. Then the officer had to renounce the authority of the pope by stating, "I do from my heart abhor, detest, & abjure as impious, & heretical that damnable doctrine & position that Princes Excommunicated or deprived by the Pope, or any Authority of the See of Rome, may be Deposed or Murdered by their Subjects." The oath further declared that no foreign prince or potentate had any jurisdiction in the realm of Great Britain.

The test oath, designed to eliminate Catholics from office, required the candidate to declare "that there is not any transubstantiation in the Sacrament of the Lords Supper, in the Elements of Bread & Wine, at or after the Consecration thereof, by any Person whatsoever." The Catholic dogma of transubstantiation taught that the elements actually became the body and blood of Christ. Finally, the candidate had to swear to justly and truly execute the office "according to the best of my skill, knowledge, and Power, without prejudice or affection."[3]

The vestry, thus duly installed, proceeded to organize the parish. In 1739, the vestry agreed to buy land for a parsonage and solicit subscriptions for funds to build it. Thus prepared, they could then apply to England for a minister. They sought advice of William Guy, pastor of St. Andrew's, about how to continue. Acting on Guy's advice, they wrote letters to the SPG; the Bishop of London; Commissary Alexander Garden, who was the bishop's representative in Charleston; and William Tredwell Bull, former rector of St. Paul's, who had returned to England. The SPG replied that the Society was not "in a Condition" to start a new mission. In fact, that organization had begun a gradual withdrawal from South Carolina. Nevertheless, the vestry continued to make preparations for a minister.[4]

Hugh Hext agreed to saw the timber for the parsonage house, kitchen, and store room; to make fifteen thousand bricks; to fell trees; and to square timbers for beams and featheredge the boards for siding. Anthony Trusha contracted to make two stacks of chimneys with two fireplaces each for the parsonage; to underpin, lath, and plaster the house; and to build a chimney for the kitchen with an oven out of doors, "which he is to do Workman Like, for the sum of one hundred and sixty pounds, and find him Self accommodations." With preparations for the parsonage well under way, the vestry agreed with the Reverend Samuel Quincy on June 28, 1742, to serve the parish.[5]

A native of Massachusetts, Quincy had officiated at Savannah, Georgia, as a missionary of the Society of the Propagation of the Gospel. Dr. Thomas Bray, founder of the Society, and James Oglethorpe, chairman of the Parliamentary committee on prisons, had cooperated on founding a colony for debtors and other indigents. Quincy was relieved of his post because he married a white man to an Indian woman. Tomochichi, the Yamacraw chieftain and friend of James Oglethorpe, gave the bride away, but despite the fact that both whites and Indians approved, the procedure got the minister into trouble. Quincy's replacement at Savannah was John Wesley, an Anglican minister who later founded Methodism.[6]

With subscriptions from many outstanding South Carolinians, Quincy published a volume of his South Carolina sermons in Boston in 1750. Historian Richard Beale Davis called Quincy one of "the most effective of the southern Anglican preachers who directly opposed the Great Awakening." Many evangelical ministers emphasized an emotional response rather than an educated understanding of doctrine. Quincy's sermons stressed the reasonable quality of Christianity. Quincy said, "The Doctrines of Christianity are founded in Truth and Reason, and capable of being supported by clear and rational Arguments." He admitted that some things were beyond human comprehension such as angels, spirits, and invisible beings, so reason was in some cases fallible. Nevertheless he insisted, "But still it is the only Guide we have to direct us in our Searches after Truth." Historian Carl Becker regarded Quincy's rational arguments as representing one of the sources of ideas leading to the Declaration of Independence. After serving St. John's, Quincy moved on to become Alexander Garden's assistant at St. Philip's before he returned to New England.[7]

The new church in St. John's Colleton was fortunate to have a man of Quincy's talents as its first minister. Since he accepted the position in June, it is possible that he had some influence on the completion of the interior of the church, but the design was apparently in place before his arrival. On August 28, 1742, the vestry agreed with Thomas Cheesman to pew the church, lay the tile floors, complete the chancel, and wainscot around the pulpit. They ordered twenty-seven pews, a pulpit, a clerk's desk, and a reading desk.[8]

A diagram of the interior provides an outline of the design of the church. Whereas most Anglican churches were rectangular, St. John's was square, with regular proportions which suggest a tradition inspired by Renaissance design principles. Two east-west aisles proceed from the west front entrances and intersect with a north-south aisle placed, not in the usual center position, but close to the chancel, which occupies a square extension from the east end. The neatness and regularity of the plan are accentuated by the compass lines projecting from the west end. The larger arc, drawn full circle, would touch the four corners of the square interior.[9]

A delicate watercolor by Charles Fraser probably painted about 1797 shows the exterior of the church. Two arch-topped doors with an arched window in the middle and square windows on either side define the front of the brick building. The north door is also visible in the painting.[10]

Except for the slightly larger front and center pews purchased by John Fenwicke and Hugh Hext, pews were of uniform size. All were sold by April of 1743 except for the four pews across the rear of the interior, which were reserved for the public. By 1743, nearly ten years after the establishment of the parish, the church and parsonage were complete, and there was a full congregation. The vestry had secured a very able rector who must have been pleased with his situation. His new position began on a note of sadness when his wife died less than a month after he arrived at St. John's. According to historian Frederick Dalcho, Mrs. Quincy "fell a victim to the climate."[11]

After the building program was complete, the vestry turned to the support of the "pore." They provided clothing for a boy whom they apprenticed to James Simpson. Nursing care for older women and burial for indigents were frequent needs, but they also allowed £50 per year to Ruth Peekham and her child. As was customary at that time, physicians' fees varied according to whether or not the patient recovered. The vestry hired Dr. John Roberts "for the cureing and providing nessesarys and house room for James Ellis. Agreed to give the said Doctor Roberts Seventy Pounds if he makes a Perfect Cure, and if not, to have Twenty Pounds." To secure funds for charity, it was essential to assess a poor tax of two shillings per head on slaves, two shillings per hundred acres, and one shilling on every £100 of interest "above what they pay interest for." Apparently interest was deductible even in the eighteenth century.[12]

Certain fines could supplement the tax. In 1744, the minute book states, "That there is in the hands of William Boone £15/15 as fines of Defaulters of Not bringing armes to Church and Meeting on Johns Island." A law requiring men to carry arms to church had been in effect at least since 1724, but in 1743, the Assembly strengthened the law by providing that churchwardens would be fined if they did not report church members who failed to comply. Travelers and men over sixty were exempt. The purpose was to be prepared in case of a slave revolt.[13]

From 1742 to 1775, nine ministers served St. John's, and interim vacancies accounted for nearly seven years. By the 1760s, St. John's had developed a reputation for ill-treating the clergy by refusing to elect them, thus denying tenure. The vestry preferred to keep the clergyman on probation and thus maintain greater control. This attitude is apparent in the will of Colonel John Gibbes, who bequeathed £1000 to be put at interest for the benefit of the church with the following provision: "Sometimes it happens that a Minister proves disagreeable to the people of the Parish, and not to be Worthy of the Interest." In such a case Gibbes's sons had the authority "not to pay the money, till he behaves to the satisfaction of the Parish."[14]

In 1770, George Hext left a substantial legacy of £1250 to the parish to be used for educating poor children. There is no record in the vestry minutes of how this legacy was administered. After the death of Benjamin Blackburn in 1775, there was no minister at St. John's until after the Revolution in 1787.[15]

In 1820, when Frederick Dalcho wrote his history of the denomination, he noted that the colonial church, which was in ruins, had been replaced in 1817 through the liberality of Francis Simmons. The new structure was a neat and commodious wooden building with a handsome portico. He stated, "St. John's, Colleton, is a flourishing and respectable Cure. It has a Glebe and Parsonage, and its funds are large and increasing."[16] Fire of unknown origin destroyed the church in 1864. Today, St. John's Colleton is still an active parish on Johns Island with the parish church, built in 1955, located on the same spot as the original.[17]

[1] Walter B. Edgar and N. Louise Bailey, *Biographical Dictionary of the South Carolina House of Representatives* (Columbia: University of South Carolina Press, 1977), II, 242-243.

[2] Thomas Cooper, ed., *Statutes at Large of South Carolina* (Columbia: A. S. Johnston, 1838), III, 374-375; Minutes of the Vestry, St. John's Colleton Parish, 1734-1874, WPA Typescript, Mf, South Carolina Department of Archives and History, June 18, 1734, p. 3; hereinafter cited as Minutes of the Vestry.

[3] Minutes of the Vestry, pp. 1, 2, 5.

[4] Minutes of the Vestry, January, 1738/9, p. 6; SPG Journal, June 15, 1739, as cited in S. Charles Bolton, *Southern Anglicanism: The Church of England in Colonial South Carolina* (Westport, CN: Greenwood Press, 1982), p. 59.

[5] Minutes of the Vestry, April 19, July 5, 1742, pp. 9-10.

[6] M. Eugene Sirmans, *Colonial South Carolina* (Chapel Hill: University of North Carolina Press, 1966), pp. 168-169; John Wesley, *The Journal of the Reverend John Wesley, A. M.*, ed. Nehemiah Curnock (London: Epworth Press, 1938), I, 168; VIII, 283-284.

[7] Richard Beale Davis, *Intellectual Life in the Colonial South*, 3 vols. (Knoxville: University of Tennessee Press, 1978), II, 756-758; Samuel Quincy, *Twenty Sermons* (Boston: John Draper, 1750), pp. 5, 8-9, 12, South Caroliniana Library.

[8] Minutes of the Vestry, August 28, 1742, p. 10.

[9] Louis Nelson, "South Carolina Anglican: the architecture of the Lowcountry plantation parishes," Draft of November 17, 1997, Diocese of South Carolina, pp. 57-58 and figure 22.

[10] Copy of the watercolor by Charles Fraser, courtesy of the Gibbes Museum.

[11] Minutes of the Vestry, April 4, 1743, pp. 12-13; Dalcho, p. 361.

[12] Minutes of the Vestry, 1744, *passim.*, pp. 14-16; October 8, 1751, p. 32.

[13] Minutes of the Vestry, 1744, p. 17; *Journal of the Commons House of Assembly, June 2, 1724–June 16, 1724*, ed. A. S. Salley (Columbia: General Assembly, 1944), p. 7; *Statutes*, VII, 417-419.

[14] Charles Martyn to Bishop Osbaldeston, St. Andrew's, February 1, 1763, abstract in William W. Manross, ed., *The Fulham Papers in the Lambeth Palace Library* (Oxford: Clarendon Press, 1965), X, 158-159, p. 154; Minutes of the Vestry, April 21, 1758, pp. 90-91.

[15] Minutes of the Vestry, [n.d.] 1770, pp. 93-94; Dalcho, p. 364.

[16] Dalcho, p. 365.

[17] Albert S. Thomas, *A Historical Account of the Protestant Episcopal Church in South Carolina, 1820-1957* (Columbia: R. L. Bryan, 1957), p. 339.

*(Top) Charles Fraser painted Sheldon Church about 1798 after it had been burned by the British in the Revolution.
(Bottom) The ruins of Prince William's Parish, Sheldon indicate the massive nature of the original building.*

PRINCE WILLIAM'S PARISH

Majestic though in ruin...
With Atlantean shoulders, fit to bear
The weight of mightiest monarchies...
Drew audience and attention still as night
Or summer's noontide air.

From *Paradise Lost* by John Milton

The warm sunlight filters through the live oaks and Spanish moss, giving a soft glow to the ancient rose-colored brick walls which are all that remain of Prince William's Parish Church at Sheldon. The building was burned in the Revolutionary War, rebuilt, and burned again in the Civil War. Though it is but a ruin, the structure recalls the dignity and reverence of a place of worship built in a classic plan in the finest manner available at the time. An occasional wedding and an annual worship service are held at the site, and visitors regularly frequent the grounds.[1] That a structure of this quality appeared in the wilderness in an area so recently the frontier of the province of South Carolina raises intriguing questions that a consideration of the historical background of the region should help to answer.

The Indian trade in deerskins was important to the economy in the early eighteenth century. In order to try to preserve the opportunities for trade while avoiding conflict, the provincial government set aside a region bounded by the Combahee, Coosaw, Port Royal, and Savannah Rivers as a reservation for the Yamassee Indians in 1707. In this area, called "Indian Land," whites were not permitted to settle. The act as passed by the General Assembly was "to limit the bounds of the Yamassee settlement, to prevent persons from disturbing them in their stocks, and to remove such as are settled within the bounds described." Despite sincere attempts by the government to regulate matters, unscrupulous traders continued to defraud the Native Americans, and conflict became inevitable.[2]

When the Yamassee and other tribes made war on the settlers in 1715, approximately 400 colonists died, and it was not until 1728 that Colonel John Palmer, a veteran Indian fighter, led a raid on St. Augustine and finally ended the Yamassee War. As a result, the fertile swamps between the Combahee and Coosawhatchie Rivers were opened to white settlement and the cultivation of rice. Because the government forbade settlement while this region was "Indian Land," large tracts became available to those who had the substantial capital necessary to establish rice plantations. The Combahee, Coosawhatchie, and Pocotaligo Rivers provided abundant acreage admirably suited to the cultivation of rice. In the 1730s, some of South Carolina's wealthiest and most prominent planter families established plantations. These included the Bellingers at Tomotley, the Blakes at Bonny Hall, the Izards and Middletons at Hobonny, James Michie at Richfield and Mount Alexander (later part of Auldbrass), and John Mulryne at what later became Green Point, now part of Nemours Plantation. These were people of education and style who brought substantial wealth to the region.[3]

Landgrave Edmund Bellinger had received a grant for the twelve-thousand-acre Tomotley Barony on May 7, 1698. The provincial government did not grant any other baronies in what later became Prince William's Parish due to the reservation for the Indians. The second Landgrave Edmund Bellinger and his two sisters, Lucia and Elizabeth, inherited Tomotley. Lucia Bellinger married Burnaby Bull, and Elizabeth married Colonel John Palmer. Both Bull and Palmer were veteran Indian fighters and pioneers of Beaufort District. Burnaby

Bull, John Palmer, and Palmer's son-in-law, Andrew DeVeaux II, all established rice plantations on lands that were part of the original Tomotley Barony.

Burnaby Bull's brothers, William and John, also began to shift their planting interests south of the Combahee in the 1730s. John Bull was a militia captain during the Yamassee War, and his first wife was a victim of the massacre of 1715. William Bull was a colonel during the same war. His wife was Mary Quintyne, and her stepfather, Thomas Nairne, was the commissioner of the Indian trade who died at the outbreak of the war after having endured torture for four days by having slivers of lightwood stuck into his flesh and set afire.[4] Mary's brother, Henry Quintyne, and his small garrison at Port Royal Island were massacred by the Indians in 1716. The Bulls and their relatives paid a heavy price for the right to settle the former "Indian Land."[5]

William Bull purchased 6000 acres in what later became Prince William's Parish, and he successfully developed Sheldon Plantation and Newbury Plantation as well as a town on the Combahee called Radnor, where John Mulryne operated a store, lodging house, and public house. Bull's ancestors had been landed gentry in Old Radnor, Wales, in the early Tudor period. In the late sixteenth century, Bull's great-grandfather moved to Warwickshire and purchased the estates of Sheldon and Kinghurst Hall. Thus, the names "Radnor" and "Sheldon" were reminiscent of the Bull family's English heritage.[6]

William Bull's investment in the region was important not only from an economic point of view but also because of his political position as a leader of the colony. He was lieutenant governor and served as acting governor of South Carolina in the absence of a royal appointee from 1737 through 1743. William Bull II was Speaker of the Commons House, and from 1740 to 1742, all South Carolina laws were signed by father and son. Although William Bull I was no longer acting governor in 1745, his son, as Speaker of the House, signed the bill establishing Prince William's Parish, which noted that it was a great hardship for people in the vicinity to undertake the journey to St. Helena's (which included a long ferry ride) in order to vote.[7]

The Commons House of Assembly passed an act in 1736 for establishing an Anglican chapel of ease between the Combahee and Pocotaligo Rivers, but plans for a chapel did not materialize. Construction began after the formal establishment of Prince William's Parish on May 25, 1745. The name was in honor of William, duke of Cumberland, the son of King George II, who became famous for his victory over Bonnie Prince Charlie at Culloden in April 1746. Elizabeth Bellinger, widow of the second Landgrave Edmund Bellinger, donated fifty acres of Tomotley barony for the parish church. The donated land was adjacent to William Bull's Sheldon Plantation settlement. William Bull, Stephen Bull, Robert Troup, John Green, and James DeVeaux served as trustees for building the church. They laid the cornerstone in 1751, and construction began, largely at the expense of the Bull family. Glazed brick headers mark out the year in large numbers on the exterior of the eastern elevation.[8]

The church must have been largely completed within two years, because in 1753, the commissioners requested funds from the Assembly to finish and adorn the interior and to sell the pews.[9] Tradition states that the Bull coat-of-arms in bronze was built into the wall over the family pew. William Bull I died at Sheldon March 21, 1755, and was buried in front of the altar.[10]

The most significant thing about Prince William's Parish Church was its architecture. Because of its remote location, its contribution to English architectural design has remained largely unacknowledged. It is possibly the first temple-form building in English or American architecture based on an ancient model. As such, it is one of the earliest contributions to archaeological neoclassicism in English and American architecture. It served as an example of the Greek Revival style which would become characteristic of the antebellum south.[11]

It is likely that William Bull II was instrumental in choosing the plan for the church. He studied in England as a boy, and he probably visited the ancestral home of the Bulls at Sheldon in Warwickshire. Later he mastered Latin and Greek and completed a medical degree at the University of Leyden in the Netherlands. He also visited other European universities and cultural centers in an approximation of the Grand Tour. Given his education in the classics, he may well have been interested in Greek and Roman architecture.[12]

The rediscovery of Greek art as the original source of classic style as well as archaeological excavations at Pompeii and Herculaneum stimulated interest in the neoclassical style in the mid-eighteenth century. A number of architects published pattern books featuring the temple-form building. In his *Vitruvius Britannicus*, first published in London in 1715, English architect Colin Campbell included a "New Design of my Invention for a Church in the Vitruvian Stile."[13] This plan shares with Prince William's the inclusion of freestanding and engaged columns. However, the columns in the Campbell design far outnumber the columns on the Carolina church, making unlikely any association between the two beyond the shared temple form. Other original designs based on antique temples appear in pattern books from both England and France throughout the eighteenth century. An example is the Temple of Fortuna Verilis in Isaac Ware's 1738 edition of Andrea Palladio's *Four Books of Architecture*. In number and arrangement of freestanding and engaged columns, none of the designs in Ware's book closely relates to Prince William's Church.[14]

The design of Prince William's was not an eighteenth-century adaptation, but rather bears a significant resemblance to an ancient Roman temple. Sebastiano Serlio, a sixteenth-century Italian Renaissance architect, published an elevation and plan of a temple described simply as located in "Tivoli by the River." A London edition of Serlio's work was published in 1611. Although the columns of Prince William's are Doric, not Ionic like those of the ancient model, the four freestanding columns supporting the pediment and six engaged columns along each long side strongly resemble the plan of Serlio's temple at Tivoli. Even the four engaged columns of the rear elevation are alike. One difference is that the plan of Prince William's added a door in the center of each side. The standard plan seen across the South Carolina Lowcountry in the third quarter of the eighteenth century included

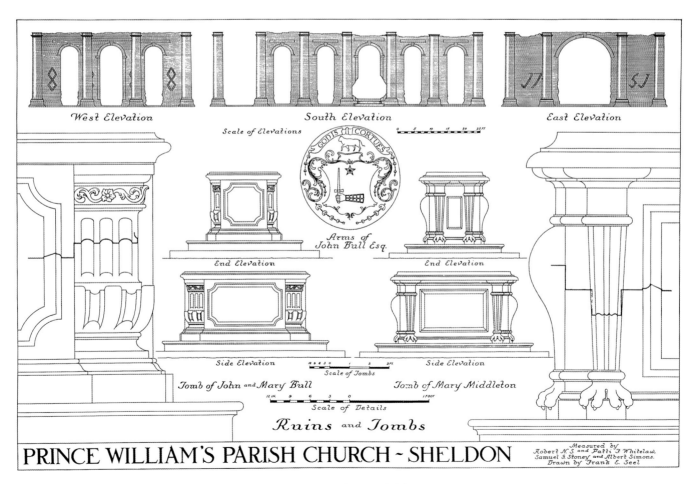

Architectural drawings of the walls and monuments at Prince William's, Sheldon.

entrances at the west end opposite the altar and at the center of each side.[15]

In addition to its importance as a prototype for temple-form neoclassical buildings in America, Prince William's Church is also significant as a product of unnamed, but highly skilled, regional craftsmen, possibly slaves, working in a remote part of South Carolina. Unlike other rural churches where the builders carved unmistakable marks in the brick, the builders of Prince William remain unknown. Intriguing figure eight marks outlined in brick headers on the west elevation raise questions as to their possible meaning. Were the four figure eights elaborate builder's marks or simply decoration? As a Christian symbol, the figure eight denoted the resurrection since it was on the eighth day after his entry into Jerusalem that Christ arose.[16]

The spaces between bricks which appear at regular intervals can be explained. Charleston architect Samuel Gaillard Stoney said that they were "put-log holes" for insertion of supports for the scaffolding used in erecting the building. Upon the completion of the building, the masons would have stopped up the holes with brickbats, but as the building decayed, these patches came out, leaving holes in the wall.[17]

Although no visual representations of the interior are available, documentation of its beauty may be found in contemporary sources. William Bull's obituary in the *South Carolina Gazette* of April 3, 1755, noted that Bull was interred in "Prince William's Parish Church (which he was the principal instrument in building and is esteemed the most elegant and compleatest Country Church in America)...." Charles Woodmason, an Anglican minister, described Prince William's in 1765. "This is the second best Church in the Province, and by many esteem'd a more beautiful Building than St. Philip's. It is far more elegant than St. Michael's, and is beautifully pew'd and Ornamented." Woodmason noted that the minister was the Reverend Mr. Frink, but he probably was not a full-time rector. Frink was a missionary from the Society for the Propagation of the Gospel assigned to Augusta, Georgia, and he sometimes performed divine services on the Carolina side of the Savannah River.[18]

It must have been a rare privilege for a frontier missionary to preach in such an impressive building. William Bull bequeathed to the church a silver communion set including a tankard and stand, two chalices and a plate, engraved in Latin which translated read, "Dedicated as sacred to the Celebration of the Lord's Supper, William Bull, Governor of the Province of South Carolina, fulfills the will of his very excellent deceased father, William Bull. Prince William's Parish, 1756."

In considering the question of why such an impressive edifice was located in the wilderness, far from any metropolitan area, several possibilities exist. One motivating factor may have been competition from dissenters. A group of followers of Reverend George Whitefield, an evangelist who led an extensive revival movement in South Carolina, formed the Stoney Creek congregation and built a meeting house on the banks of the Pocotaligo River in 1744. Whitefield's evangelism was a serious threat to the Church of England, and the Bull family may have wished to assert the presence of the establishment in the region of Sheldon.[19] Since the parish was a political as well as a religious entity, an impressive Anglican church building would make a strong statement both politically and theologically. William Bull II later commented, "...I charitably hope every sect of Christians will find their way to the kingdom of heaven, yet I think the Church of England best adapted to the kingdom of England."[20]

It is understandable that those who had lived through the Yamassee War would want to demonstrate a strong European presence in the wilderness. It is also natural that the Bull family would want to establish a countryseat complete with a local church in the fashion of their English ancestors. One author has suggested that the first immigrant, Stephen Bull, took a Native American as his wife.[21] If so, this might be another reason why the Bulls of the third generation in America wanted to affirm their heritage as English gentlemen.

In the final analysis, however, what they did was to build a temple to the Lord which even in its current state of ruin still proclaims the dignity and reverence for the Divine. Perhaps their real motivation was to praise God. Since he had studied science in Europe, William Bull II may have been familiar with the horizontal figure eight as the symbol for infinity.[22] One might interpret the four figure eights on the front wall as symbolic of God's infinite mercy, grace, wisdom, and love. In the words of the *Gloria Patri,* which was a part of the Anglican service:

*Glory be to the Father and to the Son
and to the Holy Ghost;
As it was in the beginning, is now
and ever shall be,
World without end, Amen.*

[1] For an account of the 1998 service, see *The State* (Columbia, S. C.), May 3, 1998.

[2] William L. McDowell, ed., *Journals of the Commissioners of the Indian Trade, September 20, 1710–August 29, 1718* (Columbia: University of South Carolina Press, 1953), p. 11, as cited in Lawrence S. Rowland, Alexander Moore, and George C. Rogers, Jr., *History of Beaufort County, South Carolina* (Columbia: University of South Carolina Press, 1996), I, 83.

[3] *History of Beaufort County,* 114-116; David Duncan Wallace, *South Carolina, A Short History, 1520-1948* (Columbia: University of South Carolina Press, 1951), p. 90; *History of Beaufort County,* p. 6.

[4] *History of Beaufort County,* pp. 96, 113-114.

[5] *Ibid.*, 116; Kinloch Bull, *The Oligarchs* (Columbia: University of South Carolina Press, 1991), p. 10.

[6] Walter B. Edgar and N. Louise Bailey, *Biographical Directory of the South Carolina House of Representatives* (Columbia: University of South Carolina Press, 1977), II, 120-125; Geraldine M. Meroney, *Inseparable Loyalty* (Norcross, GA: The Harrison Company, 1991), p. 6.

[7] *Ibid.*; Thomas Cooper, ed., *Statutes at Large of South Carolina* (Columbia: A. S. Johnston, 1838), II, 658-660.

[8] *History of Beaufort County,* 117; John R. Todd and Francis M. Hutson, *Prince William Parish and Plantations* (Richmond: Garrett and Massie, 1935), pp. 32-71, passim. See illustration of eastern elevation. "Headers" are bricks placed so that the small end is visible. "Stretchers" show the long side of the brick.

[9] Frederick Dalcho, *An Historical Account of the Protestant Episcopal Church in South Carolina* (Charleston: E. Thayer, 1820; rpt. Arno Press, 1970), pp. 382-383.

[10] Henry DeSaussure Bull, *The Family of Stephen Bull* (Georgetown: The Winyah Press, 1961), pp. xi, 11.

[11] A small collection of garden buildings, or follies, predates Prince William's as temple-form buildings. William Kent's Temple of Venus at Stowe (from before 1732) and Henry Flintcroft's Temple of Flora at Stourhead (from 1745) are among them. Neither depends directly on an antique model. One obvious exception is the anomaly of the church designed as a Tuscan barn by Inigo Jones in 1630-31: the church of St. Paul at Covent Garden in London. See Louis P. Nelson, "South Carolina Anglican: the architecture of the Lowcountry plantation parishes," MS, Dissertation in Progress, University of Delaware, Department of Art History, Draft of November 17, 1997, pp. 79-80. See also H. W. Janson, *History of Art* (New York: Harry N. Abrams, 2nd edition, 1984), pp. 557-563, passim. Barnard Elliott erected on his Bellevue Plantation in St. Bartholomew's Parish a 'Temple of Sport" in the Greek form with eight columns. The exact date is not known, but it was said to have predated the Revolution. See William Elliott, *Carolina Sports by Land and Water* (Charleston: Burges and James, 1846; rpt. Columbia: University of South Carolina Press, 1994), p. 152.

[12] Meroney, *Inseparable Loyalty*, pp. 15-17.

[13] Roger G. Kennedy, *Greek Revival America* (New York: Stewart, Tabori, & Chang, 1989), pp. 329-330. Kennedy notes the importance of Prince William's Church as a prototype. He attributes the plan to Colin Campbell. Other scholars have attributed it to the unused plans for St. Mary-le-Strand Church in London designed by English architect James Gibbs. See *History of Beaufort County,* p. 118.

[14] Nelson, pp. 79-80.

[15] Nelson, pp. 80-81; Vaughan Hart and Peter Hicks, translator-editors, *Sebastiano Serlio on Architecture* (New Haven: Yale University Press, 1996), p. 126. Serlio notes that the temple he copied was in ruins, so that although the footprint showing location of columns remained, it was impossible to note exactly where the original windows were. Obviously, Serlio drew the upper part of the temple as he supposed it to be. The editors also note that the plan was a reconstruction of the "Temple of the Sibyl" as cited in R. B. Bandinelli, ed., *Enciclopedia dell' Arte Antica* (E.A.A.) 7 vols. (Rome: Istituto della Enciclopedia Italiana, 1958-66), VII, p. 704 a.

[16] George Ferguson, *Signs and Symbols in Christian Art* (New York: Oxford University Press, 1954), p. 277.

[17] Samuel Gaillard Stoney, *Colonial Church Architecture in South Carolina* (Charleston: Dalcho Historical Society, 1953), pp. 4-5.

[18] Charles Woodmason, *The Carolina Backcountry on the Eve of the Revolution: The Journal and Other Writings of Charles Woodmason, Anglican Itinerant*, ed. Richard J. Hooker (Chapel Hill: University of North Carolina Press, 1953), pp. 72, 68; Dalcho, p. 197.

[19] *History of Beaufort County,* pp. 117, 132-134.

[20] "Governor William Bull's Representation of the Colony, 1770," *Records in the British Public Record Office Relating to South Carolina, 1663-1782*, Sainsbury Transcripts, XXXII, 365-406, as cited in H. Roy Merrens, ed., *The Colonial South Carolina Scene* (Columbia: University of South Carolina Press, 1977), p. 256.

[21] Meroney, p. 8. Stephen Bull engaged in the Indian trade and was made a chieftain by the Etowah tribe. He worked for fair trade practices and opposed Native American slavery.

[22] The mathematical symbol of infinity was introduced in 1655 by John Wallis. See Jan Gullberg, *Mathematics: From the Birth of Numbers* (New York: W. W. Norton, 1977), p. 30.

Cross placed by the Huguenot Society at the site of Purrysburgh on the Savannah River, near Hardeeville, South Carolina.

ST. PETER'S PARISH

And we know that all things work together for good to them that love God, to them who are the called according to his purpose.

Romans 8: 28

Purrysburgh on the Savannah River was the site of St. Peter's Parish. It began with an enthusiastic entrepreneur who promised fulfillment of a dream—free land in the new world and a chance to become rich. To poor Swiss Protestants, the promise seemed almost too good to be true, and perhaps it was. Nevertheless, they were hardworking and strong people, and most of them found a way to succeed and to make a contribution in South Carolina.

Jean Pierre Purry of Neufchatel, Switzerland, organized a settlement of his countrymen who benefited from Governor Robert Johnson's township plan. In March 1730, Johnson proposed to the Board of Trade in London a plan to establish townships on the frontier to provide a buffer between the coastal region and the various dangers from Indians, French, and Spanish. Because slaves outnumbered whites about two to one in South Carolina, another important consideration was the desire to increase the ratio of whites to blacks in the colony to help lessen the perceived danger of slave insurrection. A third objective was to increase the economic productivity of the colony. To encourage settlement the provincial government offered free land and a supply of tools and provisions.[1]

In 1732, Purry secured a promise of 48,000 acres quitrent free for himself personally if he could settle six hundred Swiss Protestants there. In addition, the provincial government agreed to pay him £400 for bringing one hundred men and two hundred women and children to live on the Savannah River in the hope that they could produce hemp, silk, grapes, and other crops and help to provide defense on the southern frontier, which was still under threat from Spaniards and Indians. With the Reverend Francis Varnod, rector of St. George's Dorchester, as his guide, Purry chose as a site for his township the Great Yamassee Bluff on the Savannah River, about twenty-two miles inland in a straight line from the mouth of the river.[2]

In his promotional literature Purry claimed, "It was formerly called the great *Yamassee Port* and is esteemed by the Inhabitants of the Province the best place in all *Carolina*." The wilderness they found awaiting them must have been a rude shock to immigrants who had read, "If you travel into the Country, you will see stately Buildings, noble Castles and an infinite Number of all sorts of cattle, If it be ask'd what has produced all this? the Answer is: *'Tis only the rich Land of Carolina.*"

Before they left London, Purry along with Joseph Bugnion, minister, and the elders of the Swiss congregation attended a meeting of the Trustees of Georgia, some of whom made contributions to the endeavor. The Trustees also ordered a library of books to be given to Mr. Bugnion for his use in the ministry. Although Bugnion spoke French and little or no English, he was able to receive ordination as an Anglican priest before leaving for Carolina.[3]

The South Carolina authorities had promised transportation from Charleston to the township site as well as tools and provisions. On December 20, 1732, the *South Carolina Gazette* noted that Colonel John Peter Purry had set out in three periaguas (enlarged cypress canoes) with eighty-seven Switzers, and at their passing, the Bastion saluted them with seven guns.[4]

Because of its shallow draft and its capacity to carry heavy loads, the periagua was the vessel of choice at that time for navigating the inland passage between Charleston and Savannah as well as transporting people and products on South Carolina rivers. The eighty-seven Switzers, accompanied by Purry and probably some professional scouts as guides, had to carry their personal goods plus the supplies and tools provided by the government of South Carolina. The three periaguas must have been heavily loaded and severely crowded. The hardships of the trip to the Great Yamassee Bluff in open boats foretold other hardships yet to come.[5]

Due to a disagreement that developed between Bugnion and Purry, Bugnion moved on to St. James' Santee, which was already an established parish and could assure the rector a salary. Purrysburg had only sixty men in 1733, and one hundred were required for parish status.[6]

Purry went back to Europe for more settlers, and in the autumn of 1734, he brought about 260 more immigrants with another Swiss minister who had been ordained in the Anglican faith. The Reverend Henry Chiffelle petitioned the Assembly for "the Pension of a Minister," but the Assembly denied him since Purrysburg was not yet an official parish. Nevertheless, Chiffelle received £100 to pay for his voyage to Carolina.[7]

In 1746, Purrysburg finally achieved parish status. The act creating the Parish of St. Peter's declared "That the church or chapel and the dwelling house at Purrysburgh wherein the Rev Mr. Chiffelle hath preached and dwelt for some years past shall be deemed...the Parish Church and parsonage house of the said Parish of St. Peter." The provincial government had supplied funds to construct the building that served the purposes of both church and parsonage, but no description of the building has been found. The act also provided £100 per year for the minister and stipulated that the parish should have one representative in the Assembly.[8]

Henry Chiffelle served St. Peter's until his death in 1758. He had a son named Philotheus ("loving God"), who became a successful merchant in Charleston and married Rebecca Hutchinson, daughter of plantation owner Thomas Hutchinson of Chehaw. Philotheus Chiffelle represented St. Peter's in the First and Second Provincial Congresses and the First General Assembly as well as in the state Senate.[9]

The Reverend Abraham Imes came to St. Peter's in 1760 and served until he died in 1766. There is no record of any Anglican minister at Purrysburg after that time. The site was not at a good point for navigation and was near a swamp in a malarial locality. Agricultural pursuits were not very productive. The settlement failed to flourish and slowly dwindled away.

Although over six hundred people came there in the 1730s, many moved into Georgia and the town of Savannah. Among the Purrysburg residents were some very substantial citizens. Daniel Vernezobre was a large landowner; Jean Baptiste Bourquin had been a surgeon in the British army; Dr. Daniel Brabant was also a physician. Hector Berenger de Beaufain moved to Charleston, where as Collector of Customs he was able to interpret the Navigation

The Savannah River from the "Great Yamassee Bluff" at Purrysburgh.

Acts so that Charleston's trade with the Spanish colonies did not suffer. Henry de Saussure, founder of one of South Carolina's most prominent families in the revolutionary and antebellum eras, moved to Coosawhatchie and opened a store and lodging house near the bridge which crossed the Coosawhatchie River. The town there grew into an important crossroad for the southern parishes and became the Beaufort County seat for fifty-one years after the Revolution.[10]

Other French-speaking families who prospered bore the names Huguenin, Jeanneret, Robert, Verdier, Borquine, Mongin, LaFitte, and Pelot. The German-Swiss families included Mengersdorff, Holzendorf, Mayerhoffer, Winkler, Strobhar, and Zubly. Among the settlers who came from the Italian piedmont, the best known name was that of Jean Louis Poyas. The authors of the *History of Beaufort County* determined that "Though the dream of Jean Pierre Purry failed, the result was, nonetheless, an infusion into the Beaufort District of a large number of the most talented, enterprising, and productive families in the long history of the South Carolina lowcountry."[11]

[1] Public Records of South Carolina, MS, XIV, 174-177, British Public Records Office, Mf., South Carolina Department of Archives and History; Robert L. Meriwether, *The Expansion of South Carolina, 1729-1765* (Kingsport, Tennessee: Southern Publishers, 1940), pp. 19-22; Julian J. Petty, *The Growth and Distribution of Population in South Carolina* (Columbia: State Planning Board, 1943; rpt. Spartanburg: The Reprint Company, 1975), p. 222.

[2] David Duncan Wallace, *South Carolina: A Short History, 1520-1948* (Columbia: University of South Carolina Press, 1951), pp. 147-150; see the essay on St. George's Dorchester in this volume.

[3] Henry A. M. Smith, *The Historical Writings of Henry A. M. Smith*, Volume 2, *Cities and Towns of Early South Carolina* (Spartanburg, South Carolina: Reprint Company, 1988), pp. 118-120; Arthur Henry Hirsch, *The Huguenots of Colonial South Carolina* (Durham: Duke University Press, 1928; rpt. London: Archon Books, 1962), p. 64. Bugnion was ordained by Dr. Clagett, bishop of St. David's, July 25, 1732. See Frederick Dalcho, *An Historical Account of the Protestant Episcopal Church in South Carolina* (Charleston: E. Thayer, 1820; rpt., New York: Arno Press, 1970), p. 386.

[4] *South Carolina Gazette*, December 20, 1732, as cited in Smith, p. 122.

[5] Suzanne Linder, "A River in Time: A Cultural Study of the Yadkin/Pee Dee River System to 1825," Ph.D. Dissertation, University of South Carolina, 1993, pp. 61-62; William C. Fleetwood, Jr., *Tidecraft* (Tybee Island, Georgia: WBG Marine Press, 1995), pp. 30-43, passim.

[6] Hirsch, *The Huguenots*, pp. 82-84.

[7] *South Carolina Gazette,* November 23, 1734, as cited in Smith, p. 130.

[8] Thomas Cooper, ed., *Statutes at Large of South Carolina* (Columbia: A. S. Johnston, 1838), III, 668.

[9] N. Louise Bailey and Elizabeth Ivey Cooper, *Biographical Directory of the South Carolina House of Representatives* (Columbia: University of South Carolina Press, 1981), III, 141.

[10] Smith, *Cities and Towns*, p. 133; Lawrence S. Rowland, Alexander Moore, and George C. Rogers, Jr., *The History of Beaufort County, South Carolina* (Columbia: University of South Carolina Press, 1996), pp. 116-117; Walter B. Edgar and N. Louise Bailey, *Biographical Directory of the South Carolina House of Representatives* (Columbia: University of South Carolina, 1997), II, 65.

[11] Rowland, Moore, and Rogers, *History of Beaufort County*, pp. 120-121.

The baroque gable with a bull's eye window dominates the façade of St. Stephen's Parish Church in St. Stephen's, South Carolina.

ST. STEPHEN'S PARISH

O Master Workman of the race, Thou man of Galilee,
Who with the eyes of early youth Eternal things did see:

Give us a conscience bold and good; Give us a purpose true,
That it may be our highest joy, Our Father's work to do.

From "O Master Workman of the Race"
Jay T. Stocking (1870-1936)

St. Stephen's Parish was originally a part of St. James' Santee. The lower part of St. James' was "French Santee," and the upper part, which became St. Stephen's, was "English Santee." By 1754, when the Assembly granted a petition of the inhabitants and formed St. Stephen's, the French Huguenot families were about as numerous as those of English background. The chapel of ease of St. James', which fell within the new parish, became the church of St. Stephen's. The building was old and in disrepair, but the parishioners were prospering by growing indigo, a plant used to make blue dye. In 1745, the British placed a bounty on indigo, and it became an important money crop. It is likely that the profits from the indigo trade contributed significantly to the building of the new church in St. Stephen's.[1]

St. Stephen's Church stands today as a monument to God and a testament to the eighteenth-century parishioners who valued quality craftsmanship and who found master workmen to build their church. The building was a community effort. Although tradition credits A. Howard and Francis Villepontoux as architects because their names are engraved in bricks, there is no documentary evidence to support this assumption. The church commissioners and the vestry probably collaborated on the plan, so that the design leaves something to be desired by strict architectural standards. Design by a group of untrained persons is not the ideal situation, and as far as is known, there were no trained architects working in South Carolina in the 1760s.

Architectural historians have criticized the building as having a roof too heavy for the structure in order to accommodate the tray ceiling, which imitates that of St. Michael's in Charleston. Likewise, the window over the chancel, a copy from Batty Langley's pattern book, is too small for the location on the wall above the altar. Nevertheless, according to architectural historian Samuel Gaillard Stoney, "Any failures the church has in other respects are more than made up for by the virtues of its workmanship...."[2]

Today, when one can go to the local builders' supply and purchase necessary materials, it is difficult to envision that gathering the materials in the eighteenth century involved such basic operations as felling trees for lumber, finding clay to make brick, forging nails from raw metal, and grinding local marl stone for mortar. It truly was a community effort. In preparation for building the church, on August 6, 1759, the vestry agreed with Peter Sinkler for 2500 bushels of sifted lime which he was to deliver April 1, nine months later. They also contracted with Samuel Cordes for making 120,000 bricks, "counted from the Kiln, ...which said Bricks to be burnt & delivered at, or near the Church as the Clay will be found," by September 1, 1760. Joseph Palmer contracted for "as many good merchantable Shingles free of Sap as will be sufficient for shingling the new Church," and Charles Cantey would "mix up the Lime when brought on the spot."[3]

With preparations already underway, the parishioners petitioned the Assembly, which passed an act authorizing the building project on May 19, 1762, and appointing John Pamor, Charles Cantey, Philip Porcher, Joseph Pamor, Peter Sinkler, Peter Porcher,

Thomas Cooper, Rene Peyre, and Samuel Cordes commissioners. When Peyre declined to serve, the vestry elected John Gaillard in his place. Of those on the commission, Peter Porcher, John Pamor, Philip Porcher, Peter Sinkler, and Thomas Cooper also served on the vestry in 1762. In addition to those who did double duty, James Sinkler and Charles Richbourg were wardens; Isaac Porcher and Philip Williams were on the vestry.[4]

When Samuel Cordes delivered the bricks in October 1762, the vestry and wardens rejected them as "not being sufficiently burnt." Peter Sinkler had 500 bushels of lime ready for plastering, but the vestry asked him to keep it until needed and proceed to prepare the rest of the lime they had ordered. In 1764, the vestry contracted with Joseph Palmer for 150,000 bricks at eight pounds per thousand, and agreed with Charles Cantey to saw all the timber, planks, boards and laths of pine and cypress. When Pamor [Palmer] delivered the bricks, the vestry again rejected them as "intirely too Bad, and are not Proper for Building a Church."[5]

Finally, Charles Cantey, who charged £9 per thousand, was able to supply bricks which met the exacting standards of the commissioners that were "equal in Bigness to Mr. Zachry Villepontouxs." Zachariah Villepontoux was famous for the bricks from his Parnassus Plantation which he had supplied for building St. Michael's in Charleston and Pompion Hill in St. Thomas' Parish. Charles Richbourg supplied the wood for burning the bricks. Laid in the Flemish bond style, the bricks have stood the test of time and are still in excellent condition today.[6]

Francis Villepontoux, nephew of Zachariah, left his initials engraved in a brick with the date September 7, 1767. "P. V." on another brick probably refers to his brother, Paul. Francis received payment for woodwork and brick work in conjunction with William Axson. Primarily remembered as a master carpenter, Axson had a shop in Charleston, and he had recently worked on Pompion Hill chapel. The vestry minutes specifically state, "By cash paid Axon & Pontoux in full for the Brick work this 13th of Nov 1767 – £538." The two were again paid jointly "in part of the wood work – £510-7-3," and in September 1768, the vestry contracted with Axson and Pontoux to complete the wooden work for £250. Axson agreed do the wood work for the gallery for £300.[7]

William Axson marked a brick with his name, the date 1767, and a crossed square and compass as he did at Pompion Hill. At that time members of Masonic orders were often masons by trade as well as ritual. Above his name, Axson placed a brick with a design that appears to be a man in a pulpit, possibly to show that he built the pulpit inside the church. Another brick marked "S Guild" with the square and compass between may refer to the Solomon's Lodge of Freemasonry established in 1734 in Charleston as the first Scottish Rite Masonic Lodge in the colony. Samuel Gaillard Stoney suggested that Axson may have belonged to the nearby Wambaw Lodge, but since he had a shop in Charleston, the Solomon's Lodge seems more likely. The pride in workmanship indicated by the signature bricks and the apparent endorsement by a Masonic lodge is illustrative of the quality demanded by the church commissioners and the vestry of St. Stephen's.[8]

The building which resulted from this cooperative effort is rectangular with the usual cross aisles and entrances on the west, north, and south. Doric pilasters decorate the spaces between the arched windows and doors and support a classical entablature of architrave, frieze, and cornice. Curvilinear baroque gable ends, reminiscent of both Pon Pon chapel of St. Bartholomew's and Prince George's Winyah, ornament each end of the gambrel roof. A bull's-eye window pierces the center of each gable.

A spectacular reredos, or panel, behind the altar dominates the interior. The dark wood paneling outlines the text of the Lord's Prayer and the Apostles' Creed. Fluted pilasters support a classical entablature, and a gilded sunburst symbolizing God's grace and blessings fills the top center of the altarpiece. Although not as intricately carved, the pulpit is similar to that executed by William Axson at Pompion Hill, which was probably based on a Langley pattern.[9]

The final steps to finishing the church were the paving of the aisles, pointing the gable ends with mortar, and capping the putlog holes. Supports for the building scaffolding extended from the putlog holes, and once the building was complete the scaffolding could be removed and the holes plugged. After ten long years of work, the church was finally complete.[10]

Parishioners called the devout and scholarly Alexander Keith, former minister of Prince George's

A Venetian window lights the altar, flanked by tablets inscribed with the Lord's Prayer and the Apostles' Creed.

The masonic mark of William Axson, master craftsman, illustrates that he did both masonry and carpentry.

Gilded sunbursts and intricate carvings decorate the ornate reredos.

The Pineville Chapel of Ease, constructed in 1810, exhibits simple, yet refined, architectural details. It is a part of the Pineville Historic District listed on the National Register of Historic Places.

Winyah, who was currently serving as assistant at St. Philip's in Charleston. Because St. Stephen's was not a mission of the SPG, the congregation offered to supplement the governmental salary with £30, the equivalent of the SPG stipend. Keith served St. Stephen's for seventeen years until he resigned in 1771. His successor was the Reverend Alexander Finlay, who continued at St. Stephen's until 1783.[11]

After the Revolution, the British bounty on indigo was no longer available, and profits declined appreciably. In addition, as settlers moved into the upcountry and cleared land along the tributaries of the river, the Santee was increasingly subject to the ravages of freshets or floods. Inhabitants realized that swampy areas were subject to malarial infection, and the population gradually shifted to the healthier pinelands. In 1794, John Palmer, Peter Gaillard, John Cordes, and Samuel, Peter, and Philip Porcher all built houses in what was to become the village of Pineville. At the period of greatest prosperity, the village contained about sixty houses, and the activities of the parish centered on the chapel of ease at Pineville. Parishioners abandoned the brick church at St. Stephen's.[12]

Writing in 1852, Frederick Porcher said of the old building, "The church tells a story of former grandeur and of present desolation; ...it is finished with neatness, with some pretensions even to elegance, and the beholder involuntarily mourns over the ruin to which it is doomed."[13] It was during the period of desertion when Squire Porcher was passing the old brick church on his return home from a club dinner that he peered into the paneless window and was terrified to see standing in the pulpit the parson's ghost in his white surplice. He left the premises as rapidly as possible, but returned with friends in the light of day to investigate. They found a huge white owl perched on the sounding board.[14]

On another occasion, Josh Couturier, a resident who enjoyed hunting, took refuge in the church during a severe summer storm. He stretched out on the pew beneath the pulpit and prepared to nap until the storm subsided. Suddenly, the door burst open and in came two savage-looking outlaws carrying their plunder. Quietly Josh stretched his long, lanky form and raised his hands above his head. In the next flash of lightning he droned, "A sto-r-m-y n-i-g-h-t." In sheer terror, the thieves dived out the nearest window, leaving their loot to Josh, who slept peacefully on his chosen pew for the rest of the night.[15]

After extensive repairs, services in the old church resumed in 1870. The Charleston architectural firm of Simons and Lapham supervised a restoration in 1934. Further work was done in 1949. Designated a National Historic Landmark in 1970, the building displays a plaque which states, "This site possesses exceptional value in commemorating or illustrating the history of the United States."[16]

Today, St. Stephen's Church has an active congregation and regular services. The fact that the building was able to survive decades of neglect to become a national landmark and to remain active for the worship of God after more than two centuries recalls the hard labor and insistence on quality craftsmanship of the builders.

[1] Thomas Cooper, *Statutes at Large of South Carolina* (Columbia: A. S. Johnston, 1838), IV, 8-9.

[2] Samuel Gaillard Stoney, *Plantations of the Carolina Low Country* (Charleston: Carolina Art Association, 1964), p. 68; Stephen P. Dorsey, *Early English Churches in America, 1607-1807* (New York: Oxford University Press, 1952), p. 110; Mills Lane, *Architecture of the Old South: South Carolina* (Savannah, GA: Beehive Press, 1997), p. 57; Batty Langley, *City and Country Builder's and Workman's Treasury of Designs*, Plate 51, Winterthur Museum, as cited in Louis Nelson, "South Carolina Anglican: the architecture of the Lowcountry plantation parishes," Draft of November 17, 1997, Diocese of South Carolina, p. 92.

[3] "Minutes of the Vestry of St. Stephen's Parish, South Carolina, 1754-1873," Anne Allston Porcher, ed., *South Carolina Historical Magazine*, August 6, 1759, Vol. 45: 159-160; hereinafter cited as Minutes of the Vestry; Samuel Gaillard Stoney, *Colonial Church Architecture in South Carolina* (Charleston: Dalcho Historical Society, 1953), p. 8.

[4] Frederick Dalcho, *An Historical Account of the Protestant Episcopal Church in South Carolina* (Charleston: E. Thayer, 1820; rpt., New York: Arno Press, 1970), p. 329; Minutes of the Vestry, April 12, October 19, 1762, pp. 162-163; April 23, 1764, p. 164.

The name "Palmer" was sometimes spelled "Pamor," as it is pronounced.

[5] Minutes of the Vestry, May 7, 1764, April 8, 1765, pp. 164-165.

[6] Minutes of the Vestry, "The 14th 1766," p. 165; see also I. Heyward Peck, "The Villepontoux Family of South Carolina," *South Carolina Historical Magazine*, 50: 29-27, passim.

[7] Minutes of the Vestry, "The 14th 1766," p. 166; September 14, 1768, April 17, 1769, pp. 170-171; Board of Church Commissioners, November 13, 1767 in vestry book, p. 168; E. Milby Burton, *Charleston Furniture 1700-1825* (Columbia: University of South Carolina Press, 1997), pp. 69-70.

[8] Jane Searles Misenhelter, *St. Stephen's Episcopal Church* (Columbia: The State, 1977), pp. 10-11; Stoney, *Plantations of the Carolina Low Country*, p. 68; Albert Mackey, *History of Freemasonry in South Carolina* (Columbia: S. C. Steam Power Press, 1861), p. 57, as cited in Nelson, "South Carolina Anglican," p. 92.

[9] Author's personal observation and Nelson, "South Carolina Anglican," pp. 90-93. See also the section on Pompion Hill Chapel of Ease in the chapter on St. Thomas' and St. Denis' Parish in this volume.

[10] Minutes of the Vestry, April 17, 1769, p. 171; St. Stephen's minutes read "putlock holes." Samuel G. Stoney called them "put-log" holes, which is a modern form of the term. See Samuel G. Stoney, *Colonial Church Architecture in South Carolina* (Charleston: Dalcho Historical Society, 1953), p. 4.

[11] Misenhelter, *St. Stephen's Parish*, pp. 6-8; Dalcho, *Protestant Episcopal Church*, p. 329.

[12] Frederick A. Porcher, "Historical and Social Sketch of Craven County, South Carolina," *Southern Quarterly Review* (April, 1852), rpts. Samuel Dubose and Frederick A. Porcher, *A Contribution to the History of the Huguenots of South Carolina* (New York: Knickerbocker Press, 1887; Columbia: R. L. Bryan, 1972), pp. 116-117.

[13] *Ibid.*, p. 95.

[14] Misenhelter, *St. Stephen's Church*, p. 23.

[15] *Ibid.*, p. 25.

[16] *Ibid.*, p. 27; Albert S. Thomas, *A Historical Account of the Protestant Episcopal Church in South Carolina, 1820-1957* (Columbia: R. L. Bryan, 1957), pp. 403-406.

Pulpit detail, St. Stephen's Church.

Old St. David's Church in Cheraw, South Carolina, was built in 1772. Although there is a new brick building for Sunday services, the old church remains a vital part of Historic Cheraw.

ST. DAVID'S PARISH

O beautiful for pilgrim feet,
Whose stern, impassioned stress
A thoroughfare for freedom beat
Across the wilderness!
America! America!
God mend thine every flaw,
Confirm thy soul in self-control,
Thy liberty in law!

From "America the Beautiful"
by Katherine Lee Bates

In 1768, the region on both sides of the Great Pee Dee River from the North Carolina line to Lynch's Creek was still a wilderness. Although indigo was the principal cash crop, stock raising and hunting for deerskins were also significant aspects of the economy. There were no courts of law within a hundred miles, and law enforcement was almost non-existent. Cheraw, a village at the head of navigation of the Pee Dee River, became the location of the church, but vestry records show that the civil functions of the parish began before the religious activities.

Most of the first settlers were Baptists who came to the upper Pee Dee region under Governor Robert Johnson's township plan, which was designed to encourage white Protestants to settle in the backcountry to provide a buffer between the coastal region and the various dangers from Indians, French, and Spanish. Other purposes of the plan were to increase the ratio of whites to slaves and to increase economic productivity of the colony.[1]

Welsh Baptists who had originally settled in Pennsylvania and Delaware decided to move to the Pee Dee about 1736 due to the free land and supplies offered by South Carolina's township plan. Land set aside by the provincial government for the Welsh tract originally encompassed some 173,840 acres. A later addition of eight miles on either side of the river to the North Carolina line made the total acreage inclusive of 100 miles of river front, and the Welsh monopoly on land lasted until 1745. A few settlers other than the Welsh had moved into the area prior to that time, but after 1745, the area was open to all.[2]

When the time came to organize a parish, the name of St. David, patron saint of the Welsh, was chosen because of the preponderance of settlers of Welsh extraction. Ironically, most of the Welsh were Baptists and did not wish to belong to the Church of England. This may have been why the petition for establishing a parish originated not with the residents, but with an itinerant Anglican priest who visited Cheraw in 1767. However, by that time, many of the most prominent citizens of the Cheraw area such as Claudius Pegues, Henry William Harrington, Eli Kershaw, Thomas Ellerbe, Thomas Powe, Francis Gillespie, and William Godfrey were Anglican.[3]

Charles Woodmason was an English gentleman of learning commissioned to serve the backcountry of South Carolina as a minister of the established church. He traveled thousands of miles and preached at remote locations. On Sunday, January 25, 1767, he preached at the Cheraws to more than 500 people and baptized about sixty children. He complained about the food. "...their Provisions I could not touch – All the Cookery of these People being exceedingly filthy, and most execrable...laid my Self down for the Night frozen with the Cold – without the least Refreshment – but fat rusty Bacon, and fair Water, with Indian Corn Bread, Viands I had never before seen or tasted." Woodmason for whatever reason was apparently not invited to any of the more affluent plantations in the vicinity where the fare would have been much different.[4]

In March 1767, Woodmason proceeded from his headquarters at Pine Tree Hill (later Camden) to Lynch's Creek, where he found the swamps full of water and the bridges carried away. He had to swim his horse over Lynch's Creek and Black Creek. The mud and water were so tiresome that his horse gave out and he was obliged to stay a day in a dirty, smoky cabin without sustenance. When he reached Thompson's Creek, it was overflowing and very rapid. He said, "I waited 2 days for subsiding of the Waters...I then mounted Horse, and rode to and fro up and down the Creek to endeavor to find some narrow place, where to fall some Great Trees, and mount over by them – But the Stream was ev'ry where too Broad."

Finally a "Bold Man" came with a very large, strong, and "High Horse." He demonstrated that the horse could swim the creek, and then he ferried Woodmason's saddle and baggage across. The minister said, "The Women then stript me Naked, and gave Him my Cloaths which he carried on his Head in like Manner – They put their aprons around me – and when he returned, I got behind Him and the Horse carried us both over very safe – but I never trembled more in my Life." There was a northeast wind and the ground was covered with ice, and he was "almost stiff and torpid with the cold." Luckily it was only twelve more miles to the place of rendezvous at the Pee Dee River. Within an hour's time of his arrival, Woodmason had a hundred people in his congregation. "In the Afternoon, I drew up for them a Petition to the Legislature for this Part of the Province to be rais'd into a Parish which petition was cheerfully sign'd."[5]

Woodmason's petition has not been found, but the act creating St. David's Parish noted that "the inhabitants residing on Pedee river...have represented many inconveniences which they are under for want of having a parish laid out and established...and prayed that a law may be passed for that purpose...."[6] Actually the Pee Dee residents had protested for many years that they needed a court nearby. In 1752, they submitted a petition stating that they resided in the "remotest part of this Province, having nigh two hundred Miles to the seat of Government." They complained, "We find the frontier here to be a place of refuge for many evil-disposed people and those of the meanest principles, ...crowding in amongst us such as Horse Stealers and other felons...."[7]

In the years since 1752, the situation had gotten even worse. Outlaw gangs roamed the backcountry, terrorizing the settlements. They tortured people with hot coals or pokers to make them reveal their valuables and raped girls as young as ten. Those who refused to cooperate with the bandits risked having their homes burned with themselves inside. The summer of 1766 brought an increase in crime, and attempts to retaliate resulted in violent retribution.

Such was the situation in the Pee Dee region when Charles Woodmason wrote the petition for creating St. David's Parish. The citizens were desperate for a local government that could establish law and order. Although Woodmason wrote the petition in March of 1767, the bill creating the parish was not passed until April of 1768. By that time citizens had already begun to organize vigilante groups known as Regulators for protection. Richard Maxwell Brown has aptly told their story in his book *The South Carolina Regulators*, and it is not the purpose of this study to retell it. The important factor is that the formation of St. David's Parish was about the quest for law and order as well as about founding the church.[8]

Claudius Pegues, Philip Pledger, Alexander Mackintosh, and George Hicks, four of the men appointed as church commissioners, were also leaders of the Regulators. Pegues was a Huguenot who at least nominally accepted the Church of England. Pledger, Mackintosh, and Hicks were members of the Welsh Neck Baptist congregation. Mackintosh declined to serve since he lived a long distance from the site of the church. Thomas Lide and James James, others appointed as commissioners, were of Welsh descent. James declined to serve, but Lide became a member of St. David's. Anglican members of the commission included Thomas Ellerbe, who had his children baptized in 1743 by John Fordyce, rector of Prince Frederick's Parish. Even though George Hicks belonged to the Baptist congregation, he also had his baby daughter baptized by Fordyce in 1744. This may be an indication that he attended the Baptist church simply because no Anglican church was available. When Fordyce visited the Cheraws in 1745, he baptized more than forty children, which seems to indicate that by the time the Welsh Tract was opened to those other than Baptists, there were already a number of Anglicans living there.[9]

While the powers and duties of the parish were quite limited, they were nevertheless important, and the parish was the basic unit of local government in South Carolina. The seven vestrymen and two war-

The vestry house is attached to the back of the building.

The interior of St. David's is beautiful in its simplicity and abundant light. The cross aisles, arched windows, and railed chancel demonstrate the regularity of Anglican architecture.

dens had civil as well as ecclesiastical responsibilities. Wardens served as election officials, maintained a list of eligible voters, and staffed the polls for two days for each election. During worship services, the wardens were responsible for the weapons of the participants. Vestry members maintained the parish church and chapels, and in other parishes, they also supervised the parsonage and the glebe lands. Since St. David's did not have a rector before the Revolution, there was no parsonage or glebe. Some parishes elected a clerk, who assumed the duty of witnessing weddings, baptisms, and funerals. The register recorded the minutes of the vestry and kept the church register of vital statistics. In small parishes the offices of clerk and register were sometimes combined, and this was the case at St. David's.[10]

After the general business of organizing, the first action of the St. David's vestry was to elect a representative to the Assembly in the autumn of 1768. One poll was at Charles Beddingfield's, about three miles east of Cheraw, and the other was at John Mackintosh's, about two miles down river from Long Bluff (later Society Hill). The vestry sent notices to militia captains and requested that they "bring their Companies under their proper Leaders to Place of Election to prevent Confusion." Parish officers sent advertisements and circular letters to leaders in various areas to announce the election. On October 4 and 5, 1768, voters cast 166 votes, unanimously electing Claudius Pegues, one of the wealthiest and most influential planters in the back-country, to the South Carolina Commons House of Assembly.[11]

Since the governor dissolved the 1768 Assembly, another election was necessary in 1769. This election was unusual because four women voted. The minutes of the vestry record that Rebecca Lide, Elizabeth Counsell, Catherine Little, and Sarah Booth cast their votes, but no details about the incident are noted. The election was an anomaly, possibly attributable to the more democratic outlook in the backcountry. The women were property owners, and met all the qualifications for voting except for gender. Two of them had family ties to members of the vestry. Rebecca Lide was a niece of vestryman Thomas Lide. In 1766, she purchased a tract of land, and in the deed she was identified as a spinster. Elizabeth Counsell, widow of Robert Counsell and mother of five children, was her husband's executrix and as such was responsible for large tracts of land. Sarah Rogers Booth was sister to churchwarden Benjamin Rogers and widow of John Booth. Through her husband's will, she received land on Neck [Naked?] Creek, a Negro man named Toby, and all the cows but three, which went to his children. Catherine Little was the widow of William Little, who had owned large tracts of land along the northwest part of the Pee Dee River, extending into Anson County, North Carolina. In 1770, entrepreneur Ely Kershaw paid her £243 for 100 pounds of purple and 20 pounds of copper indigo.[12]

Kershaw operated a store at Cheraw, and in cooperation with his brother Joseph Kershaw, a merchant in Camden, he shipped deerskins, lard, pork, tobacco, flour, and indigo by boat down the Pee Dee to Georgetown and thence to Charleston. He imported textiles, china, glassware, tools, and luxury items for sale in his establishment at Cheraw. In 1770, Kershaw donated land on the southwest side of the Pee Dee to be used for building a parish church.[13]

Thomas Bingham, "House Carpenter," received the contract for building the church, which was to be fifty-three feet long, thirty feet wide, and sixteen feet high from the foundation to the plate. The plan also specified two arched doors, one at the side and one at the west end, and thirteen arched windows of eighteen lights, each to be twelve by ten, and a cove ceiling. The two aisles lengthwise and crosswise are typical of Anglican churches of the period. The vestry required a pulpit and sounding board of polished black walnut with a clerk's desk, staircase, and banister to duplicate as closely as possible the pulpit at Prince George's Winyah in Georgetown. The building was to be painted in "plain colours." The vestry would pay Bingham "by Orders on the Public Treasurer of this Province" the sum of £2600. Bingham was obliged to complete the building, which had a jerkin head roof and no steeple, by March 1772, almost two years from the date of the contract. Anglican members of the commission apparently dominated the planning, because the architectural details clearly marked the structure as a typical and regular Anglican church. The first notice of a meeting in the church was April 12, 1773.[14]

With the parish well established and the church under construction, the congregation began having religious services. The vestry submitted a bill to the public treasurer for £20 to pay the Reverend James Foulis for parochial charges in July 1770. The church sent a call to a Mr. Hogart requesting his services as clergyman. He apparently declined, for no further mention of him is found in the records. St. David's never had a resident Anglican rector. By 1768, the SPG had ceased sending out missionaries to new parishes in South Carolina, and without the support of that organization, it was very difficult to secure the services of an Anglican minister in the backcountry.[15]

In spite of the lack of a clergyman, the vestry was active in supplying relief to the poor. In 1771, it was necessary to levy a tax on all inhabitants of the parish of two shillings and six pence for every hundred acres of land and two shillings and six pence for all slaves. William Godfrey and Charles Beddingfield would collect the taxes. The vestry allocated funds as needed. For instance, "It is ordered that James Casey be paid Fifteen Pounds For Keeping a Poor Man." Sometimes, the parishioner needed a doctor's care. The vestry paid Dr. John Ogle £50 to cure Augustine Hargrove of a venereal disease, but Ogle was apparently unsuccessful. Later, the vestry paid Dr. Roach £80 "for curing Augustine Hargrove of the Pox."[16]

A major concern for the vestry was homeless children. The solution was to bind them out as apprentices. John Husbands agreed to take John Brown, son of the deceased Stephen Brown, to teach him the shoemaking trade. The vestry agreed that "Rebecker Robertson be Bound to Paul Powers for Eight years and that the sd. Powers Give her One years Schooling and Two Cows and Calves at her Freedom & a New Sute of Good Cloaths."[17]

Children born out of wedlock presented special problems. Since their fathers were usually still alive, and the parish officers wanted to insure child support, the fathers were required to post bond. The clerk recorded, "John Downs & Joshua Lucas Bond Dated the 20 May 1773 for the Maintaining of there Bastard Children which Said Bonds are

Delivered in the hands of Claudias Pegues Esqr." The wardens and vestry agreed that "Mary Judith be allowed three Pounds Ten shillings per month...for maintaining John Manderson's Bastard Child." Additional funds for the poor became available when militia Colonel George Hicks caught James Blanton fire hunting and fined him £10.[18]

In 1777, the church was still without a rector. Elhanan Winchester, pastor of the Welsh Neck Baptist Church at Long Bluff (later Society Hill), received permission from his own church to preach at St. David's once every three Sundays provided the congregation at Cheraw would contribute to his support.[19] In June 1777, the St. David's vestry invited Winchester to preach a sermon "for happy deliverance of this State from our cruel & oppressive Enemies." Unfortunately, it would be some time before that deliverance occurred. During the Revolutionary War, the 71st Regiment of Highlanders occupied Cheraw and took possession of the church in the summer of 1780. Disease, possibly malaria but probably smallpox, claimed the lives of many of the soldiers. The graves of the British troops in St. David's churchyard remind visitors of that unhappy time.[20]

After the war, the victorious Americans reorganized their government. In 1785, the General Assembly split old St. David's Parish into three counties, Chesterfield, Darlington, and Marlboro. The civil functions of the region were no longer the responsibility of the parish, and there are no vestry minutes from 1785 to 1819. The parish organization apparently dissolved. Since the church organization which had been under the direction of the Bishop of London was disrupted, and the Pee Dee region was economically devastated by the Revolution, it is not surprising that the church went through a difficult adjustment period at that time.

St. David's church became an interdenominational meetinghouse. The Methodist circuit rider, Francis Asbury, held prayer there in February 1785. Local Baptists and Presbyterians developed a rivalry about which congregation would use the building. Tradition states that at one point, two clergymen arrived at St. David's at the same time to conduct services. After a wild race down the aisle to the pulpit, the Presbyterian minister scrambled up the pulpit stairs, slammed and fastened the door and gave out a hymn just as his opponent was halfway up the steps. A young man of the Presbyterian persuasion waved a red handkerchief out the window, signaling to his friends the denominational victory. The friends were standing by for the signal, and promptly set off a cannon in celebration of the success. Understandably intimidated by the blast, the Baptist preacher retreated, and the Presbyterians maintained a presence in the church until 1823, when the Episcopalians regained control. After that time, St. David's became a catalyst for denominational growth and members were instrumental in founding churches in Bennettsville, Society Hill, and Wadesboro, North Carolina.[21]

The story of St. David's Parish is significant in that it illustrates the importance of the parish as an organization of civil government. Women voted in at least one election, and various denominations used the parish church, suggesting that the backcountry location of the parish had a democratizing influence. The settlers who organized the parish were both democratic and pragmatic. Although the parish contained large numbers of Baptists in addition to some wealthy Anglicans, both groups saw the practical utility of an organization of local government in building a community in the wilderness. Through the established church, they were able to assert their "liberty in law."

The parish church of St. David's is now a modern brick building, but old St. David's is maintained and used, in effect, as a town ecumenical chapel. Administered by the Chesterfield County Historic Preservation Commission, it is open to the public and is a very popular site for weddings.

[1] For a discussion of the local economy, see George Lloyd Johnson, Jr., *The Frontier in the Colonial South* (Westport, Connecticut: Greenwood Press, 1997), pp. 39-64, passim; Robert Meriwether, *The Expansion of South Carolina, 1729-1765* (Kingsport, Tennessee: Southern Publishers, Inc., 1940), p. 20; Julian J. Petty, *The Growth and Distribution of Population in South Carolina* (Columbia: State Planning Board, 1943; rpt. Spartanburg: The Reprint Company, 1975), p. 222.

[2] Alexander Gregg, *History of the Old Cheraws* (New York: Richardson and Company, 1867; rpt. Spartanburg, South Carolina: The Reprint Company, 1982), pp. 47-51, 58-61.

[3] Brent Holcomb, ed., *Saint David's Parish, South Carolina Minutes of the Vestry 1768-1832, Parish Register 1819-1924* (Easley, S.C.: Southern Historical Press, 1979), pp. 1, 2, 6, 8, 20 [hereinafter cited as Minutes of the Vestry]; Charles Woodmason, *The Carolina Backcountry on the Eve of the Revolution: The Journal and Other Writings of Charles Woodmason, Anglican Itinerant,* ed. Richard J. Hooker (Chapel Hill: University of North Carolina Press, 1953), pp. xxvii, 5, 13.

[4] Woodmason, *Ibid.* "The Cheraws" referred to the region. Marlboro, Darlington, and Chesterfield Counties were formed out

of the old Cheraws District. The village was called interchangeably Cheraw and The Cheraws. Sarah Spruill, Cheraw Visitors Bureau, to the author, Sept. 22, 1998.

5 Woodmason, *The Carolina Backcountry*, pp. 18-19.

6 Thomas Cooper, ed., *Statutes at Large of South Carolina* (Columbia: A. S. Johnston, 1838), IV, 300; hereinafter cited as *Statutes*.

7 South Carolina Council Journal, March 16, 1752, South Carolina Department of Archives and History.

8 Richard Maxwell Brown, *The South Carolina Regulators* (Cambridge: Harvard University Press, 1963), pp. 34-37; *Statutes*, IV, 300.

9 Gregg, *History of the Old Cheraws,* pp. 52, 77; Welsh Neck Baptist Church Minutes, WPA, Trans., South Caroliniana Library; Johnson, *The Frontier in the Colonial South,* p. 122; *Register Book of Prince Frederick Winyah*, pp. 53, 112; John Fordyce to SPG, November 4, 1745, SPG MS, South Carolina Department of Archives and History, cited in Johnson, p. 141.

10 George Terry, "'Champaign Country,': A Social History of An Eighteenth Century Lowcountry Parish in South Carolina, St. John's Berkeley County," Ph.D. Dissertation, University of South Carolina, 1981, pp. 298-302; see also Eleanor Clarke Hannum, "The Parish in South Carolina, 1706-1868," Master's Thesis, University of South Carolina, 1970, pp. 40-59, *passim; Statutes*, II, 282-289, 338-342; III, 487.

11 Minutes of the Vestry, pp. 1-5; Gregg, *History of the Old Cheraws*, p. 167; Walter Edgar and N. Louise Bailey, *Biographical Directory of the South Carolina House of Representatives* (Columbia: University of South Carolina Press, 1977), II, 514-515.

12 Voting records in Minutes of the Vestry, pp. 6-7; Robin Copp, "The Early Settlers of St. David's Parish: Four Women Who Voted," MS, Cheraw Visitor's Bureau, pp. 5-6; Ledger Book of Ely Kershaw, 14 November 1770, South Carolina Historical Society, Charleston.

13 Kershaw Ledger, passim. Minutes of the Vestry, April 30, 1770, in Holcomb, *St. David's Parish*, p. 9.

14 Minutes of the Vestry, April 30, 1770, pp. 9-10; April 12, 1773, p. 13. In the Minutes for June 3, 1826, [p. 32], the addition of a steeple was proposed. W. R. Godfrey, writing in 1916 [see note 21], stated that the additions were copied from St. Martin's-in-the-Fields designed by Christopher Wren. Wren did design a cupola for the tower of St. Martin's in 1672, but it was demolished, and the church was rebuilt by James Gibbs in 1722. The Gibbs design for St. Mary-le-Strand, Westminster, London, which was published in *A Book of Architecture* (1728), was much more elaborate, but bears a slight resemblance in proportion to St. David's. See Harold F. Hutchison, *Sir Christopher Wren* (London: Victor Gollancz, 1976), p. 155; and Terry Friedman, *James Gibbs* (New Haven: Yale University Press, 1984), pp. 65, 47; South Carolina Department of Parks, Recreation, and Tourism Brochure on Colonial Churches, n.p.

15 *Ibid.*, 10. Governor William Bull reported in 1770, "It is worth observing that tho' we have benefices for twenty four ministers, we seldom have above fifteen or sixteen at a time here." ("Governor William Bull's Representation of the Colony, 1770," in H. Roy Merrens, *The Colonial South Carolina Scene* (Columbia: University of South Carolina Press, 1977), p. 255.)

16 Minutes of the Vestry, February 13, 1772, p. 12; February 13, 1775, p. 17; April 8, 1776, p. 19.

17 Minutes of the Vestry, February 13, 1772; April 20, 1772, p. 13.

18 *Ibid.*, February 13, 1775, p. 17; August 12, 1775, p. 19; April 20, 1778, p. 21.

19 Welsh Neck Baptist Church Minutes, p.22, as cited in Johnson, *The Frontier in the Colonial South*, p. 151.

20 Minutes of the Vestry, June 21, 1777, p. 21. The minutes record that Winchester was invited to come on the 28th of June 1776, but this must have been an error, since entries both before and after the invitation are dated 1777. Gregg, *History of the Old Cheraws*, pp. 307-308.

21 Elmer T. Clark, ed., *The Journal and Letters of Francis Asbury* (Nashville, TN: Abingdon Press, 1958), I, 482; W. R. Godfrey, *An Historical Sketch of Old St. David's Church, Cheraw, South Carolina, 1768-1916* (Cheraw: n.p., 1916), pp. 14-15; Cheraw Visitor's Bureau; Albert S. Thomas, *A Historical Account of the Protestant Episcopal Church in South Carolina, 1820-1957* (Columbia: R. L. Bryan, 1957), pp. 276-277.

The current St. Mark's Parish Church was completed in 1855. The tiled red roof provides a bright contrast to the white stucco.

ST. MARK'S PARISH

Once to ev'ry man and nation comes the moment to decide,
In the strife of truth with falsehood, for the good or evil side;
Some great cause, God's new Messiah, off'ring each the bloom or blight,
And the choice goes by forever, 'twixt that darkness and that light.

—Thomas John Williams, 1890

The story of St. Mark's Parish is in a sense a record of the Anglican church's attempt to extend its influence into the backcountry. Until the Cherokee War of 1760-61, the backcountry was primarily an Indian frontier. The threat of the Cherokees restrained white settlement. After the white victory in 1761, the chief challenge was the transition to orderly society and government. Because of wartime deaths and dislocations, abandoned property became easy prey to unemployed former soldiers. Some found that stealing was easier than working, and those people formed gangs of outlaws that terrorized law-abiding citizens. As the parish located farthest inland, St. Mark's would become the location of an itinerant minister assigned to bring established religion to the vast wilderness beyond. Charles Woodmason was a man of energy and courage who accepted the call to the backcountry as his particular cause.[1]

St. Mark's Parish, established in 1757, was west of Prince Frederick's and between the Pee Dee and the Santee Rivers. It had no westward boundary, and thus extended indefinitely. In the modern day, the central part of St. Mark's is part of Sumter County. The region, known as the "High Hills of Santee," attracted so many settlers in the 1750s one observer estimated that there were 5000 gunmen in the vicinity at that time. Some settlers, such as the Richardsons, Jameses, and Singletons, came down the Great Wagon Road through the valley of Virginia, through piedmont North Carolina and on to the high hills. Others, such as the Canteys and the Haynsworths, and Huguenots such as the Melletts, Richbourgs, and DesChamps, came from the eastern part of the province. John Dargan and his brother, Timothy, were also among these early leaders in the community who helped to bring order and stability to the backcountry.[2]

The Assembly appointed Richard Richardson; Joseph, William, and John Cantey; Matthew Neilson; Isaac Brunson; and James McGirt as commissioners for building the church. In 1759, the commissioners selected a site on Halfway Swamp, but due to the sparseness of the population, they were unable to raise enough money to build. The Assembly appropriated £700 to assist. Richard Richardson donated a glebe of 150 acres surrounding the church site, and the next year, the Assembly allocated £1000 to the building fund. Parishioners proceeded to build a church, but without a parsonage, they were unable to persuade a minister to settle in the parish.[3]

By 1767, the congregation had completed a rectory, thirty-six feet across the front with four good rooms, a lobby, and a staircase. Outbuildings included a kitchen and stables. With a garden, an orchard, and fish and wild fowl from the nearby Wateree River, a gentleman and his family might be quite comfortable. Unfortunately, along with the river swamp went malaria, and when the Reverend Thomas Morgan settled there he died within two weeks. During periods of vacancies, John Giessendanner of Orangeburg and Paul Turquand of St. Matthew's conducted services occasionally.[4]

In addition, Charles Woodmason served St. Mark's as an itinerant, or travelling, minister. Woodmason had emigrated from England about 1752 and was thus acclimated to the environment.

When the itinerant post became available, he went to England for ordination and returned to begin work in 1766. With headquarters at Pine Tree Hill, he traveled widely and preached at sites from the Great Swamp of the Santee and St. Mark's Church to Hanging Rock Creek, the Waxhaws, Dutchman's Creek, the Cheraws, and Anson Court House, North Carolina.[5]

In contrast to the gentry at St. Mark's parish church, Woodmason encountered many settlers in the backcountry who were only a few generations removed from civilized society. Their families had lived on the fringes of civilization so long that only scattered remnants of the religious and social disciplines of more settled parts of the world remained. Lack of contact with an orderly community compromised law and order, morality, and family integrity.[6]

The traveling parson estimated that ninety-four percent of the women he married were already pregnant and that nine-tenths of the settlers had a venereal disease. One of Woodmason's sermons addressed correct behavior in church. He said, "Bring no Dogs with You – they are very troublesome." He cautioned the congregation not to whisper, talk, or gaze about, and to refrain from coughing or sneezing if possible. He emphasized, "Do not practise that unseemly, rude, indecent Custom of Chewing or of spitting, which is very ridiculous and absurd in Public, especially in Women…." He warned the people that when banns, or announcements of forthcoming marriages, were published, "Don't make it a Matter of Sport; but…put up a Petition to Heav'n for a Blessing of God upon the Parties."[7]

In August 1768, a guide led Woodmason to Flatt Creek, where he found a vast multitude of all classes and complexions. "Most of these People had never before seen a Minister, or heard the Lords Prayer…I was a Great Curiosity to them – and they were Oddities to me." After the service the congregation "went to Revelling Drinking Singing Dancing and Whoring – and most of the Company were drunk before I quitted the Spot." In two years, he rode nearly 6000 miles, mostly on one horse.[8]

In contrast, at Cane Creek he found people who "behav'd very decently and orderly." Some excellent singers were present so that the service was regularly performed. When he preached to a group of Catawba Indians, they responded very quietly. At Sandy River, near Broad River, the service was "perform'd this Day with as much pomp as if at St. Pauls." On Easter Sunday, 1767, he administered communion at St. Mark's Church and found most of the eighty persons in attendance to be "Gentry from distant Parts."[9]

Woodmason's travels brought him a variety of experiences. He once attended an estate sale in Williamsburg township at the home of Rachel Rae, wife of the lately deceased Presbyterian minister John Rae. Woodmason found the widow "not so Nice." He confessed to his journal, "She courted the Writer of this to her Embrace, and wanted to Engage Him with Her on the Couch in the Study…." The widow Rae was evidently unaware of Woodmason's admitted "Incapacity for Nuptial Rites" due to an unfortunate fall and a kick from a horse.[10]

Although the Anglican cleric was very critical of the uncivilized aspects of backcountry behavior, he also learned to understand the problems of the people and to relate to their fears and frustrations. His aim was to create as quickly as possible "a replica of a stable, tranquil, law-abiding English countryside."[11]

Woodmason became a spokesperson for the Regulators, a large organization of leading citizens who banded together to fight crime and to demand courts and law enforcement. An articulate writer, he had published poetry in *The Gentleman's Magazine* of London, and he turned his talents to writing a "Remonstrance" which Regulator leaders Benjamin Hart, John Scott, Moses Kirkland, and Thomas Woodward presented to the Assembly in the name of four thousand settlers. The Remonstrance along with the threat of a possible invasion of Charleston brought quick results, and within four days an Assembly committee recommended a court system, a vagrancy act, and two companies of soldiers for three months to prevent disturbances.[12]

Implementation of these intentions did not occur overnight, but the Regulators had made their point, and the Assembly was ready to address their grievances in a positive manner. The traditional position of the Anglican Church was to support the policies and positions of royal government. In choosing to side with the Regulators, Charles Woodmason took a courageous stand and played a positive role in bringing representation and courts to the backcountry. There were a number of strong leaders in the Regulator Movement, but Woodmason was its most articulate advocate.

Woodmason realized that being a spokesperson for a vigilante group was out of the range of usual duties of an Anglican priest, but he saw himself as a missionary not only of religion but also of English civilization; he had adopted a social gospel. He asserted that he was acting for the good of mankind in general, the rights and liberties of the people, the relief of the poor and needy, the distressed, the stranger, the traveler, the sick, the orphan. He said that if advancing the good of the church; suppressing idleness, beggary, lewdness and villainy; and promoting virtue and industry be characteristic of a Christian, "I hope that I have not...deviated from what my Great Master came into this World to establish – Glory to God Peace on Earth – and Good Will among Men."[13]

St. Mark's Parish church burned in the Revolutionary War. After the war, the congregation split into Upper St. Mark's and Lower St. Mark's. The current church was completed in 1855, largely through the efforts of Colonel Richard C. Richardson and Governor Richard I. Manning. In 1999, services are conducted periodically.

[1] Richard Maxwell Brown, *The South Carolina Regulators* (Cambridge, MA: Harvard University Press, 1963), pp. 12-13.

[2] Thomas Cooper, *Statutes at Large of South Carolina* (Columbia: A. S. Johnston, 1838), IV, 35-37; Anne King Gregorie, *History of Sumter County* (Sumter: Library Board of Sumter County, 1954), pp. 8-21, passim.

[3] *Statutes*, IV, 36; Gregorie, *Sumter County*, p. 25.

[4] Gregorie, p. 25; Thomas Morgan, a native of Wales, was ordained for South Carolina by the Bishop of London in 1769. William W. Manross, *The Fulham Papers in the Lambeth Palace Library* (Oxford: Oxford University Press, 1965), p. 306.

[5] Charles Woodmason, *The Carolina Backcountry on the Eve of the Revolution: The Journal and Other Writings of Charles Woodmason, Anglican Itinerant*, ed. Richard J. Hooker (Chapel Hill: University of North Carolina, 1953), pp. xx, 21, 26. The Assembly passed an act in 1756 to provide a salary of £700 for a clergyman to preach at "Fredericksburgh, Pine Tree Creek, or such other centrical part in the Waterees...and at the most populous places within forty miles of the same." *Statutes*, IV, 21.

[6] Woodmason, *The Carolina Backcountry*, pp. xxiv-xxv.

[7] *Ibid.*, pp. xxvi, 88-89.

[8] *Ibid.* pp. 56, 63.

[9] *Ibid.*, pp. 17, 20, 21, 25.

[10] *Ibid.*, pp. 134-135, 198.

[11] *Ibid.*, p. xxx.

[12] Brown, *The South Carolina Regulators*, pp. 40-43; Hooker, *The Carolina Backcountry*, pp. 172-173.

[13] Woodmason to an English Friend, March 26, 1771, cited in Woodmason, *The Carolina Backcountry*, p. 212.

St. Matthew's Parish Church was built in 1852 on the site of an earlier structure.

ST. MATTHEW'S PARISH

Blest be the tie that binds our hearts in Jesus' love:
The fellowship of Christian minds is like to that above.

Before our Father's throne we pour united prayers;
Our fears, our hopes, our aims are one; our comforts and our cares.

—Lowell Mason, 1832

The people of the St. Matthew's Parish area seemed to have a truly ecumenical outlook. Being Christian and Protestant was more important than denominational affiliation, possibly because of the scarcity of churches. The first minister in the community, John Ulrich Giessendanner, was a German-speaking native of Switzerland who as a young man had been involved in the Pietist movement in Germany. He was not an ordained minister, but he preached to Lutheran congregations.[1] His nephew, John Giessendanner, took over the Orangeburg church when the elder minister died. The meticulous records of the two Giessendanners provide a valuable source of genealogical and church history.

The younger John Giessendanner was originally Lutheran, but he took orders in the Presbyterian Church in 1738 in Charleston. He went to London to be ordained in the Anglican Church in 1749. Preaching in both Orangeburg and Amelia townships, he obligingly spoke in either German or English according to the preference of the congregation. Throughout his career, he preached in the same churches to the same congregations, and presumably with the same theological outlook, but he held credentials that would admit him to practically any Protestant denomination.[2]

Likewise, after the Assembly established St. Matthew's Parish, the first and only minister before the Revolution was Paul Turquand, a gentleman of Huguenot descent who also traveled to London for ordination as an Anglican priest. Turquand officiated in the parish church in Amelia township and also in Orangeburg. He found favor with parishioners of Anglican, Huguenot, and Lutheran backgrounds. The New Light Baptists, however, ridiculed him by calling him a "turkey cock," playing upon his name and his rosy complexion.[3]

The blending of English, French, and Swiss colonists began in the 1730s, when Governor Robert Johnson developed the township plan to settle the backcountry of South Carolina. Johnson wanted to provide for the defense of the western fringe of occupied territory, to increase the white to black ratio, and to encourage economic development of the colony. For these purposes, the provincial government offered free land and supplies to colonists who would settle on the frontier.[4]

On July 13, 1735, a shipload of 250 German Swiss arrived in Charleston from Rotterdam. Of these, 220 settled in Orangeburg Township on the upper Edisto River. When their minister, John Ulrich Giessendanner, joined them, they established a Lutheran Church. After the elder Giessendanner's death in 1738, his nephew, John Giessendanner, became the minister. In his long and distinguished career in the ministry, he not only preached in Orangeburg, but also held services in Amelia Township in the homes of Mary Russell, William Martin, Moses Thomson, William Heatly, and Ann and Charles Russell. By 1737, he was preaching in a chapel there.[5]

Amelia Township, between Orangeburg and the Congaree River, covered roughly the present Calhoun County. Its location on the Cherokee Path, a principal thoroughfare for the Indian trade, made it an ideal situation for defense. Amelia developed into a region of large planters, many of English stock, who dominated the church organization and politics when Orangeburg and Amelia combined to form St. Matthew's Parish.[6]

The South Carolina Assembly passed an act to establish St. Matthew's on August 9, 1765. The commissioners proceeded to build a wooden church, forty by thirty feet, near a large creek, called the Halfway Swamp, on the public road from Charleston to Columbia by McCord's ferry, and a smaller chapel near present Santee. The new church opened December 7, 1766, followed by the chapel on April 26, 1767. No details about these buildings have come to light.[7]

The parish was disallowed because British policy at that time was not to increase the size of the colonial Assembly, and the act went contrary to policy by providing for two representatives from St. Matthew's. In 1768, a compromise act provided that there would be only one representative from the new parish, and the four representatives of St. James' Santee would be reduced to three, thus not increasing the total members of the Assembly. The commissioners for organizing the parish were Benjamin Farrar, William Thomson, William Heatly, Thomas Platt, Tacitus Gaillard, Thomas Sabb, John Bordell, John Caldwell, Robert Whitton, William Flood, and John McNichol. In addition to the parish church, the act provided for a chapel in Orangeburg and appointed Gavin Pou, Christopher Rowe, Samuel Rowe, William Young, and Andrew Govan commissioners for the chapel. The old church continued in use.[8]

It is significant that two of the church commissioners, Benjamin Farrar and Tacitus Gaillard, were legislators as well as leaders of the Regulator Movement, an organization of property owners to try to promote law and order. Since residency was not a requirement for holding office, both Farrar and Gaillard served in the provincial Assembly for other parishes during the period when St. Matthew's was under consideration. Their presence in the Assembly was probably very influential in making the problems of backcountry settlers known. Membership in the Regulator Movement enabled them to stay in touch with the pulse of the backcountry, and also provided a strong political base.[9]

Because of the lack of governmental organization and law enforcement, the backcountry had become a haven for outlaw gangs that terrorized the populace. The crime wave, which included rape, murder, torture, and large-scale theft, escalated in the summer of 1766. Honest citizens banded together for protection and called themselves "Regulators." In addition to law enforcement the Regulators advocated representation of the backcountry in the Assembly, the establishment of local government including courts, and provision for education. The only instrument of local government at that time was the parish, so the formation of St. Matthew's as well as St. David's, both in the backcountry, was in effect an attempt to appease the demands of the Regulators.[10]

Lieutenant Governor William Bull noted that the Regulators were not idle vagabonds, but were landholders and in general an industrious, hardy race of men, many of whom possessed cattle and slaves. He recommended redress of their grievances. Although they were vigilantes, they took the law into their own hands for conservative social purposes—to establish an orderly society. The Anglican church and its accompanying parish organization, which included representation in the Assembly, went hand in hand with the aims of the Regulators.[11]

The first minister of St. Matthew's Parish, Paul Turquand, was born in London in 1735 of French parents. He immigrated to South Carolina and became a schoolmaster in Georgetown prior to his ordination in the Anglican faith. The fact that he was Huguenot by birth was probably pleasing to church commissioner Tacitus Gaillard, who was of similar family background. Turquand arrived in St. Matthew's to preach in 1766, since the earlier act of 1765 had not yet been disallowed. He had a long and successful career in which he recorded baptizing 663 persons and performing 154 marriages. He envisioned a plan for founding a college in the parish and recruiting faculty from England and France. With this in mind, he collected classical works as well as manuscripts to be the basis of a library, but due in part to the Revolution, his plan did not materialize.[12]

The minutes of the vestry of St. Matthew's Parish, which begin on Easter Monday, April 20, 1767, are remarkably free of any record of controversy. The vestry authorized a salary of £700 for the minister and £40 for John Liviston to act as clerk. Care for the poor was a primary concern. The vestry agreed that an assessment be made of one shilling and six pence per head on all slaves and each hundred acres of land as well as money at interest. The poor tax provided funds to help Jacob Smith, a blind man unable to support himself, as well as various small children who were in need. In an incident reminiscent of the Biblical story of the Good Samaritan, Jacob Esler applied for reimbursement "for attendance and funeral of a man found in the road."[13]

The strength and continuity of Paul Turquand's guidance proved beneficial to St. Matthew's Parish. Turquand continued his leadership during the Revolution, when he served in the Provincial Congresses and the First General Assembly. As the war progressed, he realized that the British would not look kindly on the fact that an Anglican clergyman held office under the patriot government. He went to New Orleans, then ruled by the French, until the war was over, and he returned to the parish in 1785.[14]

After the Revolution, the location of the church changed several times. The current building dates from 1852. In 1998, extensive restoration took place, and services resumed in the historic sanctuary on August 16. During the building process, the contractor and church members discovered foundation timbers that they believed dated from an earlier structure. Certainly the spiritual foundations of the church have a long and very rich history. There are undoubtedly members of the current congregation who represent families of Lutheran, Huguenot, and Anglican descent. In the town of St. Matthews, which took its name from the parish and became the county seat of Calhoun County, the "ties that bind" have reached down through the centuries to be felt in a true sense of community in the modern day.[15]

[1] History of Synod Committee, eds., *A History of the Lutheran Church in South Carolina* (Columbia: South Carolina Synod of the Lutheran Church in America, 1971), pp. 46-47.

[2] Daniel Marchant Culler, *Orangeburgh District, 1768-1868, History and Records* (Spartanburg, SC: Reprint Company, 1995), pp. 4, 159.

[3] Frederick Dalcho, *An Historical Account of the Protestant Episcopal Church in South Carolina* (Charleston: E. Thayer, 1820; rpt., New York: Arno Press, 1970), pp. 333-334; Charles Woodmason, *The Carolina Backcountry on the Eve of the Revolution: The Journal and Other Writings of Charles Woodmason, Anglican Itinerant*, ed. Richard J. Hooker (Chapel Hill: The University of North Carolina Press, 1953), p. 111.

[4] Robert Meriwether, *The Expansion of South Carolina, 1729-1765* (Kingsport, TN: Southern Publishers, 1940), pp. 19-20.

[5] Alexander S. Salley, *The History of Orangeburg County, South Carolina* (Orangeburg: R. Lewis Berry, 1898), pp. 35-39, 57; Daniel Marchant Culler, *Orangeburgh District, 1768-1868, History and Records* (Spartanburg, SC: Reprint Company, 1995), p. 159.

[6] David Duncan Wallace, *South Carolina: A Short History, 1520-1948* (Columbia: University of South Carolina Press, 1951), p. 151.

[7] Thomas Cooper, ed., *Statutes at Large of South Carolina* (Columbia: A. S. Johnston, 1838), IV, 230; hereinafter cited as *Statutes*; Frederick Dalcho, *An Historical Account of the Protestant Episcopal Church in South Carolina* (Charleston: E. Thayer, 1820; rpt. New York: Arno Press, 1970), pp. 332-334.

[8] *Statutes*, IV, 298-299. See also the Sermon Book of Paul Turquand, South Carolina Historical Society.

[9] Walter B. Edgar, ed., *Biographical Directory of the South Carolina House of Representatives* (Columbia: University of South Carolina Press, 1977), pp. 240-241, 265-267.

[10] Richard Maxwell Brown, *The South Carolina Regulators* (Cambridge, Massachusetts: Harvard University Press, 1963), p. 138. For specific examples of rape, torture, murder, and thievery, see pp. 34-37. The fact that All Saints' Waccamaw, a Lowcountry parish, was disallowed in 1767, while St. David's and St. Matthew's in the backcountry were allowed in 1768, was probably due to the agitation of the Regulators.

[11] *Ibid.*, pp. 135-138. This is a broad generalization, and undoubtedly certain excesses did occur, but Richard Maxwell Brown's thorough study supports this conclusion.

[12] Dalcho, *Protestant Episcopal Church*, pp. 332-334; Arthur Henry Hirsch, *The Huguenots of Colonial South Carolina* (Durham: Duke University Press, 1928; rpt., Hamden, CN: Archon Books, 1962), pp. 35-37.

[13] "The Red Church Record," typescript by Lillian M. Cain, copy of the Minutes of the Vestry of the Episcopal Church near Fort Motte in the Calhoun County Museum, April 20 - July 11, 1767, pp. 1-3, April 15, 1770, p. 6, April 20, 1772, p. 8.

[14] N. Louise Bailey and Elizabeth Ivey Cooper, *Biographical Directory of the South Carolina House of Representatives* (Columbia: University of South Carolina Press, 1981), III, 729.

[15] *The Calhoun Times* (St. Matthews, SC), August 20, 1998.

The church of All Saints' Parish, Waccamaw, at Pawley's Island, South Carolina, built in 1916, is very similar to the 1849 building which burned. The parish has a modern complex of buildings across the street from the historic church and cemetery.

ALL SAINTS' PARISH, WACCAMAW

*For all the saints, who from their labors rest
Who thee by faith before the world confessed,
Thy Name, O Jesus, be forever blest.
Alleluia, alleluia!*

—William Walsham How, 1864

All Saints' Parish lies on the peninsula formed by the Waccamaw River on the west and the Atlantic Ocean on the east, from the North Carolina line in the vicinity of Little River south to Winyah Bay. In this century, the area has become the location of numerous resorts including Myrtle Beach. Prince George's Parish originally included the Waccamaw neck. In 1735, the Reverend Thomas Morritt wrote to the Bishop of London that the people on the neck were a part of Prince George's, but he said, "I own they labour under great hardships because they can attend divine service no other way yn [than] come by watr wch sometimes is very hazardous in blowing weather."[1]

John Fordyce, rector of Prince Frederick's Parish, preached at a chapel built on land purchased from Percival Pawley and his wife, Anna, on July 20, 1745.[2] They sold the land to George Pawley and William Poole acting on behalf of the church. The Pawley name is perpetuated in Pawley's Island, now a beach resort. Fordyce said that he preached there only about once a year as it was "at a Distance and inconvenient for Travelling," but on the first day of Lent in 1738, he reported a large congregation of religious people and about fifteen communicants. In 1741 Fordyce said, "The 19th of July Last, I preached at Wackamaw Chapel, a Distant part of Prince George's Parish having given notice of my attendance and Design a Month before." He had twenty communicants in the Lord's Supper at that visit who were "Religious and Devout People, most of them were formerly Inhabitants of St. John's Parish."[3]

In 1767, the South Carolina Assembly created All Saints' Parish with Joseph Allston, Charles Lewis, William Pawley, Josias Allston, William Allston, Jr., and John Clarke as commissioners. For the Twenty-eighth Royal Assembly in 1768, the parish elected Thomas Lynch and Joseph Allston. Lynch was also elected for Prince George's Winyah, and he chose to serve for the older parish. Allston declined to serve. The only pre-Revolutionary assembly in which All Saints' was represented was the Twenty-ninth Royal Assembly of 1769, when Thomas Ferguson and Andrew Johnston agreed to serve.[4]

The British government did not wish to enlarge the colonial assembly, so the Board of Trade disallowed the act creating All Saints' Parish in 1770. After the Revolution, it was re-established on March 16, 1778. Mouzon's map of 1775 shows a chapel on the site of the present parish church, but details about the building are unknown.[5]

---

[1] Henry DeSaussure Bull, *All Saints' Church, Waccamaw* (Georgetown: Winyah Press, 1968), p. 3. See also Alberta Lachicotte Quattlebaum, George Rowe Townsend, and Katherine Wells, *All Saints Church, Waccamaw, 1739-1968* (Spartanburg, SC: Reprint Company, 1994), passim.

[2] Charleston Deeds, F3, p. 484, South Carolina Department of Archives and History; quoted in full in Quattlebaum, Townsend, and Wells, pp. 251-255.

[3] *Ibid.*, pp. 3-4.

[4] Thomas Cooper, *Statutes at Large of South Carolina* (Columbia: A. S. Johnston, 1838), pp. 266-268; Walter B. Edgar, ed., *Biographical Directory of the South Carolina House of Representatives* (Columbia: University of South Carolina Press, 1974), I, 134-138.

[5] Bull, *All Saints*, pp. 4, 7; Frances H. Porcher, "Royal Review of South Carolina Law, 1719-1776," MA Thesis, University of South Carolina, 1962, pp. 76, 112; as cited in George Rogers, *History of Georgetown County* (Columbia: University of South Carolina Press, 1970), p. 4; Quattlebaum, Townsend, and Wells, *All Saints*, p. 260.

The Church of the Holy Trinity, located in Grahamville in Jasper County, was built in 1858. Parishioners held services as early as 1824 at this location. Originally a chapel of ease for St. Luke's Parish, the congregation incorporated in 1834, and the church is flourishing in the present day. The building is an outstanding example of carpenter gothic church architecture and as such is listed on the National Register of Historic Places.

ST. LUKE'S PARISH

Inasmuch as many have undertaken to compile a narrative of the things which have been accomplished among us, ...it seemed good to me also, having followed all things closely...to write an orderly account for you...."

Luke 1:1-3

The South Carolina Assembly passed an act on May 23, 1767, providing that St. Luke's Parish would be divided from St. Helena's. The lines of the new parish would run "from the bridge over New river or Day's creek, North ten degrees, West until it intersects the line of Prince William's parish, and from thence to be bounded by the South-west side of Coosawhatchee [sic] river, Port Royal, Broad river, the Sea, Callibogy Sound, and New river or Day's Creek, up to the bridge on the said river or creek, including all the islands to the south and west of Port Royal, Broad river and Callibogy Sound."

The act authorized building a church and parsonage house and appointed Daniel Heyward, John Heyward, Daniel Pepper, Richard Proctor, John Garvey, William Hazzard, and Stephen Drayton to be commissioners for construction.[1] In 1768, St. Luke's Parish elected two representatives to the provincial assembly. Daniel Heyward declined to serve, and Stephen Drayton never qualified. The only assembly in which representatives of St. Luke's took part was the Twenty-ninth Royal Assembly in 1769, when Thomas Bee and Stephen Drayton served.[2]

British policy was not to enlarge the South Carolina Assembly, so the Board of Trade disallowed the act creating St. Luke's in 1770 before a church was ever built. St. Luke's was re-established as an election district after the Revolution, and a church was built about 1786. St. Luke's parishioners also built a church on Hilton Head Island, and the two shared a minister. The Church of the Holy Trinity at Grahamville separated from this congregation about 1835.[3]

[1] Thomas Cooper, ed., *Statutes at Large of South Carolina* (Columbia: A. S. Johnston, 1838), pp. 266-268.

[2] Walter B. Edgar, ed., *Biographical Directory of the South Carolina House of Representatives* (Columbia: University of South Carolina Press, 1974), I, 150, 134-138; 140-143.

[3] Frances H. Porcher, "Royal Review of South Carolina Law, 1719-1776," MA Thesis, University of South Carolina, 1962, pp. 76, 112; as cited in George Rogers, *History of Georgetown County* (Columbia: University of South Carolina Press, 1970), p. 4; Frederick Dalcho, *An Historical Account of the Protestant Episcopal Church in South Carolina* (Charleston: E. Thayer, 1820; rpt., New York: Arno Press, 1970), pp. 387-388; Albert S. Thomas, *Protestant Episcopal Church in South Carolina, 1820-1957* (Columbia: R. L. Bryan, 1957), p. 325.

The multi-tiered steeple and classically inspired portico of St. Michael's Church in Charleston.

ST. MICHAEL'S PARISH

I heard the bells on Christmas Day
Their old familiar carols play,
And wild and sweet
The words repeat
Of peace on earth, good-will to men!

—Henry Wadsworth Longfellow

When the resonant bells peal the hour from the steeple of St. Michael's Church in Charleston, the sound reminds both resident and visitor that the magnificent church has stood for more than two centuries at its strategic location at the intersection of Broad and Meeting Streets. St. Michael's is a prominent landmark in downtown Charleston and has been so since its first service in 1761. Some ten years earlier, in 1751, Charleston was growing so rapidly that St. Philip's Church was "not capable to Contain half of those who are members of the Church of England, and are desirous to worship God accordingly."[1] After some negotiation, a bill was passed to divide the parish of St. Philip's at Broad Street. The part of the city south of Broad would become the new parish of St. Michael's. The act further provided that the new church be built on or near the place where the old church of St. Philip's formerly stood. Commissioners for building the church and a suitable parsonage were Charles Pinckney, Alexander Vander Dussen, Edward Fenwick, William Bull, Jr., Andrew Rutledge, Isaac Mazyck, Benjamin Smith, Jordan Roche, and James Irving.[2]

Before the first service in the new church on February 1, 1761, membership of the commission would change several times. Building such an imposing edifice in the decade of the 1750s was a tremendous undertaking. Funds were scarce, and building materials in the amounts needed were sometimes difficult to find. Each brick had to be handmade and baked, each plank or beam sawed by hand, each nail fashioned individually. The builders purchased excellent bricks from the kilns of Zachariah Villepontoux of Parnassus Plantation on Back River, and other brick from James Withers. Isaac Lesene and Robert Rivers supplied lime, said to be ground from shells of an Indian midden. Anthony Bonneau, Tacitus Gaillard, Joseph Baird, and others furnished logs, timbers, planks, and scantling. Items such as slate, glass, ironware, and Purbeck stones for paving the floor had to be imported.[3]

The consensus is that the plan of the building was probably a composite of ideas from English architects Christopher Wren and James Gibbs with modifications by local commissioners and builders. Samuel Cardy, an Irishman, was the principal contractor, and he stuck with the job until the building was complete.[4]

The vestry called Robert Cooper, then serving as assistant at St. Philip's, to be the first minister. He remained at the post until, being a Loyalist, he resigned at the outbreak of the Revolution. On February 1, 1761, Robert Pringle, one of the churchwardens, recorded in his journal that divine service was first performed in the new church of St. Michael's, and Robert Cooper "preach'd a sermon suitable to the Occasion to a crowded congregation."[5]

At the opening service the congregation saw a magnificent church with a center aisle and a high ceiling unsupported by interior posts. Originally there was a cross aisle from the north to the south door, but it was removed to make space for additional pews in 1818. The pulpit, carved by Henry Burnett complete with a "pine apple" on top, is in its original position on the south side of the middle

The interior of St. Michael's looking toward the front door, showing the organ and balcony supported by carved columns.

aisle near the east end. The pulpit was a "three decker" with clerk's bench, reading desk, and pulpit above. Thomas Elfe and Thomas Hutchinson, furniture and cabinetmakers, constructed the original woodwork in the chancel, which consisted of four large cedar columns with simple bases and capitals which rose to the entablature below the half-dome. Anthony Forehand proposed to add more elaborate carving in 1762. Between the columns was a Venetian window. Elfe and Hutchinson also supplied a wooden altar rail with banisters and a solid door. A wrought iron rail imported from England replaced the wooden railing in 1772.[6]

Outside the west door, the massive portico is supported by four Doric columns of curved brick from the kilns of Zachariah Villepontoux. Doric pilasters interspersed with two rows of arched windows adorn the north and south sides. The steeple dominates the exterior view, but what is not immediately apparent is that in the eighteenth century, the steeple was not merely decorative, it was very functional. The first square block was the bell ringers' room. A "ring of bells" required eight strong men specially trained to synchronize their motions. Just above was the actual belfry with louvered shutters called "abatte-sons," from the French, meaning to throw the sound. The louvers are angled down so that the sound will go down toward the city to call people to church, to celebrate a wedding or a momentous event, to warn of fire or danger, or when muffled, to announce a death. Before the days of modern communications, the church bells were the only method of sending a message immediately to the whole community.[7]

Above the belfry was the clock tower with a clock face on all four sides. The balustrade around the base is not only decorative, but it also provides a place for a mechanic to get outside and work on the dials. Before electrification, the workings of the huge clock were composed of massive ropes, wires, and pulleys. Keeping the clock in repair was a major undertaking, and the vestry hired a skilled workman to wind the clock and keep it in working order. In the 1760s, the town clock provided a standard for local time.[8]

Above the clock was the watchman's arcade. It was the duty of the watchman to call out the hour and to look for fires in the city. The rule of the Fire Masters stated, "If a steepleman discovers a building on fire he shall, without waiting for orders, give the alarm by ringing the bells. The whole peal of bells shall be rung until the commanding officer is satisfied that a sufficient alarm has been given...." At night, the watchman would extend a lantern on a pole to show in which direction the fire was located. The last surviving watchman, Clarence Levy, died at the age of ninety-eight in 1950. He said, "You could hear me for two or three miles when the wind direction was right."[9]

Finally, at the very top of the 186-foot spire was the weather vane. At that height, it was well out of the lower changes of air that might result from fires in local chimneys or other minor disturbances. The weather vane could demonstrate the prevailing wind. This could be important for predicting the weather or, in a seaport such as Charleston, it would be useful for making plans for sailing vessels.[10]

Visibility from the sea was also an important function of the spire. In 1755, construction of the steeple had progressed to the arcade or watchtower level. When the church builders ran short of construction funds, they petitioned the Assembly, stating that the steeple was on a massive foundation and would be constructed to such a height as to be of extraordinary use to navigation. "It is so high as to be discerned at Sea before the Land is seen, & is so properly situated as to be a plain leading mark for the Bar of this Harbour, and therefore effectually answers the Purpose and Intention of building a Beacon, which expence may be thereby saved...."

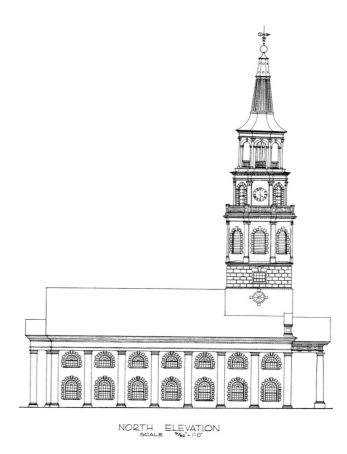

A measured drawing showing details of design of the north elevation of St. Michaels.

On May 19, 1755, the Assembly voted that £500 sterling be borrowed from the beacon fund to be paid to the church commissioners to enable them to finish the steeple and secure the outside of the church from the weather.[11]

The weather has been a recurring problem throughout the nearly 250 years of St. Michael's existence. Numerous natural disasters such as hurricanes, storms, and tornadoes, and the massive earthquake of 1886 have damaged the building, the last being Hurricane Hugo in 1989. Various remodeling projects have changed the appearance of the interior. In 1893, the Frost family presented the memorial window by Tiffany now in the chancel. The

Tiffany firm renovated the chancel in 1905, adding columns, cherub heads, and stenciling the half-dome.

St. Michael's escaped major damage during the Revolution. A British officer took the bells to England, but the church recovered them after the war. Larger guns made the Civil War much more destructive, and a Union shell smashed into the chancel, leaving a gaping hole in the wall. Other cannon fire caused extensive damage, and the looting which followed was almost as destructive. The bells, which were in Columbia for safekeeping, happened to be right in the path of the Union Army. They were damaged by the fire in the burning of Columbia and had to make yet another trip across the Atlantic for repair.

Through earthquake, fire, and storm, St. Michael's has survived to face the world with its steeple high and freshly painted. The bells, ringing loud and clear, tie the present to the past and tell of a spirit that will not be conquered. Henry Wadsworth Longfellow seems to echo the story of the bells of St. Michael's in his poem:

> Then from each black, accursèd mouth
> The cannon thundered in the South,
>   And with the sound
>   The carols drowned
> Of peace on earth, good-will to men!
>
> It was as if an earthquake rent
> The hearth stones of a continent,
>   And made forlorn
>   The households born
> Of peace on earth, good-will to men!
>
> And in despair I bowed my head;
> "There is no peace on earth," I said;
>   "For hate is strong,
>   And mocks the song
> Of peace on earth, good-will to men!"
>
> Then pealed the bells more loud and deep:
> "God is not dead, nor doth He sleep!
>   The Wrong shall fail,
>   The Right prevail,
> With peace on earth, good-will to men!"

[1] Nicholas Oldsberg, ed., *The Journal of the Commons House of Assembly, 1750-1751* (Columbia: University of South Carolina Press, 1974), p. 543.

[2] Act of June 14, 1751, quoted in full in Frederick Dalcho, *An Historical Account of the Protestant Episcopal Church in South Carolina* (Charleston: E. Thayer, 1820; rpt., New York: Arno Press, 1970), pp. 459-460. For biographical information on the commissioners, see George W. Williams, *St. Michael's, Charleston, 1751-1951* (Columbia: University of South Carolina Press, 1951), pp. 12-13.

[3] Williams, *St. Michael's*, pp. 20, 135, 137, 148. Purbeck is an island in Dorset, in the South of England, noted for the production of Purbeck marble and china clay. Gabriel Manigault employed Acadian laborers to saw the marble into squares. William Bridgwater and Seymour Kurtz, *The Columbia Encyclopedia* (New York: Columbia University Press, 1963), p. 1745.

[4] *Ibid.*, 18, 132, 151. Charles Woodmason, an Anglican clergyman, wrote in 1765, "*St. Michael's* Is a New built Church from the Model of that of Greenwich being Truss'd-Roof [e] d and no Pillars." The minister of St. Michael's in 1765 was the Reverend Joseph Dacre Wilton, who had been curate of the chapel at Greenwich. [Dalcho, p. 189] The question arises if Woodmason might have confused the minister with the source of the design.

[5] "Entries in the old Bible of Robert Pringle," *South Carolina Historical Magazine*, V, 22, 30.

[6] Dalcho, *Protestant Episcopal Church*, p. 184; Williams, *St. Michael's*, pp. 167-170, 148, 154. See drawing of reconstruction of the eighteenth-century chancel on p. 158.

[7] Samuel Gaillard Stoney, *Colonial Church Architecture in South Carolina* (Charleston: Dalcho Historical Society, 1953), p. 3.

[8] Stoney, pp. 3-4; Williams, *St. Michael's*, pp. 248-249.

[9] Stoney, p. 4; *News and Courier* (Charleston), November 1, 1950, as cited in Williams, p. 360; see also p. 276.

[10] Stephen P. Dorsey, *Early English Churches in America* (New York: Oxford University Press, 1952), p. 102; Stoney, p. 4.

[11] Williams, *St. Michael's*, p. 142; *Journal of the Commons House of Assembly, November 12, 1754–September 23, 1755*, ed. Terry W. Lipscomb (Columbia: University of South Carolina Press for the South Carolina Department of Archives and History, 1986), p. 302.

The pulpit composed of clerk's bench, reading desk, and pulpit topped by a pineapple was carved by Henry Burnett.

Interior, Pompion Hill Chapel

EPILOGUE

The worship of God is an intensely personal experience, yet since time immemorial, people have joined together in faith. Perhaps beginning with a simple pile of stones, a designated place has seemed to be an important part of the worship experience. Several factors motivated the people of colonial South Carolina to build churches. Survival in the new land was difficult, and life was extremely hazardous. A place where neighbors could come together to seek God's guidance and his blessings might help to make the uncertainties of life in America more bearable. The Anglican Church offered continuity and regularity as well. The liturgy in the Book of Common Prayer was the same in America as in the cities and villages of England, and a French translation was available for Huguenot congregations.

When building materials were difficult to assemble and settlers were working from daylight to dark clearing land and struggling to raise crops, they still expended tremendous energy in constructing churches. The examples which remain show that these settlers were building for the future. The churches they built were much sturdier than most of their homes, and they gave a sense of stability to the community. Through the church organization, people provided mutual support to neighbors in need and attended to the duties of local government. The church also provided a gathering place, a social outlet in a sparsely populated land. Although there were a number of reasons for organizing churches, the primary purpose was to form a community of faith in order to worship God.

South Carolina churches have changed in many ways since the early eighteenth century. Today some denominations boast recreational facilities, daycare for children, internet web pages, and video screens to aid in visibility within the church. Still, the basic motivation of forming a community of faith in order to worship continues. The history of Anglican parishes in colonial South Carolina serves as a reminder that the basic needs of the human heart remain the same. Those who came before, who constructed graceful houses of worship that have stood the test of time, have left more than just buildings. Their legacy is that the worship of God through a community of faith provides a firm foundation for a soul as well as for an entire society.

INDEX

—A—

All Saints' Parish, Waccamaw, 127
Allen, Andrew, 59
Allen, Eleazer, 73
Allestree, Richard, *The Whole Duty of Man* (London, 1689), 69
Allston, Joseph, 127
Allston, Josias, 127
Allston, William, 80
Allston, William Jr., 127
Amelia township, SC, 123, 124
American Revolutionary War, 1, 24, 25, 54, 57, 60, 71, 75, 80, 82, 93, 103, 114, 116, 124, 127, 129, 131, 134; impact on churches, 23, 30, 80, 88, 95, 108, 121, 125, 131, 134
Anabaptist, 47–48. *See also* Dissenters
Andrew, a slave, 11
Andrews Plantation, Charleston Co., SC, 15
Anglican Church in America (ACA): church buildings, 4–5, 7, 9–10, 15–17, 21–24, 27–28, 33, 35, 37, 44, 48–49, 54, 58, 60, 62–63, 68, 70, 75, 80, 86–87, 92–93, 96–98, 105–106, 108–109, 115–116, 119, 124, 131–134; church schools and literacy, 2–4, 11, 16, 22, 34–35, 41–43, 47–48, 68; church wardens and officers, 2, 10, 17–18, 24, 27–28, 48, 59, 69–70, 73, 91, 114–116; civil role of, 2–3, 10, 17, 24, 34, 69, 73, 92–93, 115–116; clergy, 2–4, 7–9, 10, 15–18, 21–24, 27–29, 33–35, 41–43, 47–49, 51–54, 57–61, 67–71, 80, 82, 87–88, 91–93, 98, 101–102, 106, 108, 111–112, 115–116, 119–121, 123–125, 127, 131; founding of, 1–3; function of parish, 2–3; glebe lands and parsonages in, 2, 17, 21, 24, 27, 30, 34–35, 41–43, 47, 49, 52–53, 58, 68, 73, 75, 87, 91–92, 114, 119, 129; liturgical furniture and fittings of, 4–5, 9–10, 16–17, 22–23, 28–29, 35, 37, 47, 54, 58, 60, 62–63, 75, 80, 86–87, 92, 96, 98, 106, 115, 131–132; liturgy of, 4, 10, 16, 22, 27, 48, 51–53; ministry to Indians and slaves, 3–4, 10, 11, 16–17, 22, 34, 35, 41–43, 47–48, 68, 73–75; relations with colonial government, 1–3, 7–9, 11, 15, 21–22, 27, 33, 47, 48, 61, 67, 73, 80, 114, 127, 129
Anne (queen of England), 1
Anson County Courthouse, NC, 115; courthouse, 120
Architecture. *See* Anglican Church in America, church buildings
Architecture, English influence, 5, 21, 23, 131
Asbury, Rev. Francis, 116
Ashby, Cassique John, Jr., 33–34
Ashby, Constantia Broughton, wife of John, 34
Ashepoo Barony, 47
Ashepoo River, 41, 42, 43, 44

Ashepoo-Combahee-Edisto-Basin (ACE Basin), 41
Ashepoo, 43
Ashley Hall Plantation, 18
Ashley River settlements, 1, 15–18, 73
Atkinson, Anthony, 87
Augusta, GA, 74, 98
Auldbrass Plantation. *See* Mount Alexander Plantation
Avant, Caleb, 87
Avant, Francis, 87
Awendaw Creek, SC, 27
Axson, William, Jr., 33, 35, 37–38, 106
Axtell, Lady Rebecca, wife of Landgrave Daniel, 73
Axtell, Landgrave Daniel, 73

—B—

Back River, SC, 35, 131
Baird, Joseph, 131
Ball family, 60
Ball, Keating Simons, 63
Banbury, Elizabeth (Cousin Betsy), 82
Barking Church, London, 10
Barnwell, John, 68
Barnwell, Nathaniel, 69
Baron, Rev. Robert, 44
Barton, Thomas, 27
Battle of Videau's Bridge, 25
Bearcroft, Mrs., wife of Philip, 43
Bearcroft, Philip, 43
Beaufain. *See* de Beaufain
Beaufort, SC, 16, 67–68, 95, 103
Beddingfield, Charles, 114–115
Bee, John, 9
Bee, Thomas, 129
Beech Hill Chapel, St. Paul's Parish, 49
Bellinger family (Tomotley barony), 95
Bellinger, Elizabeth, wife of Landgrave Edmund II, 96
Bellinger, Landgrave Edmund (d. 1739), 43, 47, 95
Bellinger, Landgrave Edmund II, 95
Bennettsville, SC, 116
Beresford "Bounty," 35, 37
Beresford, Richard, 35
Berkeley Co., SC, 15
Bermuda Town, Christ Church Parish, 8, 27
Bess, a slave, 82
Biggin Church, St. John's Parish, Berkeley, 57–60, 63
Biggin Hill, Kent, England, 60
Bingham, Thomas, 115
Bishop of London, 2–3, 8, 28, 33, 35, 48, 52, 53, 58, 80, 88, 91, 116, 127
Black Creek, SC, 112
Black Mingo Creek, SC, 80

Black River, SC, 79, 85–86, 88
Blackburn, Benjamin, 93
Blake family (Bonny Hall), 95
Blake, Benjamin, 73
Blake, Joseph, 75
Blanton, James, 116
Board of Trade, 101, 127, 129
Boisseau, John, 52
Boisseau, Mary Postell, wife of John, 52
Bond, Joshua Lucas, 115
Bonneau, Anthony, 131
Bonnell, John, 87
Bonny Hall, 95
Book of Architecture containing Designs of Buildings and Ornaments (Gibbs, 1728), 80
Book of Common Prayer, 4, 10, 15, 27, 43, 44, 52. *See also* Anglican Church in America, liturgy of
Boone, William, 93
Booth, John, 115
Booth, Sarah Rogers, wife of John, 114–115
Bordell, John, 124
Borquine family, 103
Boschi, Rev. Charles, 43
Bourquin, Jean Baptiste, 102
Brabant, Dr. Daniel, 102
Brailsford, Edward, 23
Bray, Rev. Thomas, 3, 92
Brickmaking, 22, 35–36, 105–106
Broad River, SC, 120, 129
Broughton, Anne Johnson, wife of Thomas, 34
Broughton, Thomas (of Mulberry Castle), 34–35, 58
Brown, John, a minor, 115
Brown, John, 87
Brown, Richard Maxwell, *The South Carolina Regulators*, 112
Brown, Stephen, 115
Brunson, Isaac, 119
Bryan, Hugh, 10, 69
Bryan, Jonathan, 69
Bugnion, Rev. Joseph, 101–102
Bull family, 96, 98
Bull, Burnaby, 95–96
Bull, John, 96
Bull, Lucia Bellinger, wife of Burnaby, 95
Bull, Mary Quintyne, wife of William I, 96
Bull, Stephen, 96, 98
Bull, William I, 17, 96, 98
Bull, William II, 96, 98, 124, 131
Bull, William Izard, 18
Bull, William Tredwell, 24, 48–49, 58, 91
Burke, Aedanus, 44
Burnett, Doct. [sic] Andrew, 88
Burnett, Henry, 131
Burnt Church, The, 44. *See also* Pon Pon Chapel
Burroughs, Seymour, 68
Butcher, Michael, 60

—C—

Caldwell, John, 124
Calhoun Co., SC, 123, 125
Callibogy [sic] Sound, SC, 129
Camden, SC, 111, 115
Campbell, Archibald ("Mad Archie"), 25
Campbell, Colin, *Vitruvius Britannicus*, 97
Campbell, Paulina Philp, wife of Archibald, 25
Cane Creek, SC, 120
Cantey family, 119
Cantey, Charles, 105–106
Cantey, George, 22
Cantey, John, 22, 73, 119
Cantey, Joseph, 119
Cantey, William, 119
Cape Fear, NC, 34, 79, 88
Cardy, Samuel, 131
Cary, Michal, 88
Casey, James, 115
Catawba Indians. *See* Native American peoples
Cattell, William, 17, 75
Cawood, John, 59
Chamberlayne, John, 52
Chapel Hill, Berkeley Co., SC, 57
Charles II (king of England), 52
Charleston Courier, 22
Charleston News and Courier, 62–63
Charleston, SC, 2–4, 6–13, 16, 22, 25, 27, 28, 34, 35, 37, 42–43, 48, 57, 59, 60, 67–68, 73, 75, 79–80, 82, 85, 87, 91, 101–103, 106, 108, 109, 115, 120, 123, 124, 130–134
Chastaigner, Alexander, 52
Cheesman, Thomas, 92
Chehaw River, 41
Chehaw, SC, 42, 43
Cheraw Indians. *See* Native American peoples
Cheraw, SC, 111, 112, 114, 115, 116, 120
Cherokee Indians. *See* Native American peoples
Cherokee Path, SC, 61, 123
Cherokee War (1760–61), 119
Chesterfield County Historic Preservation Commission, 116
Chesterfield Co., SC, 116
Chicken, Catherine ("Little Mistress Chicken"), 63
Chiffelle, Philotheus, 102
Chiffelle, Rebecca Hutchinson, wife of Philotheus, 102
Chiffelle, Rev. Henry, 102
Chikasaw [sic] Indians. *See* Native American peoples
Child, James, 60–63
Childsbury Town, 57, 61–63
Choctaw Indians. *See* Native American peoples
Christ Church, 1706–1959 (Gregorie), 27
Christ Church Parish, 8, 27–31
Church Act of 1704, 1
Church Act of 1706, 1, 2, 15, 21, 22, 27, 33, 41, 47–48, 51–52, 57
Church Act of 1742, 80
Church Flats, 48, 49. *See also* St. Paul's Parish

Church liturgical furniture and fittings. *See* Anglican Church in America
Church of England, 1–3, 7, 10, 43, 59, 98, 111, 112, 131. *See also* Anglican Church in America
Church of the Holy Trinity, Grahamville, SC, 129
City and Country Builder's and Workman's Treasury of Design (Langley), 35, 37, 105
Civil War, American, 18, 30, 43, 63, 71, 80, 88, 95, 134
Clapp, Gillson, 73
Clarke, John, 127
Clarke, Rev. Moses, 59
Cleland, John, 79, 80
Clergy. *See* Anglican Church in America
Coates, James, 60
Cochran, John, 68
Colleton County, SC, 15, 67
Colleton family, 57
Colleton, Peter, 57
Colleton, Sir John, 57–58
Columbia, SC, 124, 134
Combahee River, SC, 41, 43, 67, 95, 96
Coming, Affra, wife of John, 8
Coming, John, 8
Comingtee Plantation, 63
Commons House of Assembly, 2, 7, 8, 9, 10, 15, 17, 35, 37, 42–43, 48, 49, 51, 52, 53, 54, 57, 60, 61, 67, 75, 80, 86, 87–88, 91, 93, 95, 96, 102, 105, 114, 116, 119, 120, 123, 124, 125, 127, 129, 133
Compton, Rev. Henry (bishop of London), 3
Congaree River, SC, 123
Congregationalists, 73, 75. *See also* Dissenters
Cooper River settlement, 32–39
Cooper River, SC, 27, 32–39, 57, 58, 60, 61
Cooper, Rev. Robert, 131
Cooper, Thomas, 106
Coosaw River, SC, 95
Coosawhatchie River, SC, 103, 129
Coosawhatchie, SC, 95, 103
Cordes, John, 60, 108
Cordes, Samuel, 105–106, 108
Cotes, William, 75
Counsell, Elizabeth, wife of Robert, 114–115
Counsell, Robert, 115
Court of Pipowders, 62
Cousaponakeesa. *See* Musgrove, Mary
Couturier, Josh, 109
Craven, Gov. Charles, 9, 67
Creek Indians. *See* Native American peoples

–D–

Dalcho, Frederick, *An Historical Account of the Protestant Episcopal Church in South Carolina*, 15, 17–18, 58, 70, 80, 92–93
Dale, Richard, 70
Dargan, John, 119
Dargan, Timothy, 119
Darlington Co., SC, 116

Davidson, Alexander, 87
Davis, Richard Beale, *Intellectual Life in the Colonial South* (1978), 92
Day's Creek. *See* New River, SC
de Beaufain, Hector Berenger, 102
de Malacare, Peter St. Julien, 33
de Richebourg, Rev. Claude Phillippe, 52–53
de Saussure, Henry, 103
Deas, David, 22
Deas, Margaret Campbell, wife of Robert, 25
Deas, Robert, 25
Deep Gulley Creek (off Sampit River), SC, 87
Dennis, Benjamin, 22
DesChamps family, 119
DeVeaux, Andrew II, 96
DeVeaux, James, 96
Dissenters' meetinghouse, 10, 87
Dissenters, 1–3, 21, 28, 34, 42–43, 47–48, 75. *See also* Anabaptists, Congregationalists, Presbyterians, Quakers
Disto, Thomas, 73
Dixie Plantation, 47
Dorchester Co., SC, 73–75
Downing, Rachel, 88
Downs, John, 115
Drayton, Stephen, 129
Duharra Plantation, 44
Dunn, Rev. William, 47–48
Dupre, Josias, 87
Durand, Rev. Levi, 29–30
Durel, John, 52
Dutarque, Monsieur, 63
Dutchman's Creek, SC, 120

–E–

Earthquake of 1886, 63
Echaw Creek (on the Santee River), 52, 54
Edict of Nantes, 21, 51
Edisto Island chapel of ease, 75
Edisto Island, SC, 47, 91
Edisto River, SC, 41–42, 43, 47, 49, 123
Edmundsbury chapel of ease, 43–44
Education, free schools, 11, 16–17, 75. *See also* Anglican Church in America, ministry to Indians and slaves
Elfe, Thomas, 132
Ellerbe, Thomas, 111, 112
Ellington, Rev. Edward, 24, 25
Elliott, Thomas, 49
Elliott, William, 28
Ellis, James, 93
English Santee, 53, 75, 105. *See also* St. Stephen's Parish
Epidemics and disease, 3, 8–9, 22, 45, 59, 93, 119
Esler, Jacob, 125
Euhaws Baptist Church, 69
Eve, Abraham, 48
Exeter Plantation, 25

–F–

Fairlawn Barony, 57–58
Fairs and markets, 17, 73
Farr, Thomas, 48
Farrar, Benjamin, 124
Fayerweather, Rev. Samuel, 82
Fenwick, Edward, 91, 131
Fenwicke, John, 48, 91–92
Fenwicke Hall, Johns Island, SC, 91
Ferguson, Thomas, 127
Fidling, Francis, 10
Finlay, Rev. Alexander, 108
Fire Masters, Charleston, SC, 133
Fitch, Jonathan, 15
Flatt Creek, SC, 120
Flood, William, 124
Fordyce, Rev. John, 87, 112, 127
Forehand, Anthony, 132
Foulis, Rev. James, 115
Fraser, Charles, 44, 92
Frederick, Prince of Wales, 86
Free Schools, 11, 16–17, 75. *See also* Anglican Church in America, ministry to Indians and slaves
Freemasons, 35, 106
French Protestants, 51, 52. *See also* Huguenots
French Santee, 53, 105. *See also* St. James' Parish
French settlement, Santee, 51
Frink, Rev. Mr., 98
Frost family, 133
Fullerton, Rev. John, 29
Fulton, Rev. John, 28–29
Fundamental Constitutions of Carolina, 1, 34

–G–

Gaillard, John, 106
Gaillard, Mr., 51
Gaillard, Peter, 108
Gaillard, Tacitus, 124, 131
Garden, Rev. Alexander, 33, 35, 37
Garden, Commissary Alexander, 4, 9–10, 11, 28–29, 35, 42–43, 69, 91, 92
Garvey, John, 129
Geddy, David, 60
Gendron, Mr., 51
Gentleman's Magazine, The, 120
George II (king of England), 79, 86, 96
George III (king of England), 86
George (king of England), 91
George, Prince of Wales, 79
Georgetown, SC, 75, 79, 80, 82, 86, 115, 124
German Swiss, 101–103, 123
Gibbes family, 23
Gibbes, John, 23, 91, 93
Gibbon, William, 9
Gibbs, James, 131; *Book of Architecture containing Designs of Buildings and Ornaments*, 80

Giessendanner, John (of Orangeburg), 119, 123
Giessendanner, John Ulrich, 123
Giggerman, Emanuel, 60
Gignillat, Rev. James, 52
Gillespie, Francis, 111
Glebe lands and parsonages. *See* Anglican Church in America
Glover, Charlesworth, 74
God's Acre, 47, 49, 89
Godfrey, William, 111, 115
Goose Creek, SC, 3, 7, 21, 22, 24–25, 33, 80
Gourdin, Theodore, 88
Govan, Andrew, 124
Gowie, Rev. Robert, 42
Grahamville, SC, 129
Granville Co., SC, 67
Great Awakening, 4, 10, 68, 92
Great Pee Dee River, SC, 79
Great Yamassee Bluff, 75, 101–102
Green Point Plantation. *See* Nemours Plantation
Green, John, 96
Gregorie, Anne King, *Christ Church, 1706–1969*, 27
Gunn Church, 88. *See also* Prince Frederick Parish
Guy, Rev. William, 16–17, 29, 67–68, 91

–H–

Haddrell, Susannah, 29
Halfway Swamp, SC, 119, 124
Hall, Arthur, 48
Hampton, Wade, 60
Hanging Rock Creek, SC, 120
Hargrove, Augustine, 115
Harrington, Henry William, 111
Harris, Richard, 35
Harry, a slave, 4, 11
Hart, Benjamin, 120
Hasell, Elizabeth Ashby, wife of Rev. Thomas, 34
Hasell, Rev. Thomas, 29, 33–35, 38
Hasell, Thomas, 80
Hayes, John, 86
Haynsworth family, 119
Hazzard, William, 129
Heatly, William, 123–124
Hendlin, Edward, 87
Henry VIII (king of England), 1
Henry, Duke of Beaufort, 67
Herreford, a slave, 10
Hext, George, 93
Hext, Hugh, 92
Heyward, Daniel, 129
Heyward, John, 129
Hicks, George, 112, 116
Hill, Charles, 59
Hilton Head Island, SC, 129
History of Georgetown County (Rogers), 80
Historical Account of the Protestant Episcopal Church in South Carolina, An (Dalcho), 15, 17, 18, 58, 70, 80, 92–93

Hogart, Mr., 115
Holzendorf family, 103
Hood, Jonathan, 30
Howard, A., 105
Huger, Mr., 51
Hughes, Meredith, 80, 85–87
Huguenin family, 103
Huguenot Church, Charleston, SC, 10
Huguenots, 21, 33, 37, 52, 51–54, 63, 57, 105, 112, 119, 123, 124, 125
Humphreys, David, 73
Hunt, Rev. Brian, 59–61
Hurricane Hugo, 133
Husbands, John, 115
Hutchinson, Thomas (of Charleston), 132
Hutchinson, Thomas (of Chehaw), 102

–I–

Imes, Rev. Abraham, 102
Indians. *See* Native American peoples
Indian slaves. *See* Native American peoples
Indian trade. *See* Native American peoples
Indigo cultivation, 17, 43, 54, 88, 105, 108, 115
Insurrections. *See* Stono Rebellion and Yamassee War
Intellectual Life in the Colonial South (Davis), 92
Irving, James, 131
Izard family, 23, 95
Izard, Ralph, 22, 75
Izard, Walter, 73, 75

–J–

Jackson, Millicent, wife of Originall, 7
Jackson, Originall, 7
Jacksonborough, SC, 42
James family, 119
James Island chapel of ease, 17
James, James, 112
Jamestown, SC, 51, 53
Jeanneret family, 103
Jeffrey's Creek, SC, 88
Jenkins, John, 91
Jenys, Paul, 75
Johns Island, SC, 47, 91, 93
Johnson, Robert, 101, 111, 123
Johnson, Sir Nathaniel, 3, 33, 34, 58
Johnston, Andrew, 127
Johnston, Commissary Gideon (d. 1716), 7, 8–9, 15, 28, 33–34, 42, 48, 52, 67
Johnston, Henrietta, portraitist and wife of Gideon (d. 1729), 8–9
Jones, Rev. Gilbert, 27–28
Jones, Rev. Lewis, 68–70

–K–

Kalm, Peter, 3

Keith, Rev. Alexander, 80, 82, 106, 108
Kershaw, Ely, 111, 115
Kershaw, Joseph, 115
Kinghurst Hall, Warwickshire, England, 96
Kirkland, Moses, 120

–L–

La Motte, 54. *See also* Motte
La Pierre, John, 52
La Rochelle, France, 21
LaBruce, Joseph, 80
LaFitte family, 103
Landon, Thomas, 86
Lane, John, 86–87
Langhorne, Rev. William, 43, 75
Langley, Batty, *City and Country Builder's and Workman's Treasury of Design*, 35, 105
LaPierre, Rev. John, 33–34, 52
LaRoche, Daniel, 79, 80, 87
LaRoche, Thomas, 87
Lawson, John, 51
Lee, Henry, 60
LeGrand, Mr., 51
LeJau, Francis, 3–4, 7, 9, 15, 21–25, 52, 59, 63, 67
Lenud's Ferry (on South Santee River), SC, 51
Lesesne, James, 80
Lesesne, Isaac, 131
Levy, Clarence, 133
Lewis, Charles, 127
Lide, Rebecca, 114–115
Lide, Thomas, 112, 115
Little, Catherine, 114, 115
Little Pee Dee River, SC, 79
Little River, SC, 127
Little, William, 115
Liviston, John, 124
Logan, George, 27, 28
Logan, Patrick, 28
Long Bluff. *See* Society Hill, SC
Longfellow, Henry Wadsworth, 134
Lords Proprietors, 1–2, 4, 8, 33, 57, 67
Louis XIV (king of France), 51
Ludlam, Rev. Richard, 24
Lutheranism, 123, 125
Lynch's Creek, SC, 111–112
Lynch, Thomas, 54, 127, 129
Lynches River, SC, 79

–M–

MacCormack, Shadrack, 88
Mackintosh, Alexander, 112
Mackintosh, John, 114
Maitland, Rev. John, 48
Manakintown [sic], VA, 52
Manderson, John, 116
Manigault, Anne Ashby, wife of Gabriel, 34

Manigault, Gabriel, 34–35, 37
Manigault, Peter, 82
Manning, Richard I., 121
Markley's Old Field, Berkeley Co., SC, 57
Marlboro Co., SC, 116
Marsden, Rev. Richard, 8, 27–28
Marshall, Rev. Samuel, 7–8
Marston, Rev. Edward, 8, 27–28
Martin, William, 123
Martyn, Rev. Charles, 17
Mathews, Sarah, 70
Maule, Rev. Robert, 57–59
Mayerhoffer family, 103
Mazyck's Ferry (on South Santee River), 51
Mazyck, Isaac, 131
McCord's Ferry, SC, 124
McCorkell, Samuel, 30
McGirt, James, 119
McNichol, John, 124
Mellett family, 119
Mengersdorff family, 103
Merry, Rev. Francis, 24
Metheringham, John, 28
Methodism, 42, 69, 92, 116
Michau, William, 88
Michie, James (of Richfield Plantation), 95
Middleburg Plantation, 38, 63
Middleton family, Hobonny, 95
Middleton, Arthur, 22, 59, 75
Middleton, Henry, 75
Middleton, William, 23
Miles, Jeremiah, 49
Mills, Robert, 9–10
Missionaries. *See* Society for the Propagation of the Gospel in Foreign Parts
Mitchell, Thomas, 80
Monck's Corner, SC, 57
Mongin family, 103
Moore, James, 21, 22
Morgan, Rev. Thomas, 119
Morgue, Peter, 10
Morritt, Rev. Thomas, 80, 86, 87, 127
Morton, Joseph, 48, 73
Motte, Jacob, 27, 54
Motte, John Abraham, 27
Motte, Rebecca Brewton, wife of Jacob, 54
Mount Alexander Plantation, 95
Mount Pleasant Plantation, 27
Mulberry Castle Plantation, 34, 58–59
Mulryne, John, 95–96
Murray's ferry (on the Santee River), SC, 88
Murray's Old Field chapel of ease, 88
Musgrove, John, 41
Musgrove, Mary, wife of John, 41
Myrtle Beach, SC, 127

–N–

Nairne, Thomas, 61, 68, 96
Nanny, a slave girl, 42
Narragansett, RI, 16, 82
Native American peoples: religious practices and ceremonies of, 74, 85; slavery among, 21, 22, 34, 47–48, 61–62, 85; trade with, 4, 21, 33, 41, 53, 58, 61, 68, 85, 95–96, 98, 123; South Carolina tribes of: Catawba, 4, 120; Cheraw, 85; Cherokee, 4, 68, 74, 119; Chikasaw [sic], 74; Choctaw, 4; Creek, 4, 41, 74; Savana [sic], 74; Uchee, 75; Waccamaw, 85; Winiaw, 74; Yamacraw, 92; Yamassee, 3–4, 22, 42, 48, 58–59, 68, 85, 95, 96. *See also* Anglican Church in America, ministry to Indians and slaves
Neck Creek, SC, 115
Nelson, Louis P., 5
Neilson, Matthew, 119
Nemours Plantation, 95
New Light Baptists, 123
New River, SC, 129
Newbury Plantation, 96
Norris, John, 41, 42
Northhampton Plantation, 60

–O–

Ogle, John, 115
Oglethorpe, James, 41, 92
Old Brim, a Creek chieftain, 41
Old Dorchester State Park, Summerville, SC, 75
Old Radnor, Wales, 96
Orange Quarter, 33–34, 37
Orangeburg township, 119, 123, 124
Osborne, Rev. Nathaniel, 28, 41–42

–P–

Pachelbel, Charles Theodore, 10
Paget, Thomas, 80
Palladio's *Four Books of Architecture* (Ware, 1738), 97
Palmer, Elizabeth Bellinger, wife of John, 95–96
Palmer, John, 95–96, 108
Pamor (Palmer), Joseph, 105, 106
Pamor, John, 105–106
Parker's Ferry, SC, 42, 49
Parnassus Plantation, Back River, SC, 37, 106, 131
Parris, Alexander, 9
Pawley's Island, SC, 80, 127
Pawley, Anna, wife of Percival, 127
Pawley, George, 80, 127
Pawley, Percival, 127
Pawley, William, 127
Pearce, Offspring, 82
Peasley, Rev. William, 71
Pee Dee River, SC, 85, 111, 112, 115, 119
Peekham, Ruth, 93
Pegues, Claudius, 111–112, 114–115, 116

Pelot family, 103
Pepper, Daniel, 129
Periagua, 33, 85, 101–102
Peyre, Rene, 106
Pietist movement in Germany, 123
Pinckney, Charles, 131
Pinckney, Eliza, 17
Pine Tree Hill, 111, 120. *See also* Camden, SC
Pineville chapel of ease, St. Stephen's Parish, 108
Pineville, SC, 108
Plantation economy, 17, 21
Platt, Thomas, 124
Pledger, Philip, 112
Pocotaligo, SC, 4, 95–96, 98
Pompion Hill Plantation, 35
Pompion Hill, chapel of ease to St. Thomas' Parish, 32–39, 58, 106
Pompkinhill Church, 33
Pon Pon Chapel, St. Bartholomew's Parish, 42–43, 44, 80, 106
Ponkin Church Bluff, 33. *See also* Pompion Hill, chapel of ease to St. Thomas' Parish
Poole, William, 127
Porcher, Frederick, 108
Porcher, Isaac, 106
Porcher, Peter, 105–106, 108
Porcher, Philip, 105–106, 108
Porcher, Samuel, 108
Port Royal Island, SC, 96
Port Royal River, SC, 95
Port Royal, SC, 43, 67–68, 129
Pou, Gavin, 124
Pouderous, Rev. Albert, 53
Powe, Thomas, 111
Powers, Paul, 115
Poyas, Jean Louis, 103
Pratt, Elder William, 73
Presbyterian Church, Charleston, SC, 123
Presbyterians, 3, 15, 47, 48–49, 69, 73, 82, 116, 123. *See also* Dissenters
Prince Frederick Parish, 79, 85–89, 112, 119, 127
Prince George's Parish, Winyah, 53, 79–83 106, 115, 127
Prince William's Parish, 95–99, 129
Pringle, Elizabeth Allston, 89
Pringle, Robert, 131
Proctor, Richard, 129
Protestant (Dissenters) Church, 1–3, 10, 111, 116
Protestant settlements, 111
Purry, Peter, 75
Purry, Jean Pierre (John Peter), 101–103
Purrysburgh, Savannah River, 101, 102

–Q–

Quakers, 48
Queen Anne's War, 53, 68
Quinby Bridge, SC, 60
Quincy, Mrs., wife of Samuel, 92

Quincy, Samuel, 91–92
Quintyne, Henry, 96

–R–

Radnor. *See* Old Radnor, Wales
Rae, Rev. John, 120
Rae, Rachel, wife of John, 120
Ravenel, Charlotte St. Julien de Malacare, wife of Rene, 33
Ravenel, Madame Damaris, 63
Ravenel, Rene, 33
Regulators, 112, 120–121, 124
Religious movements. *See* Great Awakening
Reynolds, Ross, 41, 42
Rhett, William, 9–10
Rhett, William, Jr., 73
Richardson, Richard, 119
Richardson family, 119
Richardson, Richard C., 121
Richbourg family, 119
Richbourg, Charles, 106
Richfield Plantation, 95
Rivers, Robert, 131
Roach, Dr., 115
Robert family, 103
Robert, Rev. Pierre, 51–52
Roberts, John, 93
Robertson, Rebecker [sic], 115
Roche, Jordan, 131
Rocky River, SC, 79
Rogers, Benjamin, 115
Rogers, George C., Jr., *History of Georgetown County*, 80
Roman Catholic Church, 52, 91
Rose, Jennie Haskell, *The Youth's Companion*, 63
Rose, Thomas, 15
Rowe, Christopher, 124
Rowe, Samuel, 124
Russell, Ann, 123
Russell, Charles, 123
Russell, Mary, 123
Rutledge, Andrew, 131

–S–

Sabb, Thomas, 124
Salter, John, 10
Sampit River, SC, 79, 87
Sanders, Abraham, 58
Sanders, John, 22
Sandy River, SC, 120
Santee chapel of ease, 52, 124
Santee River, SC, 51–52, 53–54, 79, 88, 108, 119–120
Satur, Jacob, 9, 73
Savana [sic] Indians. *See* Native American peoples
Savannah garrison, 74–75
Savannah River, SC, 67, 74–75, 95, 98, 101
Savannah, GA, 42, 69, 75, 92, 102
Schenckingh, Benjamin, 24

School at the Parsonage, 11
Scott, John, 120
Scott, Thomas, 88
Secare, Peter, 87
Shaw, Daniel, 87
Sheldon Church, Prince William's Parish, 96–98
Sheldon Plantation, 96
Sheldon, SC, 95, 98
Sheldon, Warwickshire, England, 96
Silk Hope Plantation, 33, 37, 38
Simmons, Francis, 93
Simons and Lapham, 109
Simons, Benjamin III (Middleburg Plantation), 63
Simons, Catherine, wife of Benjamin III, 63
Simons, Ethel, 25
Simpson, James, 93
Simpson, John, 88
Singleton family, 119
Sinkler, James, 106
Sinkler, Peter, 105–106
Skene, Alexander, 11, 73–75
Skene, Rev. George, 88
Slavery, 2, 4, 10–11, 16, 22, 24, 28, 47–48, 57
Slayton, John, 37
Smith, Benjamin, 24, 131
Smith, Elizabeth, wife of Benjamin, 24
Smith, Jacob, 125
Smith, Rev. Michael, 87–88
Smith, O'Brien (Duharra Plantation), 44
Smith, William, 42
Society for the Propagation of the Gospel in Foreign Parts (SPG), 7, 9, 10, 11, 15, 17, 21–22, 30, 33, 34–35, 41–42, 47, 54, 57–58, 61, 67–70, 73–75, 91–92, 98, 108, 115; founding of, 2, 3–4; clerical controversy, 16, 24, 28–29, 43, 48, 52–53, 59–60, 87–88
Society Hill, SC, 114, 116
South Carolina Gazette, 60, 80, 98, 101
South Carolina Regulators, The (Brown), 112
South Carolina Township plan, 111
South Edisto River, SC, 47
South Santee, SC, 51
Spencer, Margaret, 88
SPG. *See* Society for the Propagation of the Gospel in Foreign Parts
St. Andrew's Parish, 1, 11, 15–19, 29, 58, 73–74, 91
St. Augustine, FL, 53, 95
St. Bartholomew's Parish, 28, 41–45, 75, 106
St. Christopher's Island, Caribbean, 4, 21
St. David's Parish, 80, 111–117, 124
St. Denis' Parish. *See* St. Thomas' and St.Denis' Parish
St. George's Parish, Dorchester, 10, 11, 17, 43, 73–76, 82, 101
St. Helena's Parish, 4, 16, 67–71, 96, 129
St. Ignatius, Antwerp, Holland, 9
St. James chapel of ease, 105
St. James' Parish, Goose Creek, 4, 7, 15, 21–25, 52, 59, 62, 67, 75, 80
St. James' Parish, Santee, 51–55, 58, 79, 102, 105, 124

St. John's Parish, Berkeley, 57–64, 127
St. John's Parish, Colleton, 47, 91–93
St. Luke's Parish, 129
St. Mark's Parish, 119–121
St. Matthew's Parish, 119, 123–125
St. Michael's Church and Parish, 37, 105, 106, 131–134
St. Paul's Cathedral, London, 3, 21, 23
St. Paul's Parish, 47–49, 75, 91
St. Peter's Parish, 75, 101–103
St. Philip's Parish, 7–12, 16, 28, 59, 67, 80, 82, 92, 108, 131
St. Stephen's Parish, 53, 80–82, 105–109
St. Thomas' & St. Denis' Parish, 29, 33–39, 52
Stanyarne, John, 91
Stevens, Robert, 22
Stobo, Rev. Archibald, 49
Stoney Creek Presbyterian Congregation, Pocotaligo River, SC, 69, 98
Stoney Landing, Cooper River, 57
Stoney, Samuel Gaillard, 24, 54, 98, 105–106
Stono Rebellion, 10
Stono River, SC, 47–48
Strawberry Chapel, St. John's Parish, Berkeley, 57, 60–63
Strawberry landing, Cooper River, SC, 57
Strobhar family, 103
Stuart, Rev. James, 82
Stuart Town, SC, 67
Summerville, SC, 49, 75
Sumter Co., SC, 119–121
Sumter, Thomas, 60
Swinton, William, 87
Swiss Protestants (Switzers), 75, 101–102, 123

—T—

Tabby construction, 70
Taylor, Rev. Ebenezer, 15–16
Tenison, Rev. Thomas (archbishop of Canterbury), 3
Thomas, Rev. Samuel, 3, 21, 33
Thompson's Creek, 112
Thompson, John, Jr., 87
Thompson, Rev. Thomas, 42–43
Thomson, Moses, 123
Thomson, William, 124
Tiffany Studios, 133–134
Tillotson, Rev. John (archbishop of Canterbury), 10
Tilly, Rev. William, 69
Tissot, Rev. John James, 34, 37
Toby, a Negro man, 115
Tomochichi, Yamacraw chieftain, 92
Tomotley Barony, 95–96
Tompkins, Rev. George, 18
Townsend Tract on Chehaw River, 41
Townsend, Stephen, 35
Townships, 101, 103, 111
Trading Post, Black River, SC, 85
Transportation, 9, 27, 48, 51, 61–62, 101, 102, 112, 119
Trinity College, Dublin, 21

Trott, Nicholas, 52
Trouillard, Florente Phillippe, 57
Troup, Robert, 96
Trusha, Anthony, 92
Turquand, Paul, 119, 123–125
Tustian, Rev. Peter, 73

–U–

Uauenee. *See* Yauhannah
Uchee Indians. *See* Native American peoples
Underwood, Samuel, 91
University of Leyden, the Netherlands, 96
Uwharrie River, 79

–V–

Vander Dussen, Alexander, 131
Varnod, Rev. Francis, 73–75, 101
Vaughan, John, 58
Verdier family, 103
Vernezobre, Daniel, 102
Vigilantism, 112, 120–121, 124
Villepontoux, Francis, 105–106
Villepontoux, Paul, 106
Villepontoux, Zachariah, 33, 35, 37–38, 106, 131–133
Villette, Rev. John, 88
Vitruvius Britannicus (Campbell), 97
Vourmerl'n, John, 85

–W–

Waccamaw Indians. *See* Native American peoples
Waccamaw River, SC, 79, 127
Wackamaw [sic] Chapel, 127
Wadesboro, NC, 116
Wadmalaw Island, SC, 47, 91
Wadmalaw River, SC, 47
Waight, Abraham, 48, 91
Walliss, John, 87
Wambaw Church, 54
Wambaw Creek (off South Santee River), 51
Wando River, SC, 27, 33
Ware, Isaac, Palladio's *Four Books of Architecture*, 97
Waring, Benjamin, 75
Waring, Thomas, 73, 75
Warren, Rev. Samuel Fenner, 54
Washington, George, 44
Wassamasaw chapel of ease, 24, 75
Wateree River, SC, 119
Waties, William, 80, 85
Waxhaw, SC, 120
Welsh Baptists, 111–112
Welsh Neck Baptist Church, 112, 116
Wesley, Rev. John, 42–43, 69, 92
Westminster Cathedral, Dean of, 3
White, Anthony, 28, 80, 87
White, John, 87
Whitefield, Rev. George, 4, 10; controversy, 11, 69, 98
Whiteside, William, 80
Whitton, Robert, 124
Whole Duty of Man, The (Allestree), 69
William III (king of England), 3
William, duke of Cumberland, 96
Williams, John, 75
Williams, Mary, 88
Williams, Philip, 106
Williams, William, 22
Williamsburg township, SC, 120
Williamson, Rev. Atkins, 7
Willtown, SC, 49
Winchester, Elhanan, 116
Wineau on Black River, 85, 86. *See also* Winyah Bay
Winiaw [sic] Indians. *See* Native American peoples
Winkler family, 103
Winteley, Rev. John, 28
Winyah Bay, SC, 79, 127
Withers, James, 131
Wood, Rev. Alexander, 15
Wood, Peter, 4
Woodmason, Rev. Charles, 17, 80, 88, 98, 111–112, 119–121
Woodward, Thomas, 120
Wragg, Samuel, 73
Wren, Sir Christopher, 21, 131
Wright, Gibbon Cawood, wife of Robert, 59
Wright, Robert, 59, 75
Wright, Robert, Sr., 60

–Y–

Yadkin–Pee Dee River, 79
Yamacraw Indians. *See* Native American peoples
Yamassee Indians. *See* Native American peoples
Yamassee Port, SC, 101
Yamassee War (1715), 3–4, 16, 22, 27, 28, 42, 48, 49, 52, 58, 67, 68, 85, 95, 96, 98
Yauhannah, 85
Young, William, 124
Youth's Companion, The (Rose), 63

–Z–

Zubly family, 103